Contents

Acknowledgements

This book has drawn heavily on our clinical experience working in forensic mental health services in the National Health Service in London. The contribution of both colleagues and clients has been central to the development of our ideas and skills. We are indebted those who have provoked debate, lent an ear and a shoulder, raised clinical challenges, and allowed us privileged access to their inner worlds.

Managing Personality Disordered Offenders in the Community

Drawing on the latest evidence from the disparate worlds of mental health and criminal justice, *Managing Personality Disordered Offenders in the Community* provides a practical guide to the management and treatment of a group who comprise some of the most troubled offenders, who provoke the most anxiety in our society.

Illustrated throughout with relevant case examples, this book provides a detailed account of key issues in the assessment of both personality disorder and offending. Dowsett and Craissati explore the current state of knowledge regarding treatment approaches, before suggesting a framework for thinking about community management, legislation, and multi-agency practice. The book concludes with a discussion of community pilot projects currently taking place throughout England and Wales.

Managing Personality Disordered Offenders in the Community is an accessible and informative guide for trainees and practitioners working in the fields of mental health, social services, and the criminal justice system.

John Dowsett is a consultant clinical psychologist currently working in private practice. He specialises in the assessment of perpetrators of physical and sexual abuse and parenting. He previously worked in the NHS as lead clinical psychologist in forensic services and managed a team of psychologists in Lambeth in South London.

Jackie Craissati is a consultant clinical and forensic psychologist. She is head of forensic psychology for Oxleas Foundation NHS Trust in South East London. She has a particular interest in the community assessment and treatment of high risk violent, sexual and personality disordered offenders. She is author of *Child Sexual Abusers* (Psychology Press, 1998) and *Managing High Risk Sex Offenders in the Community* (Routledge, 2004).

Managing Personality Disordered Offenders in the Community

A psychological approach

John Dowsett and Jackie Craissati

Routledge
Taylor & Francis Group

LONDON AND NEW YORK

First published 2008 by Routledge
27 Church Road, Hove, East Sussex BN3 2FA

Simultaneously published in the USA and Canada
by Routledge
270 Madison Avenue, New York, NY 10016

Routledge is an imprint of the Taylor & Francis Group, an Informa business

Typeset in Times by Garfield Morgan, Swansea, West Glamorgan
Printed and bound in Great Britain by TJ International Ltd, Padstow, Cornwall
Paperback cover design by Leigh Hurlock

This publication has been produced with paper manufactured to strict
environmental standards and with pulp derived from sustainable forests.

British Library Cataloguing in Publication Data
A catalogue record for this book is available from the British Library

Library of Congress Cataloging-in-Publication Data
Dowsett, John, 1966–
  Managing personality disordered offenders in the community : a
psychological approach / John Dowsett and Jackie Craissati.
       p. cm.
  Includes bibliographical references and index.
  ISBN: 978-1-58391-738-1 (hardback) – ISBN: 978-1-58391-739-8 (pbk.) 1.
Mentally ill offenders–Rehabilitation–Great Britain. 2. Special needs
offenders–Rehabilitation–Great Britain. 3. Personality disorders–Patients–
Rehabilitation–Great Britain. 4. Community mental health services–Great
Britain. 5. Community-based corrections–Great Britain. I. Craissati, Jackie.
II. Title.
  HV9346.A5D69 2007
  364.3'8–dc22
                                                          2007012879

ISBN: 978-1-58391-738-1 (hbk)
ISBN: 978-1-58391-739-8 (pbk)

Chapter 1

Introduction

On ninth of July 1996 Lin Russell and her two daughters, Megan and Josie, aged six and nine respectively, were walking down a Kent country lane when they and their dog were viciously attacked. Lin and Megan died, Josie was severely injured and left for dead. The incident gave rise to instant and justifiable national horror.

. . .

Michael Stone is one of the group of patients who are among the most difficult and challenging for the health, social and probation services to deal with. He presented with a combination of problems, a severe antisocial personality disorder, multiple drug and alcohol abuse, and occasionally, psychotic symptoms consistent with the adverse effects of drug misuse and/or aspects of his personality disorder. This complex and shifting picture made consistent and accurate diagnosis difficult.

. . .

This is not a case of a man with a dangerous personality disorder being ignored by agencies with responsibilities for supervising and caring for him. He received a considerable degree of attention over the years in question. The challenge presented by cases such as Michael Stone's is that his problems are not easily attributable to a single feature of his condition or to combinations of them. Further, he did not easily fall into the province of one agency or a combination of them. While at times there will be things that can be done for such a person to reduce any dangers he may pose to the public and to help him cope, at other times there will be little that can be offered by any of the services.

(*Report of the Independent Inquiry into the Care and Treatment of Michael Stone* (NHS South East Coast, 2006, pp. 4–8))

In December 2005 Damien Hanson and Elliot White were convicted of the murder of John Monckton and the attempted murder of his wife Homeyra Monckton on the 29th of November 2004, at the time when both men were under the supervision of London Probation Area. The dreadful circumstances of these crimes were widely reported and very understandably caused much public concern.

. . .

With Damien Hanson, a high Risk of Harm offender, there was an overall collective failure within London Probation Area, both to identify the nature of his risk to others and to keep that Risk of Harm to a minimum.

(*An Independent Review of a Serious Further Offence Case: Damien Hanson and Elliot White* (HM Inspectorate of Probation, 2006a, pp. 2, 4–7))

In October 2005 Anthony Rice was convicted of the murder of Naomi Bryant on the 17th of August 2005, at the time when he was being supervised on a life licence by Hampshire probation area. A number of other agencies had been working jointly with the probation service on this case through the Hampshire MAPPA (Multi-Agency Public Protection Arrangements).

. . .

Although managing offenders from start to end of a sentence is in many ways a science it is not an exact science. . . . Nevertheless we find evidence to conclude that on balance Anthony Rice should not have been released on Life Licence in the first place, and once he had been released he could and should have been better managed . . . a sequence of deficiencies in the form of mistakes, misjudgements and miscommunications at all three phases of the whole process of this case had a compounding effect so that they came to amount to what we call a cumulative failure.

. . .

They did not have full knowledge of his past offending behaviour. . . . They received cautiously encouraging but ultimately over-optimistic reports of Anthony Rice's progress under treatment . . . their own earlier decision in 2001 to transfer him to open prison conditions in our view set in motion a momentum towards release . . . created in this case a set of expectations that release had now become a matter of 'when' not 'if'. . . . People managing this case started to allow its public protection considerations to be undermined by its human rights considerations, as these required increasing attention from all involved, especially as the prisoner was legally represented.

(*An Independent Review of a Serious Further Offence Case: Anthony Rice* (HM Inspectorate of Probation, 2006b, pp. 4–8))

John Barrett was convicted of three serious assaults in January 2002. He committed the offences under the influence of abnormal mental processes. A restricted hospital order was imposed under the Mental

Health Act 1983 on the grounds that his detention was considered necessary for the protection of the public from serious harm.

. . .

In October 2003 John Barrett was conditionally discharged from detention under the Mental Health Act by a mental health review Tribunal. He was readmitted to hospital informally on two occasions in 2004. On the second of September 2004, the day after the second readmission, he was at large in Richmond Park where he stabbed to death a stranger, Denis Finnegan.

. . .

This report shows that many aspects of John Barrett's management as a patient of forensic mental health services were not attended to with sufficient thoroughness. Too much confidence was placed in clinical judgments unsupported by evidence and rigorous analysis. Ways of working did not facilitate effective discussion and challenge of clinical views. There was a tendency to emphasize unduly the desirability of engaging John Barrett rather than intervening against his wishes to reduce risk.

. . .

We criticized the team for not fully implementing the care plans during this period when John Barrett was subject to conditional discharge.

. . .

We conclude that during the period he was a patient of forensic service deficiencies in systems, processes and governance arrangements put patients and the public at risk.

(Report of the Independent Inquiry into the Care and Treatment of John Barrett (NHS London, 2006, pp. 9–11))

These are four extracts from the Executive Summaries of four independent inquiry reports, all of which were published in 2006. Catastrophic violence, personality functioning, risk assessment, standards of management and the culpability of the agencies and/or professionals involved were all features of the inquiries.

Why personality disordered offenders?

Personality disordered offenders have become a more high profile group in the UK in the last ten years. There are several reasons for this but it is undoubtedly due to a number of cases which attracted strong media and public interest. Perhaps the most well known of these is that of Michael Stone, who was convicted of the murder of a mother and her daughter in a quiet village in Kent in 1998. The public was gripped by the horror of this story, including the survival of the mother's other daughter who sustained life-threatening hammer injuries during the attack. The extra dimension that was highlighted (and inevitably simplified) by the media was that the perpetrator was assessed by the local forensic mental health clinicians and deemed untreatable. This in turn drew the media's attention – at the time – to the potential resistance of the mental health services to engaging with this group (this was rather in contrast to the muted response to the Inquiry report (NHS South East Coast, 2006) which provided a more considered view).

The Stone case came on the back of an increasing public awareness of, and concerns about, paedophiles returning to the community, which itself culminated in a well publicised vigilante-style response in some communities in the UK. The paedophile cases raised the issue once again of indefinite detention of those members of society who have paid the price of their crimes in prison but are still considered to be highly dangerous.

DSPD proposals

Partly as a result of such high profile cases, the UK government set out their proposals for the management of the risks posed by so-called dangerous severe personality disordered (DSPD) individuals, in a joint Home Office and Department of Health paper (Dept. of Health and Home Office, 1999), which was circulated for consultation. The working definition for DSPD was designed to cover those individuals:

- Who show significant disorder of personality
- Who present a significant risk of causing serious physical or psychological harm from which the victim would find it difficult or impossible to recover (e.g. homicide, rape)
- In whom the risk presented appears to be functionally linked to the personality disorder

The proposals contained a variety of options, including amendments to existing criminal justice legislation to allow for greater use of discretionary life sentences, and amendments to the Mental Health Act to remove the 'treatability criterion' for civil detainees. Suggestions were made to develop new powers in civil and criminal proceedings for the indeterminate detention of DSPD individuals in a new service separately managed from mainstream prison and health services. It should be noted that the UK is not the first western country to go down this route, and there are important forerunners in the Dangerous Offender statutes in the United States (see American Psychiatric Association, 1999) and the TBS system in the Netherlands.

As well as being triggered by a series of high profile cases, these proposals recognised a number of issues and obstacles in this field:

- Gaps in service provision specifically targeted at this group
- The possibility that more appropriate and effective legislation was necessary

- The lack of a robust research base for effective treatment in this area
- The lack of relevant training of mental health and criminal justice professionals
- Problems in the wider field of risk assessment
- Negative attitudes towards working with this client group

There is no doubt that the proposals for detention (as well as better treatment resources) for personality disordered offenders were a further response to the concern about dangerous individuals in general.

Why is it important to identify personality disorder in the management of offenders?

It is quite possible to classify offenders without reference to the diagnosis of personality disorder, and indeed the criminal justice system has largely adopted the need to focus upon offence-specific or criminogenic needs in its approach to offenders, rather than the more ephemeral idea of personality disorder. The question therefore arises as to what is gained by focusing on the individual's personality, disordered or not. We would argue that an understanding of personality deviation or disorder does add considerable incremental knowledge about a number of key issues in relation to offenders. These include issues about the motivation to offend, risk assessment (Webster *et al.*, 1997), predictions about course or prognosis for the individual (Black, 1999), and finally the likely impact and success of any multi-agency risk management strategy (Craissati, 2003). In relation to this last issue, we will argue that a failure to understand an individual's personality may run the risk of certain interventions being at best redundant and ineffective and at worst destabilising and actually liable to increase the risk.

Aims of the book

The aim of this book is to be a practical guide to the management and treatment of personality disordered offenders in the community. There are several authoritative volumes on the general field of personality disorder (Livesley, 2001, 2003), and we do not seek to emulate the range of expertise they include. The reader is referred to these in several places for more in-depth analysis. These do not, however, focus on offending and therefore may not be entirely applicable in addressing the practical issues of dealing with this client group in the community. The aim of our book is to be more pragmatic – it is aimed at clinicians/probation officers – rather than focusing on theoretical issues and controversies.

We do recognise the important role that medical treatments such as medication have to play in the client group, but will not discuss this in great detail as it is outside our professional training and field of practice.

There are several other comorbidities which can complicate the already difficult mix of personality disorder and offending. These include the presence of learning disability, substance misuse and mental illness. Female and adolescent offenders also raise particular issues in terms of epidemiology and service provision. While we have acknowledged some of these issues in places and included them in some of the case examples, we feel these represent specialisms within this field which would take us away from our core themes.

We will also focus on violent and sexual offending. This is because much public concern centres on these crimes, and the relational or interpersonal dimension involved may be closely related to the perpetrator's personality.

Finally we should note that we have aimed to include relevant case examples to illustrate certain points. Though based on real cases, we have ensured that they are sufficiently disguised to protect patient confidentiality.

Although we wanted to give a basic theoretical and empirical background to the subject, we also wanted to focus the reader on thinking about intervention both within and outside the boundaries of what is understood as treatment. The untreatable individuals also need to be assessed and managed. Related to this, we wanted to include the role of other agencies in the multi-agency framework that many of these clients find themselves in. It is vital that both mental health and criminal justice agencies have a clear understanding of the ethos and limitations of each other's role. It is hoped that the book will therefore have something to say to the police or probation officer dealing with these clients from their own perspective.

The rest of this chapter will present an overview of the chapters that follow, with particular reference to some of the social and political factors that may be relevant in this field.

Chapter 2 will focus on definitions and conceptual issues related to the question of personality disorder. While sociological models of offending have often held sway, the notion that many offenders have an underlying personality pathology or clinical condition has never been far away. Something about personality disordered offenders was known even in classical times. Aristotle (2002) in his 'Ethics' developed a hierarchy of virtue and vice. At the top of the ladder, there is the *virtuous* person who aims for good things: he is not conflicted, in modern parlance, because there is no war between virtue and vice in his soul. Next comes the *continent* person who behaves well but is always struggling successfully to control his vices. Then comes the *incontinent* person, who knows what is right but too frequently fails in his struggle. At the bottom of the hierarchy is the *brute* – our psychopath. Like the virtuous person, he too is not at war with himself, and not conflicted. Unlike the virtuous person, here vice and not virtue rules. Aristotle thought that there was something different in the physical makeup of such people; this accords with recent brain scans suggesting that some psychopaths do have altered brain structures and functioning (Blair, 2005).

The more recognisable conceptions of personality disorder can be dated to the early part of the twentieth century. Schneider's *Psychopathic Personalities* published in 1923 was particularly influential (Schneider, 1950). In the UK the Mental Health Acts of 1959 and 1983 recognised a category of 'Psychopathic Disorder' and this remains a medico-legal 'diagnosis' which allows for the indefinite detention of those so labelled in psychiatric hospital.

Forensic mental health services progressed from the centralised maximum security hospitals such as Broadmoor, Ashworth and Rampton, to the development of more local, initially regional, medium secure services in the 1970s and 1980s, and, more recently, forensic community-based services. During this development there is evidence that forensic clinicians became more cautious about admitting personality disordered offenders to mainstream secure provision, partly because of concerns regarding intractible behaviours, and partly because of the destructive effect of mixing mentally ill and personality disordered offenders on wards.

Despite this, forensic mental health services have always inherited a small group of personality disordered offenders from maximum security hospitals. A body of experience and expertise has therefore been built up in the treatment and supervision of these individuals in the community, often within the framework of a Home Office Restriction Order. The assumption was always that this subgroup of offenders stood out from the mainstream of criminals in the criminal justice system because of their obvious abnormal personalities which required the expertise of mental health professionals to diagnose and manage them. In fact prior to Coid's (1992) study there appears to be relatively little in the way of systematic research to characterise this group and clarify how and to what extent their personalities were abnormal.

It may, of course, be that many social and political factors influence how offenders are understood at any one time. There are, however, important implications for prevention as well as treatment and management of offending behaviour. Sociologists argue that the medicalisation of offenders and offending tends to downplay the role of social factors in crime, whilst mental health professionals are more focused on individuals and believe there may well even be individual genetic vulnerabilities towards offending (Raine, 1993).

The antisocial personality disorder (ASPD) is particularly relevant here, as this is considered a mental disorder and may be considered to be the paradigm personality of the habitual career criminal. Although the defining criteria of this condition include a history of offending, there are a number of important personality traits that constitute the disorder, including impulsivity, irresponsibility, deceitfulness, and a lack of empathy. Despite this, it has been criticised by a number of influential writers in the field, including both Kernberg (1984) and Millon and Davis (1996), for placing too much reliance on behavioural criteria and not enough on the underlying personality structure.

However, the disorder is relatively well researched and considered to have significant diagnostic validity (Moran, 1999). Studies of offender samples suggest that there may be up to 80 per cent prevalence of ASPD in samples of incarcerated offenders, and, in this sense, it could be argued that a majority of offenders are in fact personality disordered. This clearly has implications for any proposal that personality disordered offenders are a distinct subgroup.

The medicalisation of offenders is something that many mental health practitioners as well as legal professionals are concerned about (Gunn, 1998). In part this is because the National Health Service in the UK has not been a particularly safe or containing place in which to learn about management of these difficult individuals. The development of the concept of psychopathy, for example, has suggested that this may be a clinical disorder for which a treatment could be developed. Similarly, the concept of a sadistic personality disorder was mooted in one version of an influential classification system, but subsequently left out of the current DSM-IV classification, in part because of concerns that the discourse of psychiatry should not intrude inappropriately in the moral framework of the law (Pincus et al., 1992).

Chapter 3 will focus on assessment issues. There have historically been serious problems in the reliability and validity of assessing personality disorder. In the context of individuals engaging voluntarily in treatment this is less of a problem than the potential situation where individuals are 'labelled' and detained on the basis of a diagnosis of personality disorder.

It could be argued that one of the political factors influencing the new proposals and legislation is aimed at controlling particularly dangerous offenders under the umbrella of a medical disorder that legitimates preventative detention. Whilst the criminal justice system has always been able to detain, or easily recall to prison, certain subgroups of offenders (e.g. life-sentenced prisoners), there has, until recently, been some reluctance to extend the provision to wider groups of offenders on the basis of their presumed dangerousness. The notion of 'just deserts' has held sway for many years in penal policy, and this argues against locking people up for crimes they might commit in the future. Furthermore the European Convention on Human Rights legislation which came into force in 2000 also sets limits on the circumstances in which liberty can be taken away (Article 5). One of these is the 'lawful detention of persons of unsound mind'. By medicalising certain offenders, the UK government may feel the Human Rights legislation can be circumvented, and that preventative detention is more ethical in supposedly humane settings such as hospitals rather than in prisons. As Maden et al. (2004) note, however, indefinite detention in hospital is an expensive option to manage risk.

The problems with preventative detention have been further highlighted by arguments suggesting that existing risk assessment tools may often be inaccurate, and in particular generate an excessive number of false positives. These are individuals considered to be dangerous who in fact would not offend if they were given the opportunity.

The statistics around preventative detention were criticised by Buchanan and Leese (2001). They reviewed published reports in which the accuracy of a clinical judgement or a statistically derived rating of dangerousness was validated by its use to predict violent behaviour of adults in the community. Buchanan and Leese went on to calculate the sensitivity and specificity of the procedures used in each study. Using a total of twenty-one studies they deduced that six people would have to be detained to prevent one violent act. They added that in practice the accuracy of the predictions would be even lower given that there are often some differences between the samples used in research and clinical practice and in reality there is often missing information.

As has been noted by many others in relation to base rates and the inherent inaccuracies of risk assessment, Buchanan and Leese (2001) comment:

> there is no value at which predication can be said to be of reasonable accuracy. The decision as to what rate of error should be deemed acceptable from the point of view of preventative detention is ultimately a moral one which will be affected not only by the likely number of mistakes, but by the conditions under which people are to be detained. . . . If those conditions are deemed to be therapeutic, it will presumably be more acceptable and appropriate for mental health professionals to be involved in risk assessment.

Chapter 4 will focus on the issue of treatment and treatability. This has both clinical and medico-legal dimensions. The Mental Health Act 1983 is the current legislation in England and Wales for dealing with mental disorder. The Act recognises four categories of 'mental disorder', one of which is Psychopathic Disorder. This is defined in the Act as:

> A persistent disorder or disability of mind, whether or not accompanied by low intelligence, that results in abnormally aggressive or seriously irresponsible conduct.

In practice this definition is as broad or as narrow as psychiatrists want to make it, and the use of this category has been explicitly tied into the notion of treatability (Berry et al., 1999). The 1959 Mental Health Act did not have an explicit treatability criterion but this was added in the 1983 Act because of concerns that the law would be used for preventative detention where no meaningful treatment could be offered. 'Legal psychopaths' have therefore only been deemed appropriate for transfer to the mental health services if there is some realistic prospect of treating the disorder or at least preventing a further deterioration in its course. It is probably fair to say that psychiatrists have exercised a considerable degree of caution in diagnosing psychopathy, understandably not wanting to be held responsible for the actions of individuals who may be unable or unwilling to address their offending behaviour.

Unhappiness with several aspects of the 1983 Act, including the unique status accorded to psychopathic disorder, has led to proposals for a new Mental Health Act, which has already stalled several times.

The proposed changes to the Mental Health Act represent the first major overhaul of this legislation in nearly fifty years. Although it is not possible here to assess the overarching considerations in the proposals, the Bill includes a number of specific issues in relation to personality disorder (Department of Health website, 2006). It introduces a single definition of 'mental disorder'. This means that personality disordered individuals will no longer be excluded from compulsory treatment on the grounds that they are untreatable, provided they meet the criteria for compulsion. The treatability criterion is also being weakened by replacement with the more general qualification 'and a medical treatment is available'. The Bill will also highlight the need for new community and inpatient services for people with personality disorder.

The Department of Health has addressed a number of what it calls 'common myths' about this legislation. These include the idea that the government needs it to control dangerous personality disordered people, that it creates new powers to detain people who have not committed an offence, and that it effectively removes the treatability criterion for psychopathic disorder in the 1983 Mental Health Act.

In addressing these concerns, the Department of Health suggests that:

- The DSPD programme is proceeding successfully under the 1983 Act, and does not require a change in the law.
- The power to detain people who have not offended, but who are in need of treatment to protect them or others from the harmful effects of their disorder, has been present since the 1959 Act.
- In relation to the treatability criterion, all mentally disordered individuals (and not just those detained under the psychopathic disorder criterion) will have the benefit of a more explicit and individual treatability test.

At the same time as this previous caution and ambivalence in the mental health services, the criminal justice system was pushing ahead in its own attempts to 'treat' offenders. There has been substantial progress in the last ten years in the development of accredited treatment programmes within this system, and in many ways the criminal justice system is clearly ahead of the mental health services (Blud, 2003). In particular, psychological models of offending are now prominent and most of the treatment programmes are based on a cognitive-behavioural orientation. Despite this, it is clear that a significant minority of offenders may be unresponsive or unwilling to engage in such treatment, and it is likely that many of these are personality disordered men who will need a more individually tailored combination of treatment and management, and require particularly close working between relevant agencies in the community.

Chapter 5 addresses the important developments in the criminal justice system and other multi-agency arrangements that have taken place in recent years. The mental health services in reality only deal with a tiny proportion of those individuals committing criminal acts or who could be described as dangerous. The justice system comprising the police, court, prison and probation services is primarily responsible for the detection, arrest, judgment, punishment and rehabilitation of criminals. This system deals with offenders largely without reference to the diagnosis and conceptualisation of personality disorder, although many of the more dangerous offenders are undoubtedly personality disordered by some definition.

There have been a number of legislative changes in the last few years that are particularly relevant to personality disordered offenders. These include the Sex Offenders Act 1997 which introduced registration for the more serious sex offenders convicted post-1997 and also gave more explicit permission for appropriate authorities (usually police) to use disclosure about particular offenders. Although not specifically framed with regard to personality disorder, this legislation began a new wave of thinking more explicitly about risk management in the community.

The Crime and Disorder Act 1998 continued this trend in introducing the Sex Offender Order, a civil order that can be used to control and limit the freedom of movement of sexual offenders deemed to pose an imminent risk of further offences. Applications for the order are made by senior police officers to a magistrates' court, and prohibitions and restriction can be tailor-made for that individual, bearing in mind his previous *modus operandi* and current risk environment.

More recently the Sex Offences Act 2003 updated the 1997 Act and added four new civil orders relevant to sexual offenders, including the Sexual Offences Prevention Orders which replace the previous Sex Offender Order, and the Risk of Sexual Harm Order, which could, for example, be used to stop an adult grooming a child by sending child pornography or indecent text messages by mobile phone.

A key development in the last few years has been the establishment of Multi-Agency Public Protection Arrangements (MAPPA). The most visible aspect of this has been the creation of Multi-Agency Public Protection

Panels (MAPPPs). MAPPPs were established by the Criminal Justice and Court Services Act (2000). Sections 67 and 68 of the Act provide the police and the probation service with a statutory duty to make joint arrangements for the assessment and management of the risks posed by sexual, violent and other potentially dangerous offenders (National Probation Service, 2003). The role of mental health services has been relatively undeveloped, but should include liaison, consultation and advice on the assessment and management of personality disordered offenders for criminal justice agencies via the MAPPP.

One of the ideas underlying the work of MAPPA is the assumption that it is possible to identify a subgroup of individuals who are both highly dangerous and small in number. This group has been referred to as 'the critical few'. The idea that a number of highly prolific offenders are responsible for a disproportionate volume of crime has been influential in criminological circles. It has received empirical support from two primary sources.

First, evidence is cited from longitudinal studies on the career of criminals, one of the most well known of these being the Cambridge Study (Farrington and West, 1990). This comprehensive series of studies, which are still ongoing, tracked the life histories of 400 boys from a defined working-class catchment area in London. Extensive assessments and collateral information were obtained at various points in their development and now extend into the men's fifth decade. The results have indicated that over 50 per cent of the total crimes committed by this group are by about 6 per cent of the group.

The UK Home Office also suggests that 50 per cent of crimes are committed by fewer than 10 per cent of offenders; this group have been designated as Persistent and Prolific Offenders (PPOs). However it is not clear that this group are particularly responsible for the serious violent and sexual offences that are of particular concern at the present time.

Second, the body of research on offenders with high psychopathy scores tends to promote the view that it is empirically possible to identify a subgroup of offenders who are particularly prone to reoffend (Hare, 1991). Not only have these psychopaths been suggested as prolific and particularly damaging in their criminal activity, but there is a strong suggestion that they have biological anomalies in their functioning and are highly refractory to most criminal justice interventions.

The government proposals set out in the DSPD paper may also have wanted to emphasise the idea that they were targeting a very small group of dangerous offenders who were not adequately managed by existing arrangements. They went on to suggest that about 250–300 of these individuals existed at present in the community in England and Wales (Dept. of Health and Home Office, 1999). This group has been dubbed 'the critical few' and should include most of those individuals discussed at the highest level of MAPPP meetings (Level 3). The guidance provided by MAPPA suggests the following criteria for a 'critical few offender' who:

- is assessed under OASys as being high or very high risk of causing serious harm; *and*
- presents risks that can only be managed by a plan which requires close co-operation at a senior level due to the complexity of the case and/or because of the unusual resource commitments the case requires; *or*
- athough not assessed as a high or very high risk, the case is exceptional because of the likelihood of media scrutiny, and/or public interest in the management of the case is very high and there is a need to ensure that public confidence in the criminal justice system is sustained.

It should be noted that these criteria conflate risk with other issues such as inter-agency liaison and media interest. A recent report on the working of MAPPA suggested that there may be a tendency to overinflate risk in some of the Level 3 cases identified, perhaps to attract more immediate resources than was possible at Level 2 (Home Office, 2005a).

Chapter 6 will aim to provide more practical illustrations of how psychological models can inform working with different types of personality presentation. Being psychologists, our approach and emphasis are on a psychological model of community management. This means recognising how the individual personality may respond differently to different kinds of intervention, including treatment, supervision, environmental manipulation, etc. It also means being aware of how different types of offenders affect both individual professionals and local agencies, with an understanding of the central role of managing the anxiety created by the offender.

In reviewing the evidence-base for intervention with this population, one is struck by the paucity of well controlled studies. It would seem the evidence-base for addressing antisocial and psychopathic offenders in the UK has moved on little between the Dolan and Coid review in 1993 and the Warren *et al.* review in 2001. Our approach has therefore been to cite empirical evidence where available, but to also develop theoretically driven ideas about intervention which could be effective, based on our current understanding of different disorders. At the very least this should aid in the making of defensible decisions – no small achievement in a context where many professionals are anxious about taking responsibility for these individuals.

Chapter 7 will briefly review the development of the current pilot projects in the community to date. The current range of pilot projects attempts to address many of the tensions and uncertainties described above, and followed consultation among experts and other relevant service providers. This will ultimately lead on to a discussion of what it means to provide a community PDO (personality disordered offender) service.

What may be neglected in any focus on dangerous individuals or specialist services is a consideration of the relevance of how community factors may either escalate or protect against violent and abusive behaviour. Indeed later in the book we will highlight environmental planning as an important strategy when weighing up the management options in any given case. Some authors would suggest that the management of a few high risk individuals through the surveillance/control model is fundamentally misguided and represents an attempt by society and communities to ignore and disown social factors that promote offending. In line with this view, some authors (e.g. Twemlow and Sacco, 1996) have described interventions at the level of whole communities, and these interventions could be seen to also represent an attempt to address the situational determinants of violent behaviour. One of the few interventions at the level of communities that has been debated is the controversial issue of community notification of sex offenders. This happens in the United States but not in the UK except in exceptional circumstances (Craissati, 2003; Fitch, 2006).

In the context of the inner-city environments we work in, we are struck by the importance of a range of community factors that come up on a regular basis in MAPPA discussions and provide an important context to risk management decisions. These include:

1   The presence of gang-related crime, particularly the patterns of robbery, substance misuse and sexually coercive behaviour towards young women.
2   The availability of and crime associated with street drugs.
3   The lack of appropriate housing provision for dangerous offenders.
4   The multi-ethnic composition of many inner-city boroughs.
5   The way deprived housing estates foster the development of antisocial personality traits.
6   The increasing availability of lethal weapons including knives and guns.

Other relevant factors at this level identified by Twemlow and Sacco (1996) may include the perception of the police by the community, the role of the media, and local levels of socio-economic deprivation. Although we try to embrace the relevance of these situations and community factors in one of the management strategies we identify, we feel that this is an area which deserves much wider consideration in the context of multi-agency panels where the focus tends to be very much on the individual rather than the neighbourhood.

Chapter 2

Theory

Introduction

The aims of this chapter are to highlight a number of conceptual and theoretical issues in relation to personality disordered offenders. This covers issues of definition, classification, epidemiology and causal origins. Models that draw together the potential links between personality disorder and offending are then described. A number of useful typologies and motivational models are outlined.

Definition of personality

Whilst many definitions of personality could be given, one that highlights both the form and content of the concept is that of Livesley:

> Personality refers to regularities and consistencies in behaviour and forms of experience. These enduring features are usually described in terms of traits that vary across individuals such as dependency, suspiciousness and impulsiveness. They also agree that personality is not just a collection of traits; instead most approaches emphasise the integrated and organised nature of personality. . . . Hence a central task for personality research is to explain this coherence and organisation of personality and describe the means by which people forge a coherent sense of self that gives direction and meaning to their lives from the diversity of their experiences.
>
> (Livesley, 2001)

Most attempts at definition highlight the need to be clear about whether one is talking about symptoms (e.g. hallucinations, low mood), behaviour (e.g. aggression to others, deliberate self-harm) or traits (lack of empathy, suspiciousness, dependency). It can be seen from the criteria used in many of the psychiatric categorical systems (DSM/ICD) that there is often a mixture of these different clinical concepts. As a result, some authors

(Kernberg, 1984; Millon and Davis, 1996) suggest that there should be greater attempts to delineate the traits, and that this is really what is meant by personality. The difficulty, of course, is that traits are more difficult to observe, and involve a level of inference beyond both symptoms and behaviour. Consequently the reliability is lower for traits.

Normal and abnormal personality

The relationship between normal and abnormal personality is an important theoretical as well as clinical issue, and relates to the arguments about the relative merits of categorical versus dimensional approaches discussed later in this chapter. It is a fact of everyday experience, backed up by psycho-metric measurement, that normal individuals vary in important personality traits. Researchers have differed as to how such a classification system should be constructed, but there is now at least some convergence on the major overarching dimensions of normal personality. Implicit in these systems is the idea that a comprehensive set of traits can be identified that is valid across cultures, although there may be some cultural variation in the expression and behavioural manifestation of these traits.

There are broadly two lines of enquiry that influence classification and diagnosis. The first comes from the clinical tradition of trying to identify important personality types seen in clinical practice. These have evolved unsystematically over the years and have been based on different theoretical conceptualisations and clinical orientations. The other paradigm has been the psychometrically based study of personality dimensions by academic psychologists. Their approach has been more atheoretical, but is often based on lexical analysis of words used in different languages to describe personality traits, as well as assumptions about the ultimate continuity between normal and abnormal personality. Several authors have made attempts to map one system onto the other, and locate the clinical disorders along dimensions of normal personality.

What is a personality disorder?

The above discussion about normal and abnormal personality is naturally relevant to the definition and conceptualisation of personality disorder. Personality disorders are chronic conditions which become manifest in late adolescence and early adulthood. They refer to patterns of perceiving, thinking and relating to others that are considered rigid and maladaptive. They are considered to be clinical conditions with diagnostic criteria in the same way as other mental disorders such as schizophrenia or anxiety. They are included in the international systems of psychiatric classification such as the International Classification of Diseases (now in version 10) and the Diagnostic and Statistical Manual (now in version 4).

The American Psychiatric Association defines personality disorder as 'an enduring pattern of inner experience and behaviour that deviates markedly from expectations of the individual's culture, is pervasive and inflexible, has an onset in adolescence or early adulthood, is stable over time and leads to distress or impairment' (APA, 1987).

The International Classification of Diseases (ICD-10) system highlights that the personality deviation must be manifest in one or more areas of:

1   Cognition
2   Affectivity
3   Impulse control
4   Relating to others

- The deviation must be pervasive in the sense of manifesting itself as behaviour that is inflexible, maladaptive, or otherwise dysfunctional across a broad range of personal and social situations.
- There must be personal distress or adverse impact on the social environment, or both, clearly attributable to the deviation.
- There must be evidence that the deviation is stable and of long duration, having its onset in late childhood or adolescence.
- The deviation cannot be explained as a manifestation or consequence of other adult mental disorders.
- Organic brain disease, injury, or gross dysfunction must be excluded as a possible cause.

Classification systems for personality disorder

Before introducing the main classification systems relevant to personality disorder, the reader should be aware of the broad distinction between categorical and dimensional models of classification.

Categorical vs. dimensional models

Diagnosing abnormal personality has presented many challenges for clinicians and researchers alike. The diagnosis of problematic personality traits is inherently difficult compared with other diagnostic decisions. This is because diagnosis is not based on symptom clusters linked to discrete episodes of abnormality. More importantly, abnormality is not judged against previously normal functioning or against criteria such as recency, frequency and duration, as is the case in Axis I mental illness diagnosis.

Rivalry between categorical and dimensional models of personality disorder has been prominent in the research literature. The categorical model, based largely on clinical psychiatry, has held sway partly because of its practical value to clinicians. Despite its imperfections it remains useful in planning treatment and management. The categories have, however, been criticised on a number of grounds.

First, as Saulsman and Page (2003) suggest, the categorical system has translated problematic personality traits into discrete symptomatology, as indicated by the behavioural criteria commonly used to make diagnoses. This has achieved diagnostic reliability at the expense of validity. Defining the core of the psychopathology, i.e. the abnormal personality traits, has been avoided.

Second, by allowing numerous combinations of these same behavioural criteria to characterise the same disorder, the system accommodates heterogeneity into the classification process rather than minimising it. Third, arbitrary cut-off scores are used to classify the disorder. Fourth, categorical approaches waste some of the information in the profile that dimensional scores do not.

There is also the more fundamental issue as to whether disordered personality should be conceptualised as a qualitative distinction captured by distinct categories of personality, or as a quantitative distinction captured by continua of functioning reflecting normality through to abnormality.

Before progressing to the main examples of scientific classification, it is worth noting the anomaly of the current medico-legal definition of personality (psychopathic) disorder. The Mental Health Act 1983 category of Psychopathic Disorder is not really a clinical diagnosis based on personality traits but an administrative label allowing considerable discretion and flexibility to the individual clinician (psychiatrist).

It is defined as:

> A persistent disorder or disability of mind, whether or not accompanied by low intelligence, that results in abnormally aggressive or seriously irresponsible conduct.

Studies by Blackburn (1975) and Coid (1992) indicate that a heterogeneous group of individuals have been detained in UK secure hospitals over the years and it is likely that all sorts of individual case factors were involved in these decisions in addition to the issue of treatability (Berry et al., 1999).

The legal category of Psychopathic Disorder has often been criticised as simply being an administrative label without any clinical substance which has contributed to the mystification of personality disordered offenders. There has also been increasing reluctance on the part of psychiatrists to use the label and detain individuals on this basis, as evidenced by the declining numbers of legal psychopaths in special hospitals and the almost insignificant level of civil admissions under this category. However, thanks to the work of Coid and Blackburn, we now know something about what differentiates these admissions from those who remain in the criminal justice system – i.e. more evidence of borderline pathology.

Table 2.1 Eysenck's personality traits

Psychoticism (P)	Aggressive Antisocial	Egocentric Unempathic	Impersonal Creative	Impulsive Tough-minded	Cold
Extraversion (E)	Sociable	Carefree	Sensation-seeking	Assertive	Lively
	Dominant	Venturesome	Active	Surgent	
Neuroticism (N)	Low self-esteem	Guilt feelings	Emotional	Irrational	Moody
	Depressed	Anxious	Tense	Shy	

Dimensional models

Dimensional models have often been developed from a combination of historical ideas about normal personality types, lexical analysis of how language is used to describe personality traits, and the psychometric analysis of questionnaires given to normal rather than clinical or forensic populations. As well as potentially being more comprehensive in their coverage of personality traits, they may avoid some of the sensitivities that psychiatric (categorical) systems have to a variety of clinical, forensic, professional, international and public health issues (Widiger and Trull, 1994).

(1) Eysenck's model

Many dimensional models of normal personality are still traceable to Eysenck's influential model proposing three independent factors of normal personality (see Table 2.1).

These factors are: Extraversion (E), i.e. the degree to which the individual likes to socialise and experience stimulation; Neuroticism (N), the tendency to experience negative emotion such as anxiety, guilt, or depression; and Psychoticism (P), which, despite its connotations of mental illness, is best understood as tough-mindedness, a certain kind of callousness.

Offenders have been shown to be more likely to score higher on the Psychoticism and Extraversion factors (Eysenck, 1998). There is some evidence that different subtypes of offender may differ on these personality dimensions. For example, violent offenders may differ from sexual offenders in levels of Neuroticism and Extraversion (Gudjonsson and Sigurdsson, 2000).

(2) Five-factor model

The five-factor model (Costa and McCrae, 1992) has been proposed as a potential solution to the problems of categorical approaches. The model now enjoys a reputation as a comprehensive descriptive model of normal personality. The five factors include the Extraversion and Neuroticism of the Eysenck model, but the Psychoticism factor is replaced by three factors labelled Agreeableness, Openness to Experience and Conscientiousness. Extraversion and Neuroticism refer to similar constructs to those in the Eysenck model. Agreeableness refers to a general tendency to get along with others. Openness means a willingness to embrace new ideas, experiences, etc.; and Conscientiousness refers to a tendency to be dutiful, competent, persistent, and motivated to control one's impulses.

The initial derivation of the five-factor model was based on the rationale that the most important and fundamental traits of personality would be identified through an empirical (lexical) analysis of the natural language (Widiger and Trull, 1994). Many such lexical analyses have been conducted and the findings have consistently supported the five-factor model (Digman, 1990).

A large body of evidence is now accumulating studying the relationship between the five factors of the model and the traditional personality disorders used by clinicians. In relation to offenders, Widiger (1994) found that antisocial personality disorder was associated with low scores on Agreeablenesss, Neuroticism and Conscientiousness. It is suggested by Widiger and Trull (1994) that the range of facets within the five-factor model may tease out different combinations of risk factors of violence and other criminal behaviour, in a way that is not possible in the current psychiatric systems.

Further studies of the five-factor model have also shown that there are small declines in Neuroticism (N), Extraversion (E) and Openness (O), and small increases in Agreeableness (A) and Conscientiousness (C) as individuals age from 20 to 40, but that there is little change thereafter. In other words, over the third and fourth decades, individuals improve in their psychological adjustment by developing more social concerns and increasing their sense of responsibility, although they also become less sociable and more rigid (Duggan, 2004).

(3) Blackburn's model

This model is included in view of its special reference to forensic populations. Blackburn (1975) profiled a sample of seventy-nine men detained in English maximum security (special) hospitals under the legal category of Psychopathic Disorder, using the MMPI. Cluster analysis revealed four profiles. Two of the types showed a high frequency of violent behaviour and were impulsive, under-socialised and aggressive. They differed on dimensions of anxiety, guilt and social withdrawal. Blackburn referred to them as primary and secondary psychopaths. By contrast, the two other groups showed low levels of aggressiveness and impulsiveness. They offended infrequently but when they did it was often very serious. Again the two groups differed in terms of social withdrawal and were labelled as 'controlled' and 'inhibited'.

Blackburn went on to look at the DSM clusters of personality pattern that may correlate with his four original groups identified with the MMPI. In the Blackburn and Coid (1999) study, violent male offenders in maximum security hospitals and special units in prison (N = 164) were interviewed with the SCID-II. The technique of cluster analysis of the personality disorder criteria sets identified six diagnostic patterns: (1) antisocial–narcissistic; (2) paranoid–antisocial; (3) borderline–antisocial–passive aggressive; (4) borderline; (5) compulsive–borderline; and (6) schizoid. Offenders in the first three groups had more extensive criminal careers, and most were identified as psychopaths by the PCL-R. Substance misuse was more common in these groups. A history of anxiety and affective symptoms was more common in groups 3 and 5, and a majority of group 2 had a history of psychotic disorder.

Not only does this study highlight the heterogeneity in personality of violent offenders, it also suggests that single DSM categories are less likely to make useful distinctions than recurring patterns of co-varying traits. Blackburn's work is also important in identifying that cluster A and even cluster C personality traits may be associated with dangerous behaviour, something that is not immediately obvious from their defining criteria.

Categorical models

(1) DSM-IV and ICD-10

The system of categorical diagnoses still most commonly used by clinicians is based on the DSM-IV and ICD-10 classification systems (see Table 2.2). These systems have evolved over the last few decades subject to various revisions. They represent the accumulated experience of clinicians, and the range of personality disorders come from a variety of different clinical traditions, for example psychoanalytic (borderline and narcissistic), social learning theory (avoidant), psychiatric (antisocial). The American DSM-IV system has been particularly influential in its advocacy of a multi-axial classification of psychological functioning, where personality disorder is referred to as the Axis II diagnosis.

The DSM-IV system separates personality disorders into three groups or 'clusters'. Cluster A personality disorders focus on odd, eccentric features; cluster B personality disorders focus on dramatic, emotional or erratic features; and cluster C personality disorders focus on anxious or fearful features. The rationale for the clustering is that disorders in cluster may show similar psychological features and tend to present together (Morey, 1991). However, there is often comorbidity across clusters as well. There is

Table 2.2 A comparison of DSM and ICD definitions of personality disorder

DSM-IV diagnosis	ICD-10 diagnosis	Main clinical features
Cluster A		
Paranoid	Paranoid	Distrust and suspiciousness
Schizoid	Schizoid	Detachment from social relations Restricted range of emotional expression
Schizotypal	Schizotypal disorder	Acute discomfort in close relationships, cognitive or perceptual distortions, eccentricities of behaviour
Cluster B		
Antisocial	Dissocial	Disregard for and violation of the rights of others
Borderline	Emotionally unstable, borderline subtype	Instability in interpersonal relationships, instability in self-image, instability in affects and impulsivity
Histrionic	Histrionic	Excessive emotionality and attention-seeking
Narcissistic		Grandiosity, need for admiration, lack of empathy
	Emotionally unstable, impulsive subtype	
Cluster C		
Avoidant	Anxious	Social inhibition, feelings of inadequacy, hypersensitivity to negative evaluation
Dependent	Dependent	Submissive, clinging, excessive need to be taken care of
Obsessive-compulsive	Anankastic	Preoccupation with orderliness, perfectionism, and control
Not otherwise specified	Unspecified or mixed	Meets general criteria for personality disorder but not any of the above specific criteria

some evidence that, in general terms, treatability may vary across clusters, with perhaps cluster C the easiest to treat and cluster A the most difficult (Perry and Bond, 2000). Some theoretical models (e.g. Kernberg, 1984) see the cluster C disorders as based fundamentally on a less disturbed, more 'neurotic' personality organisation.

The most important cluster in terms of forensic populations is cluster B, which includes the antisocial, borderline, histrionic and narcissistic personality disorders. The characteristics of these disorders will be briefly described.

Individuals suffering from antisocial personality disorder (APD or ASPD) display the following symptoms: failure to conform to social norms regarding behaviour, deceitfulness, lying, use of aliases, impulsivity, history of physical violence, reckless disregard for safety, irresponsibility and lack of remorse.

Central features of borderline personality disorder (BPD) include frantic efforts to avoid real or imagined abandonment. These individuals demonstrate unstable and intense interpersonal relationships. In severe cases, they present with identity disturbances and recurrent suicidal gestures and threats. They are affectively unstable, often with wildly vacillating moods. This pattern is not apparent among the mood disorders which generally change over weeks and months. Finally, individuals with BPD have feelings of emptiness and intense anger and can develop stress-related paranoid ideation.

Individuals with histrionic personality disorder (HPD) become uncomfortable if they are the centre of attention. They are inappropriately sexually seductive, with rapidly shifting shallow emotions, and often use their physical appearance, often eroticised, to create attention. They consider relationships to be more intimate than they really are. They are often dramatic in their emotional expression.

The final cluster B disorder is narcissistic personality disorder (NPD). These individuals demonstrate a grandiose sense of self-importance and are preoccupied with fantasies of power, brilliance, beauty and ideal love. They often think they should be treated as 'special'. They require excessive amounts of admiration and are interpersonally exploitative; they lack empathy and are often envious of others.

The other particularly important disorder from a forensic perspective tends to be paranoid personality disorder (PPD) belonging to cluster A. Individuals with PPD are suspicious and mistrustful of others. They have great difficulty trusting others, often read neutral situations as threatening or demeaning towards themselves, and may be suspicious about partner infidelity. Their paranoia often makes them combative, antagonistic, and rigid.

Schizoid personality disorder is also a cluster A disorder. It may have particular relevance for understanding the role of fantasy in personality disordered offenders, something that was highlighted in Chapter 1 as crucial in the assessment and presentation of some of the high profile cases discussed there. In schizoid personalities there may be a very limited interest in real interaction with other people, sitting alongside a well developed fantasy life. It is also thought that some psychopaths are closer to the schizoid personality than the antisocial. One of the most important and interesting theoretical questions is why for some individuals the fantasy life is *compensatory* – i.e. it enables the individual to deal with self-esteem issues without major acting out towards others – and in others it is a *rehearsal* to more dangerous and predatory behaviour.

These pathology-focused systems have frequently been criticised on the basis that coverage (of abnormal personality) is not complete and arbitrary cut-off criteria are used (Livesley, 2001, pp. 60–83). They are also criticised by both Kernberg (1984) and Millon and Davis (1996) for reliance on behavioural criteria rather than underlying traits or personality structure. However, despite attempts to replace them with more dimensional empirical models, they retain their clinical usefulness and focus on pathology rather than health.

(2) Psychopathy

The concept of psychopathic personality has a long history dating back to the label being applied to personality disordered individuals in the early part of the last century. The classic monograph of Cleckley (1976), *The Mask of Sanity*, provided a rich descriptive profile of these individuals who clearly stood out as different from other offenders. It has been the critical work of Hare (1991), however, in developing a psychometric tool to measure the relevant characteristics, which has led to the massive importance of the concept in the personality disorder field in the last twenty-five years.

Psychopathy, according to the Hare framework, can be differentiated from other personality disorders on the basis of its characteristic pattern of interpersonal, affective and behavioural symptoms (Hare, 1991). Interpersonally, psychopaths are grandiose, egocentric, manipulative, dominant, forceful and cold-hearted. Affectively, they display shallow and labile emotions, they are unable to form long-lasting bonds to people, principles or emotions, and they are lacking in empathy, anxiety, and genuine guilt or remorse. Behaviourally, psychopaths are impulsive and sensation-seeking, and tend to violate social norms: the most obvious expressions of these predispositions involve criminality, substance misuse, and a failure to fulfil social obligations and responsibilities. A more active, aggressive subtype and a more passive, parasitic subtype were described by Henderson (1939):

Robert Hare's first experience with a psychopath

Hare received his master's degree in Psychology in the early 1960's and before he could continue with his PhD, he needed to work for a while. Thus he became the sole psychologist for the British Columbia Penitentiary, a maximum security prison near Vancouver. He had no particular training in this area or any keen interest in criminology and to his chagrin the prison gave him no introduction to his duties. 'I started work completely cold' he writes in 'Without Conscience.' He had to feel his way and make the most of it.

Some of the prisoners soon spotted his naivety, and they took subtle advantage of it by doing things like making him a prison uniform that did not quite fit and asking for unauthorised favours. The first prisoner to do this was a man called 'Ray.' This inmate, who possessed an intense and direct manner, came into Hare's office with an issue that he had to discuss. He then pulled out a knife, startling Hare, but he said that he was going to use it on another inmate.

This declaration immediately placed Hare in a bind. If he ratted, the word would get around that he couldn't be trusted; if he didn't, he violated the prison rules. In other words, in that moment, he had lost his standing in one of the areas. When he did not report the incident, he realised that he had been caught in Ray's clever trap. Ray needed this new psychologist who was a soft touch and his manipulations continued.

Hare remained at the prison for 8 months, and during that time, Ray plagued him with requests for favours, offering reasons which generally turned out to be lies. 'He lied endlessly about everything and it disturbed him not a wit, whenever I pointed something out in his file that contradicted one of his lies.' Whenever Hare resisted him, Ray turned nasty. It wasn't easy to know what to do with this man.

This was Hare's first extended encounter with what he would later realise was a psychopath and it didn't stop there. Leaving the prison to return to the university to work on his doctoral degree, he eventually began to do research on his dissertation. That's when he came across publications that described the kind of person that Ray clearly was: a psychopath. Still Hare did not make the connection, at least not then. After finishing his degree and getting a teaching position in the University of British Columbia, Hare was seated at the pre-registration desk when he heard a familiar voice. It was Ray. The former inmate now standing in line with the other students was bragging about how he had been Hare's assistant and confidant at the prison, especially on difficult cases. Hare was astonished so he confronted the impostor. To his further amazement Ray never broke his stride, he greeted Hare and smoothly steered the conversation in a new direction.

Hare later wondered just what it was in this man's psychological makeup which allowed him to so effortlessly engage in manipulation without any pangs of conscience or embarrassment. It wasn't long before he was fully engaged in studying that very personality type and it was to become his lifelong preoccupation. There were many more people both in prison and outside.

(www.crimelibrary.com/criminal_mind/psychology/robert_hare)

It should be noted that PCL-R psychopathy stands outside the current psychiatric classification systems of DSM and ICD. It is considered by some experts to be a 'superordinate' diagnosis that may comprise elements of several cluster B disorders. Other authors, however, view it essentially as a highly disordered dangerous subtype of antisocial personality disorder.

Menninger and Mayman (1956) distinguish between psychopathy and sociopathy, and refer to identification with an antisocial peer group in the latter and the complete absence of values and identification in the former. This is also roughly the same distinction between severe and moderate psychopathy or between primary and secondary psychopathy. Psychodynamic formulations of the psychopathic personality have been put forward by Kernberg (1984) and Meloy (1988). Most experts believe there is a biological basis to primary psychopathy (Blair, 2005).

Today, psychopathy enjoys a pre-eminent status among criminological researchers as the most ominous and important personality type to identify in criminal populations. High psychopathy levels predict increases in quantity and variety of offences committed (Hare and Jutai, 1983), frequency of violent offences (Hare and McPherson, 1984), reoffence rates (Hare et al., 1988), poor treatment response (Ogloff et al., 1990; Rice et al., 1992) and institutional misbehaviour (Gacono et al., 1997). These findings remain stable even when culture, gender and the presence or absence of a major mental disorder are controlled (Cooke et al., 1998).

The concept has, however, been criticised by a number of authors. Some criticism relates to the suggestion that PCL-R psychopathy is not as accurate as other instruments in predicting future risk, and that its usefulness in this context has been overstated (Freedman, 2001). Blackburn (1997) and Gunn (1998) have both criticised the concept as conflating a series of personality traits and characteristics that are important in their own right, in a way that actually obscures understanding and the potential to develop effective interventions. Gunn (1998) has also made the case that the concept is in danger of confusing the moral perspective with the psychiatric approach and inevitably invites rejection of these individuals on the part of clinicians. Finally, there remains the concern that such offenders are deemed exonerated by suffering from this clinical condition. That was the fate of the sadistic personality disorder, as discussed in Chapter 1. Hare (1998) himself recognises that, from the point of view of the criminal justice system, the presence of psychopathy should be seen as an aggravating factor, and that any attempt to cast it as a mitigating factor would, as a corollary, require long-term civil detention to manage the risk.

Epidemiology

Introduction

It is vital to know something of the epidemiology of personality disorder if new services are being developed, and the relative abnormality of any individual presentation is to be gauged. Surveys demonstrate that personality disorder is a highly prevalent form of mental disorder which affects a significant subgroup of the general population and the majority of individuals in prison. The following data illustrate the important influence that different clinical and criminal justice settings have on prevalence rates.

True prevalence (community) studies

There have been several studies, mainly in North America, providing data on the prevalence of personality disorder. Nestadt *et al.* (1992) reported the results of a follow-up assessment for personality disorders in the Epidemiological Catchment Area (ECA) study, in a series of reports. They reported a prevalence of 5.9 per cent for a definite diagnosis of personality disorder in different US sites, and a prevalence of 9.3 per cent for their combined 'definite' plus 'provisional' diagnostic categories. Casey and Tyrer (1986) found a prevalence of 13 per cent of personality disorder in a smaller community sample, and Reich *et al.* (1989) found a prevalence of 11 per cent using a self-report instrument in a postal survey. Maier *et al.* (1992) estimated a prevalence of 10.0 per cent in a sample from Germany.

There is some evidence that in general population samples cluster C personality disorders (anxious) form the majority of diagnoses, compared with cluster B in hospital-treated subjects (Kantojarvi *et al.*, 2004).

General psychiatric services

General psychiatric service populations are also thought to have significant numbers of personality disordered individuals in their caseloads, although a distinction needs to be made between cases with a comorbid Axis I disorder (e.g. schizophrenia), which may be the primary treatment focus, and pure Axis II presentations. Ranger *et al.* (2004) approached patients on the register of an assertive outreach team and asked them to give informed consent for an informant interview with their principal worker to determine their personality status, using the informant-rated ICD-10 version of the Personality Assessment Schedule (PAS). Of the 73 patients, 62 of whom had a psychotic diagnosis, 67 (92 per cent) had at least one personality disorder, with 36 (51 per cent) having a complex or severe personality disorder.

Secure psychiatric services

Although there is increasing information on personality disorder among patients detained in secure forensic psychiatric facilities, few studies have used research diagnostic instruments. Coid (1992) used the SCID-II to survey female patients detained under the legal category of Psychopathic Disorder in three special hospitals between 1984 and 1987, and male patients under the same legal category in Broadmoor Hospital between 1984 and 1986.

Legally detained individuals with a psychopathic disorder contrasted with prisoners in that in both males and females borderline personality was the most prevalent of all Axis II disorders, compared with antisocial personality disorder in prisoners. There was a higher prevalence of narcissistic personality disorder and conditions such as schizotypal and histrionic disorders, which had a low prevalence in the prison sample.

Rates of personality disorder are thought to be particularly high among women in secure psychiatric settings. This observation is thought likely to reflect the fact that thresholds for admission into secure care for personality disorder are comparatively high, and women who are admitted with this diagnosis are more likely to be defined as needing high levels of security. However, Coid (1992) examined women detained in English high secure hospitals under the Mental Health Act (1983) classification of psychopathic disorder. While 97 per cent met the criteria for one or more category of DSM-III personality disorder, the same proportion also met the criteria for one or more lifetime Axis I (psychiatric) disorder, mainly depression, suggesting that high levels of comorbidity might at the very least hinder the clear appraisal of personality disorder symptoms, leading inevitably to multiple diagnoses (see also Mulder *et al.*, 1994).

Prison populations

The recent survey of psychiatric morbidity among prisoners in the UK provides a representative picture of a full range of Axis II disorders. The Office for National Statistics (Singleton *et al.*, 1998) conducted a major study of prisoners in all prisons in England and Wales. A sample of over 30,000 prisoners was interviewed by lay interviewers who administered a screening version of the SCID-II interview. A one in six subsample was then randomly selected for re-interview by trained clinicians using the SCID-II. Antisocial personality disorder demonstrated the highest prevalence of any category: 63 per cent of male remanded prisoners, 49 per cent of sentenced prisoners and 31 per cent of female prisoners. Paranoid personality disorder was the second most prevalent condition: 29 per cent of male remand prisoners, 20 per cent of male sentenced prisoners and 16 per cent of female prisoners.

Singleton *et al.* (1998) reported that personality disorder was diagnosed (using the Structured Clinical Interview for DSM-IV Axis II personality disorders) in 50 per cent of female prisoners in England and Wales, compared with 78 per cent of male remand and 64 per cent of male sentenced prisoners. Antisocial personality disorder was the most commonly diagnosed personality disorder, followed by borderline personality disorder in women and paranoid personality disorder in men. These prevalence estimates for personality disorder diagnoses in UK samples of imprisoned women are comparable with those reported in American studies (e.g.

Gacono and Meloy, 1994), although smaller prevalence rates – nearer 20 to 30 per cent – have been reported by researchers on both sides of the Atlantic (e.g. Daniel *et al.*, 1988; Maden *et al.*, 1994).

Correlates of having a personality disorder (PD) diagnosis

Having a personality disorder diagnosis is, by definition, associated with various problems of adjustment in the important domains of relationship, occupational, psychiatric and residential functioning. Although an individual's level of functioning is often described with a single indicator such as the Global Assessment Scale, it is important to recognise that this is a simplification and also that individuals with the same diagnosis may show a considerable spectrum of ability.

Jackson and Burgess (2004) generated a random sample of households in Australia and 10,641 individuals were interviewed, a response rate of 78 per cent. Each interviewee was asked fifty-nine questions indexing specific ICD-10 PD criteria. Analyses identified that some specific PDs, notably borderline PD, were more strongly associated with having one or more Axis I conditions, greater mental disability and lost days of total and partial role functioning than was having NO PD, and that others, notably anankastic PD (obsessive-compulsive PD), were less likely to be associated with the same variables. Some specific PDs, again most notably borderline PD, were more associated, while others, again most notably anankastic PD, were less associated with having sought mental health consultations from GPs, psychiatrists and psychologists. By contrast, PD associations with gender, physical disability, physical conditions and general health consultations were weaker.

Another recent study (Cramer *et al.*, 2003), this time in Norway, pooled data from twelve previous community studies of the prevalence of personality disorders. A number of socio-demographic variables were related to PD: first and foremost living alone, and living in the centre of the city. Lower education was also related to a number of PDs, whilst gender and age were related to different groups of personality disorder. An investigation of the relationship between quality of life and dysfunction on the one hand, and number of criteria fulfilled for different PDs on the other hand, displayed a perfect linear relationship.

Morbidity/trajectory of personality disorders

Assumptions about the natural history of personality disorders are inherent in their broad description. ICD-10 diagnostic guidelines refer to abnormal behaviour patterns which are 'enduring' and which appear during childhood or adolescence and continue into adulthood (Moran, 1999). In relation to natural history and outcome of personality disorders, Stone (2001) suggests that these divide into two broad groups:

> one that relates primarily to fairly well-functioning persons who if they seek psychiatric help at all, do so within the confines of private offices or outpatient clinics and a sicker group of individuals who sometimes require institutional (including forensic hospital) care.
>
> The former group include mainly inhibited persons of the sort who may be likely to be treated by psychoanalysts and by practitioners of verbal psychotherapy. This group included the majority of avoidant, compulsive, dependent, hysteric and masochistic persons belonging at least in spirit to DSM's anxious Cluster C. The more dysfunctional personality disordered patients often exhibit either uninhibited personality styles (e.g. antisocial, psychopathic, sadistic) or else the socially awkward styles of DSM's eccentric Cluster A disorders.

There has been a prevalent and perhaps optimistic view that many individuals with maladaptive personality traits improve in middle age and the second half of their lives. This has been primarily studied in relation to borderline and antisocial personality disorder.

Stone (1990) has been an influential figure in suggesting that there is actually quite a spectrum of outcome in borderline patients and that this is influenced by important comorbidities (such as antisocial traits, substance misuse) and other heterogeneous individual factors including physical attractiveness and personal talents. There may thus be quite a broad range of outcomes associated with any individual personality disorder.

The question of trajectory in antisocial personality disorder has been of particular interest to criminologists. Moran (1999) notes that 'the available evidence does not entirely support the burn-out hypothesis, although neither does it entirely refute it'. One of the most influential (and relatively sparse) studies, by Black *et al.* (1995), indicated that 42 per cent of a sample of seventy-one antisocial men were unimproved at twenty-nine-year follow-up. The core personality traits associated with the Hare conception of psychopathic personality also seem to be refractory, with PCL-R factor 1 scores showing less diminution than factor 2 (Harpur and Hare, 1994). In writing about one of his follow-up cases, Black commented:

> Russ is a testament to what can happen when an antisocial finds the support – both internal and external – necessary to change his life. Though still relatively young at follow-up, Russ was one of the men in my study who showed considerable progress. . . . A combination of factors including health problems, a stable relationship and recovery from alcoholism likely contributed to his improvement. . . . Ultimately

change for Russ seemed to come from within, perhaps at a fortuitous time when he was poised for progress. The blend of personal motivation and circumstance is essential to any discussion of ASPD treatment since there are no proven methods for overcoming the disorder.

(Black, 1999, pp. 126–127)

Do psychopaths really get any better when they are older?

Robert Hare notes that:

> we look at the twenty items in the PCL-R and the scores are a function of the age at which offenders were assessed, and what we find, quite dramatically, is that across the age span, from adolescence to 50–55, there are no appreciable changes in interpersonal and affective characteristics of psychopathy, like egocentricity and lack of empathy. We also find that social deviant behaviour, such as impulsivity, the need for stimulation, and irresponsibility, actually do decrease with age. So we have about 7–8 PCL-R features of psychopathy that are capable of changing with age. There may be a biological basis for these changes.
> (www.crimelibrary.com/criminal_mind/psychology/robert_hare)

For example, as testosterone levels go down with age, aggressiveness may also decrease. We can take features that change with age and use them to speed up the progress. We know we are not going to instil in a psychopath the sense of empathy or a strengthened conscience but we can possibly work with characteristics related to their social behaviour, such as impulsivity, stimulation, and irresponsibility.

In addition, Hare believes that appeals to their self-interest can be successful and make use of the best available cognitive-behavioural programmes. Yet this requires very active participation:

> you say to them, most people think with their hearts, not with their heads and your problem is you think too much with your head. So let's change the problem into an asset. They understand that, they say 'Oh Yer too rational like Spock on Star Trek.'

Origins of personality disorder

There are many theoretical models as to the origins of personality disturbance. However, there is a broad consensus that a 'biopsychosocial' model is appropriate (Paris, 1996). In this framework, it is important to consider interactions between biologically based vulnerabilities, early experiences

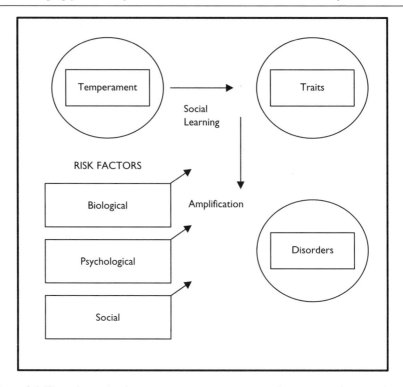

Figure 2.1 The relationship between temperament, personality traits, and personality disorders. From Paris, J. (1996). *Social Factors in the Personality Disorders*. Cambridge, UK: Cambridge University Press. Copyright © 1996 Cambridge University Press. Used with permission.

with significant others, and the role of social factors in buffering or intensifying pathological personality traits (see Figure 2.1). A number of specific models could be described for individual disorders, but we have chosen to focus on some examples of how interactions between factors might set the scene for the development of disorders. Our emphasis here has not been to be theoretically rigorous or comprehensive, but more to give basic examples of the kinds of interactive models that can be developed.

(1) Genetic/biological vulnerability

There is considerable evidence that personality traits are heritable. First, the broad personality dimensions are valid in all cultures all over the world (Eysenck, 1990). Second, some personality traits are associated with specific biochemical markers, either blood groups (Eysenck, 1990) or variations in levels of neurochemical activity (Siever and Davis, 1991). For example, there is evidence that the personality trait of impulsivity is modulated by low levels of the brain neurotransmitter serotonin (Siever and Davis, 1991). Third, there is evidence that even infants vary in basic behavioural dispositions such as activity, sociability and emotional reactivity (Thomas and Chess, 1977). Overall, it is suggested about half the total variance in personality trait scores is directly attributable to genetic difference between individuals (Bouchard, 1997).

Paris (1996) is one of a number of authors who propose an interaction between genetically based predispositions and environmental factors. He suggests that it is particularly important for clinicians to recognise the major role that genetics plays in personality traits and, by implication, personality disorder. Two examples relating to different disorders could be given.

Linehan (1993), in the context of borderline personality disorder (BPD), talks about the role of a biologically based vulnerability to emotional instability as a necessary but not sufficient condition for the development of BPD.

Similarly, Lykken (1995), in relation to the development of antisocial personality disorder and psychopathy, suggests that some children are biologically and temperamentally more difficult to socialise because of their temperament. Examples of this may be a child with a relatively fearless or hyperactive temperament who is perhaps constitutionally impulsive, distractible and energetic (Hechtman and Weiss, 1983). Lykken suggests that difficult children will need more competent parenting if they are to be socialised, i.e. develop a non-antisocial pattern of functioning. He suggests there is an interaction between temperament and quality of parenting, and the worse outcomes, for example psychopathy, may result from a combination of a difficult-to-rear child and incompetent parenting.

(2) Attachment experiences

The fundamental premise of attachment theory is the presence of a biologically rooted and species-characteristic attachment behavioural system that brings a child close to its caretaker. A behavioural system includes external, observable behaviour and intraorganismic components (Ainsworth *et al.*, 1978). Attachment theory is a dominant paradigm in child development research, with increasing implications for adult personality functioning. It is not possible to do this rapidly developing field justice here – for a review, see Bartholemew *et al.* (2001).

It is possible to classify children from about 1 year on into a certain attachment pattern – originally one of three patterns denoted by 'Secure', 'Anxious/insecure' and 'Anxious/avoidant'. Further research has identified a fourth 'Disorganised' pattern, although there is some debate as to whether this is a pathological form of the other established patterns rather than a distinct pattern in its own right. There is some evidence for the temporal stability of these patterns and their impact on cognitive development, peer status and interpersonal functioning.

It is a postulate of the model that the childhood attachment pattern crystallises in childhood and may remain relatively stable until there is perhaps an opportunity for cognitive revaluation in adolescence or later. More recently it has been clarified that adults also have a specific internal working model (IWM) of attachment which affects their interpersonal functioning and in general may contribute to their adult personality. The development of assessment tools such as the Adult Attachment Interview (George *et al.*, 1987; Main *et al.*, 1985) has led to the classification of adult patterns, such as 'Autonomous', 'Preoccupied' and 'Dismissing' – categories thought to parallel the childhood versions of Secure, Ambivalent and Avoidant, respectively.

There are theoretical and now empirical reasons to think that these adult attachment styles may map to some extent on the different personality disorders within the categorical models such as DSM-IV. In particular, borderline individuals are more likely to have a Preoccupied pattern, associated with their unstable and at times contradictory attitudes to support and intimacy with others. By contrast, more antisocial individuals would be expected to show a Dismissive pattern characterised by a rejection or minimisation of the importance of affectional relating to others (Frodi *et al.*, 2001).

Crittenden (2000) has gone on to suggest that the categories based on infant patterns are unlikely to do justice to the complexity of adult attachment systems. As individuals develop, they show increasing complexity in their self-protection strategies. For example, infants are unable to selectively inhibit or disguise their feelings in the way older children and adults can. Crittenden has developed an alternative set of categories which may be more applicable to clinical samples, including personality disorders.

(3) Trauma-related models

The role of psychological trauma in the development of adult personality was one of the original cornerstones of Freudian (psychoanalytic) theory. Early analytic thinkers saw traumatic experiences at different points in development as having a key role in the development of particular character traits (Freud, 1916). While many aspects of this theory have been difficult to substantiate, there is evidence that some early traumas are possibly linked to certain personality disorders. This has been most extensively researched in relation to borderline personality disorder (BPD). Individuals with BPD have increased likelihood of being physically or sexually abused as a child (Herman *et al.*, 1989). Whilst some authors such as Paris (1996) suggest that the causal role of such experiences has been exaggerated, there is general recognition that they represent a risk factor in a more complex, multi-factorial explanation of personality disturbance.

Bollas (1995) suggests that in some cases the cumulative impact of traumatic experiences amounts to an 'emotional death' in the individual. Although the individual functions physically, the true authentic self has been effectively annihilated. Bollas (1995) comments that biographical studies of serial killers describe how the individual has experienced the repeated killing of the self throughout his childhood: 'The serial killer – a killed self – seems to go on living by transforming other selves into similarly killed ones, establishing a companion of the dead.' This developmental process may therefore indicate one pathway to the lack of emotional functioning in the psychopath.

Bateman and Fonagy (2004) also make the point that trauma is particularly disruptive in individuals who have had poor attachments. Because they have not developed the capacity for mentalisation, such individuals are largely unable to think about and therefore potentially achieve some distance from the concrete and overwhelming aspects of the traumatic experience.

(4) Social factors

Paris (1996) has suggested that the behavioural expression or pathological amplification of personality traits is influenced not only by early developmental experiences, but also by the current social context and buffers. This includes local factors such as employment, housing, social stability, etc., but also wider societal and cultural factors that may promote social cohesion as opposed to individuality or narcissism (Twemlow and Sacco, 1996). One commonly cited example of this is the apparently low prevalence of antisocial personality in some of the East Asian countries such as Taiwan and Japan (Paris, 1996). It is suggested that this may be related to the strong family cohesion in these cultures, with fathers who are strong and authoritative. Robins (1966), in her classic study of antisocial personality disorder, also found a low incidence in Jewish families, which she attributed to their strong family structure.

Cooke and Michie (1999) have made an interesting comment about socio-cultural factors in the context of psychopathy. Using a mathematical technique called item response theory, they have shown that, in Scotland, psychopaths may present with lower average PCL-R scores than in North America. Although the underlying trait or traits of psychopathy exist in both cultures and are presumed to be essentially genetic, the behavioural expression of the disorder is different and this affects scores on those items of the PCL-R that are scored at a behavioural level.

Outcomes

It is an assumption of the biopsychosocial model that the four types of factor discussed above interact in complex ways in shaping adult personality and its disturbance. In many of the severely personality disordered offenders seen in forensic practice, there is likely to have been a troublesome combination of three or four of these factors. Furthermore the interaction between any pair of factors is likely to be 'bidirectional'. For example, although it is likely that certain biological characteristics predispose an individual child towards relatively secure or insecure attachment (Thomas and Chess, 1977), there is also evidence that attachment experiences affect brain functioning and the activation of important neuropsychological functions such as those underpinning the ability to process emotional cues and experiences (Schore, 2001).

The interaction of these different types of factor means that causal models are likely to be multi-factorial. Further research is needed to establish whether broad groups of risk factors (e.g. biological vulnerability, social milieu) act in an interactive or additive manner. However there are already some interesting findings. Raine (1988), for example, found that children from higher socio-economic groups were less likely to suffer from the environmental risk factors for antisocial behaviour than children of lower socio-economic status. Thus there seems to be a greater biological contribution to the antisocial behaviour of those growing up in less risky environments.

Outcomes from the interaction of these factors include the way certain brain structures and functions are organised, the characteristic underlying cognitive templates for processing information (schemas), and the way that affect and emotion are experienced and managed by the individual.

(1) Brain functioning

The development of more sophisticated functional imaging techniques in recent years allows researchers to look at how different brains use different locations and networks when performing certain tasks. This research has led to the identification of particular brain systems used in certain social and emotional tasks, such as being able to think about emotional states or 'mentalising' (Bateman and Fonagy, 2004).

More pertinent to offending is the identification of the neural circuits underlying different forms of aggression. There is increasing evidence that there are different systems for mediating reactive versus instrumental aggression (see p. 39), which may in turn be differentially associated with different personality disorders (Blair, 2005). In the case of psychopathy, there is increasing evidence that there is a deficit in the way that fear and possibly other emotions are processed (Blair et al., 1997).

(2) Schema organisation

The schema model is conceptually derived from cognitive-behavioural models which see the individual's thinking patterns as of primary importance and shaped around a set of templates for perceiving, filtering and processing social information about the self and others (Young, 1999). Individuals are described as displaying a number of dominant templates or schemas, any of which may become problematic if they are used pervasively and inflexibly. Such schemas are hypothesised to develop in childhood and early adolescence, based on the interaction between innate temperamental factors and interactions with significant others. Schemas are also seen as fundamental in directing interpersonal and other goal-directed behaviour. The concept has obvious links to the attachment concept of 'internalised working models of relationships' and the analytic idea of 'internal object relations'.

Examples of schemas include those of defectiveness, control, rejection, entitlement, etc. Particular personality disorders are likely to be associated with particular schemas. For example, paranoid personality disorder would be expected to be relatively prevalent in those with 'Mistrust' schemas, whilst antisocial and narcissistic personalities would be more associated with 'Entitlement/Grandiosity' schemas.

Case example

Samuel was seen for an assessment at the request of the probation service. He was diagnosed with paranoid personality disorder with prominent antisocial and border-line traits. He had been physically and sexually abused in childhood in the context of poor primary attachments. He had every reason at that time therefore to perceive the world as a dangerous, hostile and unpredictable place. He was placed in a hostel where he perceived almost everyone as 'having a go at me' or 'trying to provoke me'. At the same time it was clear that he brought some negative reactions on himself by threatening others and constantly accusing them of things. This was associated with high levels of anger, rumination about revenge and a sense of justification about his own actions.

In treatment sessions, the psychologist noted that he seemed completely in the grip of this Mistrust schema in the early part of the interview. She had to wait for the affect to subside before Samuel was able to hear anything she said about this or for him to show any capacity for reflectiveness.

In this case it was extremely easy to elicit a very powerful and self-defeating schema which was very understandable in the context of childhood abuse but generated very self-defeating behaviour patterns and interactions as an adult.

The skill is in knowing when the individual may be able to step back for a moment and be receptive to the idea that it is their own belief system and not primarily the external world that is maintaining their problems.

(3) Affect expression and regulation

The way the individual experiences and processes 'affect' (the immediate emotional colouring of any mental experience) is a fundamental characteristic of any individual personality. In a forensic context the way that the individual deals with sexual and aggressive feelings or impulses is of vital importance to consider.

The antisocial, borderline and histrionic disorders of cluster B are known for their 'dramatic' or emotional aspects. For example, borderline personality disorder is characterised by a deficit in regulating or modulating emotion, encompassed in the symptom of 'affective instability'.

By contrast, some of the cluster C disorders, sometimes referred to as the 'inhibited' group, show inhibition or over-control of emotions, such as in obsessive-compulsive and avoidant personalities. Here there is a deficit in accessing emotion spontaneously, which may be related to anxiety or mental conflict about being able to control these feelings.

This is different again from the schizoid personality of cluster A where the affect is described as 'constricted', meaning that there is a narrow range and very muted intensity of emotional experience. This is one of the aspects of cluster A personality disorders that contributes to their perceived 'odd' quality.

Theories of offending and their relevance to personality disorder

It is not possible in a text such as this to cover the range of overarching theoretical models on the causes of violent or sexual offending. In relation to violence the reader is directed to Glasser (1998), Gilligan (1996), de Zulueta (1996) and Berkowitz (1993). In relation to sex offending, helpful overviews are provided by Marshall and Marshall (2000), Ward *et al.* (2005) and Quinsey *et al.* (1998).

However it is helpful here to consider a number of influential typologies of offenders that relate to the personality disorder framework. Many of these models could be described as motivational in the sense of trying to put forward the underlying motive in a particular individual committing a particular offence. In this sense they may address the issue of the functional link between offending and personality disorder. The reader will recall that this was one of the defining criteria for identifying those individuals who may form the proposed DSPD population.

(1) Violence

One of the common clinical and motivational models of violence or aggression is the distinction between reactive or anger-related aggression and instrumental or predatory aggression (Berkowitz, 1993). The former kind of aggression is considered to be driven by the emotional state of anger, itself triggered by experiences of frustration, threat or shame. The aggression is likely to be less agreeable to the individual's value system or 'ego-dystonic'. By contrast, instrumental aggression reflects a learnt and deliberate use of aggression to secure other goals, of status, of immediate material reward or perhaps in the service of other emotional rewards. There is increasing evidence that distinct neural circuits mediate these different forms of aggression and they can be distinguished developmentally (Blair, 2005). In addition, it seems clear that a range of psychiatric conditions are associated with an increased risk of reactive aggression whereas instrumental violence is much more specifically associated with antisocial personality types.

Many instances of violence and aggression may be classifiable into one of these categories, but on close inspection the distinctions are not so simple, and even the same act of aggression may combine elements of both or display a progression from one type of violence to another. It is certainly common to see elements and examples of both in men who are both antisocial and have anger management difficulties. One study, however, found that instrumental offenders could be reliably distinguished from reactive offenders on the basis of violent crime behaviour and psychopathy (Cornell et al., 1996).

Account of a violent incident

I was in Broadmoor for the criminally insane in a dormitory and Gordon Robinson was in the next bed. He was bugging me. I'd hit the fucking idiot once before but I knew that our paths would cross and there he was in the next bed.

My mother and father had just been to see me. I was feeling happy. After the visit I went back to the ward and found Robinson with his key in my locker. The toe-rag was trying to open it. A locker thief! Prison rule by cons, number one – do not steal from other cons. I pushed him away, then I chinned him. But that wasn't enough for me. I wanted to kill him, he deserved to die. He was going to die.

I've got a silver tie that my dad had given me some years ago. My favourite tie. I locked myself in the toilet and tested its strength on the toilet cistern. To my surprise, it held my weight. I decided to strangle Gordon Robinson that very night. I was excited. It was the same buzz I got from doing armed robberies. I walked into the dormitory in my pyjamas with the tie round my waist, out of sight. I climbed into bed and waited.

Robinson's left eye was almost closed from where I punched him earlier. His other eye was alert. I smiled my best smile.

The night patrol nurse looked in every half-an-hour through the observation slit in the door. I only needed a couple of minutes. Fuck the night watchman! There was no saving the thief. I lay still, deep in thought, the tie wrapped around my wrist under the blankets, just waiting. Like a spider waits for the fly. Time was plentiful, I had all night long. This was my night, my fly – I was buzzing. Twelve o'clock, one o'clock, I waited patiently watching every bed, watching every movement. Then it happened, as if I'd sent the thief a telepathic message. He moved. He sat up. He bent over to put his slippers on. He was probably going for a piss.

I leapt out of bed. In a second, the tie was wrapped around his ugly neck. I was strangling the locker thief. It felt magic, it felt right. Surprisingly, there was very little noise – a sigh, a groan at first, but then nothing. I pulled tighter, and leant over to watch.

(quoted in Kray, 2002)

In relation to the diagnosis of personality disorder, there is a natural affinity between reactive aggression and borderline, paranoid and narcissistic personalities. The diagnosis of BPD includes an anger management problem as one of its defining characteristics. The paranoid personality encompasses a distorted preoccupation with threat which can readily predispose to reactive aggression. The narcissistic personality disorder includes the proneness to rage criterion when narcissistic needs are not met.

Whilst both antisocial and psychopathic personalities also show a predilection for reactive aggression, they tend to exhibit instrumental aggression just as easily. This is facilitated by their lack of empathy and seems to be specific to these personality types.

Within anger-related aggression, a further important distinction can be made between under-controlled and over-controlled anger. This was first highlighted by Megargee (1966), and taken up by Blackburn (1975) in his analysis of men detained under Psychopathic Disorder in special hospitals.

Megargee (1966) proposed that under-controlled offenders have weak inhibitions, and are likely to respond aggressively to provocation with some regularity. They are also likely to be identified as impulsive and/or psychopathic personalities.

Over-controlled offenders in contrast have very strong inhibitions and will aggress only when instigation is sufficiently intense to overcome inhibitions. They are therefore expected to attack others rarely but with extreme intensity if they do so. In a series of studies, Blackburn (1975) has shown that over-controlled offenders tend to present as inhibited, controlled and defensive on psychological tests.

Existing models and accounts of dysfunctional low levels of angry experience and/or expression are limited but have been reviewed by Davey *et al.* (2005). There have been several important psychoanalytic attempts to understand the way in which some of these over-controlled personalities may behave in a catastrophically violent manner (Meloy, 1997; Gallwey, 1985; Cartright, 2002; Schlesinger, 1996). These typically emphasise the extent to which the individual has 'split off' his aggressive feelings and impulses from his conscious mental experience. It is often observed that the build-up to the offence involves the following elements:

1   The offender is confronted with a complex interpersonal situation that he seems poorly equipped to deal with.
2   The offender experiences the victim as being overly intrusive or perhaps alternatively abandoning.
3   The offender may then go into a state of acute psychological tension which may manifest itself as an Axis I condition such as anxiety or depression.
4   The offence may be experienced as a massive release of tension and the offender may return to premorbid stability and functioning.

Case example

George was a 42-year-old man working as an IT consultant in a local firm. He had never been involved in an intimate relationship and had a very limited social life. He had never been in trouble with the police and had no history of mental health or substance misuse problems.

A new female colleague joined the firm and over the first few months had several work-related conversations with George. She was a bubbly, extrovert person who was quite friendly with everyone. George found himself feeling increasingly attracted to her and had thoughts that he might want a closer relationship with her. He experienced a mixture of anxiety and excitement about this in a way that made it increasingly difficult for him to sleep and to do his job effectively.

He decided one night to follow the woman home and thought about asking her on a date. He followed her increasingly closely and planned to ask her out there and then in the street. As he caught her up, the woman turned and let out a scream of shock and fear. George assaulted the woman several times and ran off, and when arrested was at a complete loss to explain why he had been so violent.

A final distinction to be aware of within violent offending is that of the organised versus disorganised pattern. This has been particularly important

Table 2.3 Organised versus disorganised offenders

Disorganised	Organised
Below average intelligence	Average to above average intelligence
Unskilled worker	Likely to be a skilled worker
Sexually incompetent	Sexually competent
Father's employment unstable	Father's employment stable
Anxiety during crime	Controlled mood during crime
Minimal situational stress	Precipitating situational stress
Lives/works near crime scene	Mobility, with car in good condition
Socially inadequate	Socially competent
Low in order of birth	High in order of birth
Harsh discipline as a child	Inconsistent childhood discipline
Minimal use of alcohol	Alcohol use associated with crime
Living alone	Living with partner
Minimal interest in news media	Interest in news media reports of crime

in American profiling work relating to serious serial offenders (Ressler *et al.*, 1988). Crime scene analysis will often give important clues as to the relative degree to which the offence was planned and premeditated as opposed to chaotic or opportunistic. For example, the rapist who comes prepared with special equipment, chooses his victim and crime location carefully and appears to enact a stylised fantasy is an organised offender. It would be suggested that this man is relatively high functioning, may be capable of holding down reasonable employment and shows a degree of planning and organisation of his life. On the other hand, the disorganised attacker may lead a much less productive, chaotic life, possibly on the fringe of society or in contact with mental health services. Diagnoses of mental illness or chaotic borderline personality disorder may be relevant. Generally, poor ego functioning is implicated. It is proposed that this distinction is particularly helpful in investigative work where a profile of the offender's lifestyle and functioning may be helpful (Ressler *et al.*, 1988).

(2) Sex offending

Sex offenders can be divided into two broad categories based on their victim group: rapists who offend against adult women (females over the age of 16); and child molesters who offend against children of both genders under 16. In fact the use of the term 'rapist' is misleading as rape may of course be perpetrated on minors. Equally, some sex offenders, for example psychopathic, are versatile and have both adult and child victims.

The distinction is helpful to make as a number of typologies have been devised for each group, which have implications for and connections to personality disorder diagnosis. The most well known of these are the Massachusetts Treatment Centre (MTC) typologies (Knight and Prentky, 1990). Typologies have been developed for both rapists and child molesters.

For example, the MTC: R3 rape taxonomy is based on four primary motivations for the offence: opportunity, pervasive anger, sexual gratification and vindictiveness. The MTC: R3 subdivides men who have committed contact sexual offences against women into nine types as follows.

Types 1 and 2 are opportunistic. The offender has an extensive history of impulsive and antisocial behaviour in multiple domains. The offence is unplanned, impulsive and related to situational factors, and only sufficient force is used to achieve immediate sexual gratification. There does not appear to be a link between the offence and protracted or stylised sexual fantasy or preoccupations. Gratuitous force is not used but the offender is indifferent to the welfare of the victim. Type 1 is an offender with high social competence and Type 2 with low.

Type 3 is pervasively angry. The offender has an extensive history of impulsive, antisocial behaviour in multiple domains with evidence of undifferentiated anger associated with violent behaviour towards both men and women. Highly expressive aggression during the sexual offence may cause serious physical injury to the victim. The offence is not related to sustained sexual fantasy and the violence itself (unlike the sadistic type) does not appear to be eroticised.

Types 4, 5, 6 and 7 are sexual. The key feature is that the offender has protracted sexual fantasies or preoccupations which appear to motivate his sexual offence and influence the way in which the offence is carried out. Type 4 is sadistic overt; the offender has sadistic sexual fantasies, which influence the way the offence is carried out, and features of excessive violence or humiliation during the offence are evident. Type 5 is sadistic muted; protracted sadistic fantasies are present but features of sadism are not acted out behaviourally. Type 6 is non-sadistic; the offender is a man of high social competence with no sadistic fantasies or preoccupations that motivate the assault and his sexual arousal; the assault may be associated with distorted masculine cognitions about women, feelings of inadequacy about his sexuality, and dominance needs. There are low levels of expressive aggression during the offence and the offender may flee in the face of victim resistance. Type 7 is a non-sadistic offender of low social competence; the conditions for type 6 above again apply.

Types 8 and 9 are vindictive. Women appear to be the central and exclusive focus of the offender's anger. There is no undifferentiated anger (e.g. fights with men) and less lifetime impulsivity than that shown by the pervasively angry type. No protracted sexual fantasies or preoccupations motivating offences are evident. The offence may involve degrading behaviour and high levels of violence resulting in victim injury, but physical aggression does not appear to be eroticised. Type 8 is a vindictive offender of high social competence; type 9 is a vindictive offender of moderate social competence.

Although there are no studies directly examining the personality styles associated with these motivations, types 1, 2 and 3 are clearly related to antisocial personalities. It seems possible that types 6 and 7 may be associated with under-assertive and cluster C types, whilst the vindictive features of types 8 and 9 may form part of a paranoid personality structure.

In suggesting these links, we do not wish to go beyond the available evidence, simply to give an example of how a motivational taxonomy such as the MTC: R3 may map onto the classification of personality disorders.

A parallel framework has been proposed for classifying child molesters, based on the variables of fixation, social competence, amount of contact with children, meaning of contact, level of physical injury and degree of sadism (Prentky and Burgess, 2000). Prentky and Burgess took note of the widely influential distinction between fixated and regressed child molesters:

> A fixated offender has from adolescence been sexually attracted primarily or exclusively to significantly younger persons. Sexual involvement with peer-age or older persons where this has occurred, has been situational in nature and never replaced the primary sexual attraction to and preference for underage persons.
>
> In contrast a regressed offender has not exhibited any predominant sexual attraction to significantly younger persons during his sexual development – if any such involvement did occur during adolescence, it was situational or experimental in nature. Instead this individual's socio-sexual interests have focused on peer-age or adult persons primarily or exclusively.
>
> (Prentky and Burgess, 2000)

Whilst there is some support for this distinction from both offending history analysis and psychometric assessment (Beech et al., 1999), the MTC group noted that fixation and level of social competence were potentially independent. There are a number of other problems with the typology. These include the strong sexual response to children shown by some regressed offenders on physiological testing, and the fact that this group also offends outside the family. This taxonomy also maps onto the related but not synonymous distinction between the paedophile and the incest offender.

In terms of personality correlates, there is heterogeneity across both fixated and regressed groups, and it is not obvious that any one personality disorder is more common in either type. There has, however, been a suggestion that the paedophilic (fixated) offender shows some characteristics of the PCL-R psychopath:

> The overt modus operandi is more specialised in the paedophile (i.e. sexual behaviour with a minor) but the deeper aim – to assuage one's inner emptiness by dominating or controlling someone weaker and less

able to manage the situation – seems strikingly similar to the style of the psychopath.

(Dorr, 1998)

More generally paedophilia is often considered a narcissistic disorder in that there is an (unconscious) narcissistic identification with the child victim, although this aspect should not be equated with the narcissistic personality disorder.

(3) Other areas of specific interest

Although there is a large range of specific offences that could be covered here, three are considered that may have particular interest to the issue of personality disorder.

Domestic violence

Investigating psychopathology in male batterers has been considered collusive in some quarters and potentially undermining the prevailing feminist construction of the causes of domestic violence. Despite this, some studies have been attempted, and a heterogeneous range of personalities has been found.

Hamberger and Hastings (1988), for example, found that in men referred to batterer programmes in the US, only 12 of the 99 subjects showed no evidence of personality disorder, but no single abuser personality was found. Three major personality categories among abusers confirmed a previous study by the authors in 1985 indicating that schizoidal/borderline, narcissistic/antisocial and passive dependent/compulsive personality disorders were common. They concluded that the high degree of replication between these studies confirms that psychopathology is demonstrable in male spouse abusers.

There were important implications for such a classification in terms of risk and treatability, with narcissistic and aggressive features on the Millon personality scale indicating poor prognosis (Hamberger and Hastings, 1990). Another recent review found, not surprisingly, that general antisociality, psychopathy, substance misuse and a history of assault/psychological control were the best predictors of recidivism (Hilton and Harris, 2005).

It has to be said that other reviewers such as Gondolf (1998) have looked at similar studies and are less impressed with their relevance to conceptualisation and intervention. Gondolf suggests that, despite suggestions of different types, the vast majority of batterers may be acting out a similar mindset based on an egocentric perspective that holds one's needs and desires as primary and sees their behaviour as 'a righteous crime'.

Stalking

Stalking can be defined as the wilful, malicious and repeated following or harassing of another person which threatens his or her safety. It has attracted a good deal of psychological investigation in recent years. Stalkers are best thought of as a heterogeneous group whose behaviour is motivated by various forms of psychopathology, including psychosis and severe personality disorder (Kamphuis and Emmelkamp, 2000).

There is a need to arrive at a consensus on a typology of stalkers, but studies have typically thrown up about five motivational descriptors: rejected, intimacy-seeking, incompetent, resentful and predatory (Mullen *et al.*, 1999). Personality disorders were noted in Mullen *et al.*'s Australian study to be particularly common among the rejected stalkers. However it is likely that a range of personality traits, such as paranoid, dependent, obsessional and narcissistic, are relevant to different stalkers. In another study involving a follow-up of 148 stalking and harassment offenders court-ordered to mental health evaluation, the strongest predictors of recidivism included the presence of a personality disorder, and in particular a cluster B personality disorder (Rosenfeld, 2003).

Firesetting

There are various typologies of firesetters in the literature. Again, most of these focus on the motivation of the firesetting rather than the underlying personality structure of the offender. Quinsey *et al.* (1998) describe a typology based on the Oak Ridge study. Using cluster analysis they identi-fied four subtypes which were internally homogeneous and clearly distinct from one another. The largest group (33 per cent) were labelled psychotic and the motive for firesetting appeared to be primarily delusional. The second largest group (28 per cent) were labelled 'unassertives'. They had the highest level of premorbid functioning prior to hospitalisation and lowest rates of recidivism. They were the least assertive and resembled the individuals described in other studies as high in over-controlled hostility. They tended to set their fires out of anger or revenge.

The multi-firesetters had the worst childhood histories and came from unstable homes. They were also very under-assertive and tended to have spent long periods in psychiatric hospital even though they were not psychotic. There was some evidence that there were two clusters within this group: one motivated by anger and revenge, and the other by a need for excitement or attention-seeking. They had high levels of recidivism for all crimes.

The fourth group was a smaller group consisting of more traditional criminals. They had extensive criminal histories and poor childhood back-grounds marked by unaccepting, abusive parents. They were most likely to have been diagnosed personality disordered, least likely to have known the victim of the fire, most likely to have set the fire at night, and least likely to have confessed to the fire.

In terms of personality profile, the last group would appear to be a more obvious ASPD group. However the second and third groups are likely to have significant personality pathology. The unassertives may correspond to an avoidant personality type, whilst the third particularly dangerous group may have a combination of borderline, histrionic and narcissistic traits, i.e. cluster B but not ASPD.

Personality disorder and risk

It is clearly possible to find evidence of different personality disorders in offender samples. Looking at the converse proposition, it is helpful to consider what in the definition of different disorders actually contributes to risk. Violent behaviour is in fact a defining feature for the antisocial personality disorder, and an anger management problem a defining feature for borderline personality disorder. However, hostile, antagonistic traits are evident in seven of the DSM-IV disorders (paranoid, antisocial, borderline, histrionic, narcissistic, schizotypal and obsessive-compulsive), whereas complementary traits of agreeableness are prominent in just one – the dependent personality disorder.

Very few studies, however, appear to have been done to try to answer the question as to how common violence or other offending is in different disorders. Even the two most well researched personality disorders (antisocial and borderline) have not been extensively studied in this regard. However, Robins et al. (1991) reported that 85 per cent of the 628 people diagnosed with ASPD in the NIMH Catchment Area Study had a history of unspecified violence. Bland and Orn (1986) suggested, on the basis of an epidemiologic study of randomly selected residents of a large Canadian city, that the diagnosis of ASPD provided a significant risk factor for violent behaviour towards a spouse or child, particularly combined with an alcohol or depressed mood disorder.

In relation to BPD, there are fewer studies. Stone's long-term follow-up of borderline patients suggested that 11 per cent of the BPD patients were victims of parental abuse, and 26 per cent of the abused borderlines were perpetrators of abuse (Stone, 1990). This rate was not significantly higher than for some other diagnostic groups such as schizophrenia and bipolar disorder. It seems more likely that a more general impulsivity is much more common in BPD, but this could be manifest in a range of ways including promiscuity, criminal activity, substance abuse and self-harm.

Outside of the fairly predictable domains of antisocial personality, psychopathy and impulsivity, it is difficult to be confident about the relationship between various personality traits and risk. Even within ASPD,

Table 2.4 Gradations of antisociality (Stone, 2000)

1	Some antisocial personality traits which are insufficient to meet DSM criteria; some antisocial traits occurring in another personality disorder
2	Explosive irritable personality disorder with some antisocial traits
3	Malignant narcissism
4	Antisocial personality disorder with property crimes only
5	Sexual offences without violence (i.e. voyeurism, exhibitionism, frotteurism)
6	Antisocial personality disorder with violent offences (some psychopathic traits may be present but are insufficient to meet Hare's PCL-R criteria (score > 29))
7	Psychopathy without vioence (e.g. con artists, financial scams)
8	Psychopathy with violent crimes
9	Psychopathy with sadistic control (e.g. unlawful imprisonment of a kidnap victim while awaiting ransom)
10	Psychopathy with violent sadism and murder but no prolonged torture
11	Psychopathy with prolonged torture followed by murder

Stone comments that there is little evidence to suggest that the number of antisocial traits diagnosed is correlated with risk (Stone, 2000).

However, Stone (2000) has proposed that there are gradations of anti-sociality (elsewhere he refers to this as gradations of evil). This is an interesting and potentially helpful concept, as a diagnosis of ASPD is so common in offender samples that one needs to be able to identify those subgroups that are capable of particularly severe levels of harm to others.

It can be seen from Table 2.4 that the concept of sadism is included along with other factors such as level of violence and psychopathy. It is likely that there is a significant association between psychopathy and sadism (Holt *et al.*, 1999). Sadism comes in two forms: psychological (repeatedly humiliating and degrading others) and physical (subjecting others to torture). Stone (2000) suggests that either form has a poor prognosis, and it is unclear whether there are biological roots to sadism in those cases where there has been no obvious maltreatment or cruelty inflicted on the individual as a child. Sadistic personality disorder was included in DSM-IIIR but has been taken out in the current DSM-IV, as noted above. Within the very high risk groups now identified by multi-agency panels, it is nevertheless important to identify a potential for sadism and cruelty.

Conclusions

Work with personality disordered offenders requires an understanding of the issues of classification, epidemiology, and the theoretical models that have been proposed for linking personality disorder, risk and offending. One of the central problems diagnostically may be that the dominant diagnosis of antisocial personality disorder identifies heterogeneous populations and not a specific pathology that can be addressed in a specific way.

Some cases of ASPD may have a predominantly biological basis, others a more environmental causation.

It should be clear that some personality disordered offenders are likely to be more dangerous and some more treatable than others. To some extent this reflects the extent to which the individual is internally conflicted about his antisocial behaviour. As Hering (1997) notes, the truly 'evil' individual demonstrates a capacity for unmitigated destructiveness where the 'hate-full' part of the personality has become predominant:

> This part has managed to ensure that its fantasy and desire for total destruction will be fully and concretely satisfied; such an organisation of one's psyche amounts to a total take-over of the rest of the person-ality including all its intact mental faculties.

Chapter 3

Assessment

Introduction

As we have seen from Chapter 2, personality disorder is a complex and controversial phenomenon, fraught with theoretical uncertainty. This is mirrored in the range of approaches to the assessment and diagnosis of personality disorder, and concerns regarding the construct validity and inter-rater reliability of both clinical and psychometric assessments. Risk assessment is a less troubled area, with an acceptance, these days, of the importance of an evidence-based approach to determining the probability of an offence re-occurring. Nevertheless, practitioners are understandably confused as to the rights and wrongs of particular measures of risk, and often fall back on clinical judgement as a preferred approach. In this chapter, we aim to describe the main approaches to the assessment of personality disorder and risk assessment – psychometric and clinical – separating the two areas of interest in a somewhat artificial manner, in the interests of clarity.

Psychometric assessments refer to standardised tools of assessment which are based on empirical and clinical evidence, and which have been subjected to validity testing – to greater or lesser degrees of rigour. There is a myriad of tools available, and we have pre-selected those tools which are well known to the authors and have been chosen by the newly developed personality disordered offender services (see Service Level Agreements for DSPD and community PD (Home Office, 2005b), following lengthy discussions by experts in the field. The readers may well have their own preferred tools which perform well, and we would not wish to undermine individual choice in the matter. However, there should be simple criteria to which practitioners adhere, which should include a knowledge of the population on which the psychometric tool was designed to be used, as well as a knowledge of the basic psychometric properties of the tool, including the proper administration and interpretation of the tool. Psychometrics vary, both in terms of how they are administered (from files, self-report questionnaires or semi-structured interviews), and in the time they take to administer and the training which is required to use them, and we have tried to indicate this where possible. The second focus of assessment is on clinical approaches, which, in reality, often approximate to the variables encountered in psychometric tools. That is, the more a practitioner has an understanding of the research basis to risk prediction or to the criteria implicated in personality diagnosis, the more his or her clinical assessment will accord with a psychometric one. However, clinical approaches do allow practitioners to individualise their assessments and to take into account particular and peculiar factors in an individual's presentation which alter the assessment and may be missed from the more generalised psychometric approaches.

Choosing the approach to assessment depends on its purpose. For those who aim to research personality disordered offenders, perhaps in the evaluation of services, then some standardised psychometric approaches are crucial. Where advice is being sought about risk and diagnosis, then the practitioner does have a duty to ensure that opinions are not idiosyncratic but represent a fairly standard view based on the best evidence available; this probably means adherence to some standardised procedures. In other instances, it is a question of determining treatment need, and a practitioner may feel able to rely on clinical judgement alone, depending on the circumstances. Again, there are resource implications, and in a busy out-patient clinic, lengthy assessment procedures may not be possible. In the absence of the all-encompassing perfect tool, specialist practitioners in personality disorder services will probably need to draw on a range of psychometric and clinical approaches.

Setting the scene

Practitioners tend to think of assessment, treatment and management as separate entities. In reality, the moment an offender makes contact with a practitioner, an intervention is taking place. Even if the assessment involves a single episode of contact, never to be re-visited, the quality of the contact will affect both the quality of the assessment and the way in which an offender approaches such contacts in future. If he feels himself to be understood as an individual and engaged in a collaborative approach to achieve that understanding, this may sow the seeds of interest in a more reflective approach to solving his problems; this is not the same as the practitioner and the offender agreeing on the nature of his problems and the risk he poses. Alternatively, an adversarial assessment which creates an atmosphere of accusation and confrontation in which the offender feels that something is being done to him, and despite him, is likely to reinforce pre-existing persecutory feelings about authority figures. In saying this, we realise that there are difficult circumstances to many assessments, and agendas – such as public protection – in which the offender has little influence. The section in Chapter 4 on motivational interviewing may provide some guidelines for optimising the quality of assessment interviews.

In setting the scene, the assessor should always try to have as much corroborative information available as possible. This may take the form of criminal justice documentation – previous convictions, pre-sentence reports, victim statements – or information about previous contact with mental health services. Some psychometric tools advocate talking with key informants, including family members – the offender may give permission for this, although some key informant information (such as a report on housing problems or previous child protection concerns) will already be available via the mechanism of the MAPPP.

One component of a strategy for establishing a collaborative rapport in the assessment interview is to consider the sequencing of the assessment. Some practitioners like to administer psychometrics initially, and some offenders respond well to a more concrete formal approach which avoids overly intrusive interpersonal discussion. Others will only co-operate with psychometric tools once the interview is well underway, and their answers to the psychometric questions will be more thoughtful and honest once they have some feeling of confidence in the interviewer. It is a common mistake to commence questioning in relation to the offences or difficult behaviours which brought the offender into the assessment, but their defensiveness is likely to be lessened when they feel that the interviewer has already shown an interest in them as a broader personality – preferably having elicited their areas of strength or their own experiences of having been victimised. Being understood as a victim in his own right is the single most powerful tool in enabling the offender to think more clearly about his offence victims. Yet practitioners are nervous about colluding with an offender's minimisation of or justification for his offending. However, empathy is not the same as collusion, just as understanding is not the same as excusing.

Some personality disordered offenders have been subjected to multiple interviews and interviewers, and this is something that is often glossed over by others. It is deeply aggravating to be asked the same questions repeatedly, yet assessors often want to obtain a qualitative understanding of the offender's responses for themselves. This can be managed by simply acknowledging and apologising for the need for repetition; alternatively the assessor could acknowledge the facts which are contained in previous reports, and ask the offender to comment on them with the benefit of hindsight; psychometrics which were administered previously could be accepted without the need to repeat them, although for this to occur, practitioners do need to be transparent about their assessments and to share them more willingly. For example, if a Psychopathy Checklist (see below) has been completed, it should be clear on what variables the offender was thought to score high, thus making the information transferable.

The example of a psychopathy assessment raises the question of confidentiality and transparency in the assessment process. An offender has the right to know, at the outset, why he is being seen, and for whom the assessment is being completed; this should include an understanding of the purpose of any of the psychometrics used, and an explanation as to the findings. For the majority of cases, there should be little or no reason why an assessment report cannot be discussed with the offender and a copy given to him. Many practitioners are nervous about exposing the 'secrets' of psychometrics, fearing that this will undermine their validity, or that the offender will try to fake such assessments in future. However, if an offender is rated high risk on the basis of historical criminogenic variables, there seems little reason not to let him know exactly why his rating was high, and what percentage likelihood of reoffending is applied to that rating. If, for example, an offender meets the criteria for schizoid personality disorder on a self-report scale, he can be shown the profile, and it can be explained to him, in terms of 'this is a label which is applied to people who report certain types of thoughts, feelings and behaviour, as you did on this questionnaire. What it really means is that you are someone . . .'

Many offenders are incensed at being described as 'psychopathic' and are – as implicated in the criteria – prone to antagonistic and even litigious interpersonal responses. Clearly the practitioner needs to be meticulous in their competent use of controversial psychometrics with such offenders, but they may also need to adopt a strategy of deliberate transparency (rather than withdrawing into professional secrecy, which is the more natural response): allowing a psychopathic individual to know that he scored high on callousness, shallow affect and impulsive behaviour is unlikely to taint assessments in years to come – arguably he will already know that he is supposed to show good victim empathy, and his attempts to fake this in future will inevitably have a hollow ring, and be limited by his earlier history of unempathic attitudes.

In summary, setting the scene involves knowing – as far as possible – who you are dealing with, and approaching the assessment as though it may turn into a long-term therapeutic relationship. This involves establishing a collaborative approach as far as possible, with an emphasis on creating an atmosphere of transparency and honesty, even if this means, ultimately, agreeing to disagree.

Assessing personality disorder

If personality disorder diagnosis encapsulates the three 'P's – pathological, pervasive and persistent – then a broad diagnosis can be derived quite simply from file information: for example, where an individual has a history, throughout his adult life span, of impulsive antisocial behaviour, difficulties in relationships with others, and repeated periods of emotional turmoil and social destructiveness. Further investigation into the details of the diagnostic categories needs to take into account Cooke and Hart's (2004) six principles:

1 *Personality disorder is a culture-bound concept*, defined in relation to cultural concepts such as self, abnormality and gender. Much of the work in this area has been on psychopathic personality, but is likely to be relevant to other categories; for example, personality disorder may be more prevalent in highly individualistic cultures where the development of self-identity is independent of relationships with others; and while affective deficits are stable across cultures, the expression of the interpersonal and behavioural features vary across settings.

2 *Personality disorder is a higher-order, inferential construct*: that is, a construct used to describe regularities in clients' patterns of behaviour, affect and cognition.

3 *Personality disorder is inherently relational*, and it is therefore impossible to diagnose based solely on self-report, and observers are likely to have perceptions of clients that differ from each other and from those of the clients themselves.

4 *Personality disorder reflects enduring patterns of dysfunction*, and therefore evaluators' inferences regarding the disorder will be reliable in reflecting adjustment to problems across time, situations and interpersonal interactions.

5 *Personality disorder symptomatology is diverse*, and symptoms may differ in severity and over time, necessitating comprehensive assessment approaches which are repeated at different points in the life span.

6 *Personality disorder is independent of acute mental disorder*, although this can be difficult to distinguish. Comorbidity has various meanings: personality disorder can co-exist with severe mental illness, and in order to assess this, the mental illness must be diagnosed – and treated – first; this is particularly important where there is a history of aggressive and disruptive behaviours in an individual where a psychotic illness has been undiagnosed or insufficiently treated for long periods of time. Comorbidity can also be a feature of the personality disorder *per se*, that is, anxious and depressive disorders can be a feature of certain personality disorders; however, they may be over-reported in personality disordered offenders, or may mask the features of personality disorder.

The comorbidity of personality disorders – as shown in Chapter 2 – is frequently observed, introducing complexity to the diagnosis, and a loss of face validity to traditional categorical approaches. Diagnostic overlap is common in antisocial and borderline personality disorders, as violent behaviour can be a defining feature of both (McMurran, 2003); the same is

Table 3.1 Severity of personality disorders (from Tyrer, 2000)

Level	Criteria	Classification
0	No personality abnormality	No personality disorder
1	Sub-threshold criteria for personality disorder	Personality difficulty
2	One or more personality disorders within the same cluster	Simple personality disorder
3	Two or more personality disorders from different clusters	Complex personality disorder
4	Two or more personality disorders from different clusters that create gross societal disturbance	Severe personality disorder

true of schizoid and avoidant personality disorders, both of which share traits of problematic social and interpersonal functioning. Comorbidity of personality disorders may be one way of determining the severity of personality disorder, and this approach has been operationalised by Tyrer (2000), and is laid out in Table 3.1.

Personality disorder – psychometric assessments

Psychometric assessments of personality disorder fall into two categories: those based on self-report paper-and-pencil questionnaires, and those based on semi-structured interviews. Inevitably, there is a complication, in that some semi-structured approaches have a self-report screening questionnaire (IPDE) or allow for a purely file-based approach (PCL-R). There are limitations to psychometric approaches, including the negative influence of adverse mental or emotional states on responding style; and the extent to which validity scales are able to determine socially biased responses. Some scales are able to distinguish between impression management (a state) and self-enhancement (a narcissistic trait); however, if this is an important component of the assessment, it is recommended that the latter be assessed by means of self-deception questionnaires.

Self-report questionnaires are too numerous to describe in detail, but the more commonly used ones include the Millon Clinical Multi-Axial Inventory (MCMI-III, 3rd version; Millon *et al.*, 1994), the Personality Assessment Inventory (PAI; Morey, 1991), the Personality Diagnostic Questionnaire (PDQ; Hyler *et al.*, 1988), and the Minnesota M Personality Inventory (MMPI; Butcher, 2005)

The *Millon Clinical Multi-Axial Inventory – III (MCMI-III)* is a 175-item self-report instrument used for the clinical assessment and diagnostic screening of individuals who evidence problematic emotional and interpersonal symptoms. It assesses the extent to which the individual has problematic personality styles through eleven clinical personality patterns and three scales measuring severe personality pathology. The instrument also reports the prevalence of symptoms typical of Axis I disorders, or 'clinical syndromes'. The MCMI-III also provides an impression of the test-taking attitude of the individual, with three validity scales, indicating whether there is an attempt to produce an overly positive or negative impression. The questionnaire has good internal consistency (more than .80 for twenty of the scales) and test-retest reliability (from .82 to .96). The MCMI-III requires thirty to forty minutes to complete, and a further twenty minutes for scoring and interpretation (although a computerised scoring and interpretation system can be purchased); it does not require training, but there is a manual which needs to be read and there are useful books to assist interpretation (for example, Choca, 2004).

The *Personality Assessment Inventory (PAI)* is a 344-item self-administered objective test of personality and psychopathology, developed to provide measures of constructs central in treatment planning, implementation and evaluation. The PAI comprises four validity scales, eleven clinical scales, five treatment considerations and two interpersonal scales. Subjects are required to rate the intensity of their experience for each item on a four-point scale. The PAI provides an interpretation relative to a standardisation sample of 1,000 community-dwelling adults. The internal consistency alphas for the PAI full scales are satisfactory (Morey, 1991); test-retest reliability is .86. The PAI requires up to one hour to complete, and the answer sheet can be scanned into the computer; an interpretative report is provided by the computer package. There is also a manual to read.

The MCMI and the PAI are economical and efficient, but do require a reasonable level of literacy and fluency in the language, and are therefore not suitable for individuals with marked reading difficulties or learning disability. They represent a form of self-presentation which is a function of self-perception, insight and compliance with the assessment process (Cooke and Hart, 2004). They have been found to overpredict the presence of personality disorder, but do have other strengths, notably, tapping into problems which are not publicly observable and presenting a very personalised account of difficulties. For example, a practitioner may consider an offender to meet the criteria for paranoid personality disorder, and note the presence of some depressive features secondary to this; the offender may score very high for depressive traits but low for paranoid traits: this reflects the offender's lack of insight into his distorted and rigid thinking style but emphasises the misery and hopelessness he experiences at being unable to change the hostile nature of the world around him. Alternatively, consider the predominantly schizoid offender who scored high for both avoidant and schizoid personality traits, apparently contradictory phenomena: he reported common social and interpersonal difficulties which overlap between the disorders, but the assessor considered his avoidance of such situations to be driven primarily by a wish to avoid embarrassment and complex demands, as a response to the interpersonal *deficits* of schizoid functioning, rather than an anxiety that was fed by feelings of inadequacy, that is, the interpersonal *conflicts* of avoidant functioning.

The *Personality Diagnostic Questionnaire* (PDQ-4+) (Hyler *et al.*, 1988) is a self-report measure which assesses the presence of criteria for the ten subtypes of personality disorder described in DSM-IV. A cut-off score of more than 30 is suggested by the author as indicating a substantial likelihood of significant personality disorder. A more useful indicator of the severity of disorder may be the number of different PD diagnoses generated by this instrument (Dolan and Coid, 1993).

Although the instrument has been found to generate an excess of false positives, this may make it helpful as a screening instrument for the presence of personality disorder in large offender samples. The study of Davison *et al.* (2001) suggested that this was indeed the case, finding that a cut-off total score of 25 or above yielded near optimal sensitivity and specificity in a prison population.

Young's Schema Questionnaire (Young and Brown, 1990, 2001) is not a diagnostic tool, but is mentioned here as an interesting and useful operationalisation of a key theoretical model (see Chapter 2). It was designed to identify important schemas collaboratively with the patient for clinical use. It comprises 205 self-statements based on eighteen key schemas, with a six-point Likert scale ranging from 'completely untrue of me' to 'describes me perfectly'. A final score is not computed, but the practitioner explores, with the patient, the meaning of those items scored high (usually 5 or 6); if a patient has three or more high scores on a particular schema, then that schema is usually relevant to the patient. It can be completed and scored in around one hour, and does not require training or the purchase of materials; it does, however, require an understanding of schemas and their theoretical basis, and access to a core text (Young *et al.*, 2003).

The *International Personality Disorder Examination (IPDE)* is a semi-structured clinical interview designed to assess for personality disorders (the only tool which has the flexibility to assess either the eleven DSM-IV categories or the ten ICD-10 categories). The ninety-nine questions are organised thematically, and cover six main areas: work, self, interpersonal relationships, affects, reality testing and impulse control. Items are scored on a three-point scale, and responses can be clarified through further enquiries and utilisation of informant data. Inter-rater reliability coefficients for the number of criteria met range from .71 to .92 for the DSM-III-R version. The IPDE was validated on a large and wide-ranging psychiatric population. Personality disorder can be scored as possibly present, and definitely present.

The *Structured Clinical Interview for DSM-IV Personality Disorders (SCID-II)* comprises a similar semi-structured interview which is organised symptomatically to cover the eleven DSM-IV personality disorders. There is a SCID-II personality questionnaire which is available as a screening tool to shorten the time it takes the clinician to administer the SCID-II.

The IPDE and SCID-II assume that there has been an assessment of acute psychopathology prior to the interview. They can be lengthy to complete, requiring an interview of between two and five hours, but are then quick to score and interpret. The manual and test materials can be purchased and administered without training. However, the tests do assume experience in and knowledge of personality disorder, and require practice in order to gain confidence in their administration.

Psychopathy Checklist – Revised (PCL-R; Hare, 1991)

Although the PCL-R is one of the most rigorously validated and most widely used of actuarial instruments, the construct of psychopathy has been widely misrepresented and inaccurately used. It is frequently confused with antisocial or dissocial personality disorder, and the category of 'Psychopathic Disorder' which assesses personality deviation generally; the PCL-R relates to a specific form of personality disorder. Psychopathy has an early onset, is characteristic of the individual's long-term functioning, and results in social dysfunction. Symptoms are usually evident by middle to late childhood and the disorder persists well into adulthood. Psychopathy can be differentiated from other personality disorders on the basis of its characteristic pattern of interpersonal, affective and behavioural symptoms.

There is a range of studies establishing the psychometric properties of the PCL-R, too numerous to report. Essentially, indices of internal consistency (.80), inter-rater reliability (.80–.90) and all aspects of validity are high. Although it measures a unitary construct, it has a stable two-factor structure. Factor 1 consists of items to do with the affective/interpersonal features of psychopaths: egocentricity, manipulativeness, callousness and lack of remorse. Factor 2 reflects features associated with an impulsive, antisocial and unstable lifestyle. It is factor 2 which is most strongly correlated with antisocial personality disorder and substance misuse. Factor 1 items are most likely to occur at high levels of the construct (high psychopathy scores) and are most likely to differentiate psychopaths from non-psychopaths. As one might expect, research suggests that scores on factor 2 decrease sharply with age, whilst scores on factor 1 appear to remain stable with age. Research on the three-factor model of psychopathy (Cooke et al., 2004) has not yet influenced the structure of the PCL-R, and its official interpretation.

The PCL-R is a twenty-item clinical construct rating scale, completed on the basis of an interview and detailed collateral or file information. Each item is scored on a three-point scale: 0 = the item does not apply; 1 = the item applies to a certain extent or there is uncertainty that it applies; 2 = the item definitely applies. The twenty items can therefore produce a score ranging from 0 to 40. In North America, average PCL-R scores in male and female offender populations typically range from 22 to 24, and in forensic psychiatric populations are slightly lower at around 20. The recommended cut-off point for researchers identifying psychopathy is a score of 30. However cross-cultural research in Scotland (Cooke, 1998) suggests that there is a lower prevalence of psychopathy in the United Kingdom. For example, a PCL-R score of 25 in Scotland is metrically equivalent to the diagnostic cut-off score of 30 in North America. Even utilising this lower cut-off, only 8 per cent of offenders within Scottish prisons were found to be psychopathic, compared with approximately 29 per cent in North American samples.

There is increasing evidence for the reliability and validity of the PCL-R with female offenders and psychiatric patients. With slight modifications, it can also be useful with adolescents (PCL – Youth Version; Forth *et al.*, 2003). The PCL-R is potentially cumbersome to rate as it requires hours, rather than minutes, to complete. Ratings cannot be made on the basis of interview alone, and adequate collateral information is a prerequisite. Indeed, if there are discrepancies between the interview and the file information, greater weight is given to information from the source most suggestive of psychopathology. Furthermore, items are rated on the basis of the person's lifetime functioning and not on the basis of the individual's present state; that is, across the life span and across domains of functioning. For example, a sex offender may demonstrate a lack of responsibility, empathy and remorse in interview, in relation to the index offence, but may not have displayed these characteristics over the period of their adult life.

Some PCL-R items are quantifiable, such as 'many short-term marital relationships' or 'juvenile delinquency'. However, the majority require a clinical appraisal in line with the extensive PCL-R manual guidelines. For example, in rating 'impulsivity', the item describes

> an individual whose behavior is generally impulsive, unpremeditated, and lacking in reflection or forethought. He usually does things on the 'spur of the moment' because he 'feels like it' or because an opportunity presents itself. He is unlikely to spend much time weighing the pros and cons of a course of action, or in considering the possible consequences of a course of action, or in considering the possible consequences of his actions to himself or others. He will often break off relationships, quit jobs, change plans suddenly, or move from place to place, on little more than a whim and without bothering to inform others.
>
> (Hare, 1991, p. 25)

Given the importance of the PCL-R in predicting violent recidivism and its potential role in detaining offenders within restricted settings, the potential for harm is considerable if it is not used correctly. Training is recommended but not mandatory. However, Hare recommends that the assessor should be a registered psychologist or psychiatrist, should have experience with forensic populations, should limit their use of the PCL-R to those populations in which it has been fully validated, and should ensure that they have adequate training and experience in its use. Specifically, he recommends that the scores of two independent raters should be averaged so as to increase the reliability of the assessment, and that five to ten practice assessments should be completed in order to ensure acceptable levels of inter-rater reliability.

There is a screening version available (PCL:SV), which is less onerous to complete and can be used for screening psychopathy in forensic populations. It is the instrument of choice for non-offending populations. It has the same factor structure as the PCL-R and comprises twelve items, with scores ranging from 0 to 24. A cut-off score of 18 is recommended for diagnostic purposes (warranting further evaluation with the full PCL-R), and those scoring 12 or less can be considered non-psychopathic. An evaluation of the PCL:SV (Cooke et al., 1999) found that it has structural properties similar to the PCL-R. It also found that the interpersonal and affective features of psychopathy were assessed as reliably as the impulsive and antisocial behavioural features, although there was a higher threshold for the interpersonal and affective features of psychopathy, suggesting that these features were more central to the construct.

Mental health difficulties (Axis I disorders) are associated with personality disorder diagnoses, as has been stated previously. Some of the above measures – notably the MCMI and PAI – contain items within the questionnaires relating to clinical syndromes. Other simple measures of mental health functioning could include the Symptom Checklist (SCL-90-R), and its shorter version, the Brief Symptom Inventory (BSI; Derogatis, 2003). Semi-structured interview measures are varied, but include the Structured Clinical Interview for DSM-IV Axis I Disorders (SCID-I; American Psychiatric Association, 1997), available in paper-and-pencil and computer format.

Finally it is worth mentioning projective tests, which have enjoyed a mixed history in clinical experience. Their title derives from the principle that they use ambiguous stimuli, for example ink blots, onto which the examinee is believed to 'project' their own subjective and to some extent subconscious interpretations and preoccupations. These tests were often developed from psychoanalytic theories and have been seen as lacking in scientific credibility. However, the most famous of these tests, the Rorschach ink blot test, has been comprehensively normed in recent years by Exner and his colleagues (Exner, 1993; Exner and Weiner, 1995).

Authors such as Meloy and Gacono (1998) have argued that such tests might be particularly suited to study antisocial populations because they have very low face validity (i.e. are ambiguous) and partially bypass volitional controls. Unlike self-report measures which Hare (1991) has argued are inherently unreliable with psychopaths, Meloy and Gacono (1998) argue that the Rorschach ink blot test in particular is uniquely situated to map the psychostructure of personality disordered individuals. They claim that the instrument is able to give a unique as well as quantitative measurement of issues such as narcissism, thinking clarity, impulse control and management of affect. These instruments require some understanding of the underlying theoretical principles, and training and practice in the interpretation of results. As yet, there are no definitive recent studies in offender populations, but the renewed popularity of projective testing is likely to yield some interesting publications in the future.

Clinical approaches to personality disorder assessment

Practitioners have their own approaches to clinical assessment, varying in emphasis from background developmental variables to medical histories and offence-specific questions. Our aim is not to start from the basics, but to highlight the more complex or subtle areas of assessment which are particularly pertinent to the assessment of personality disorder. These guidelines are entirely driven by the theoretical underpinnings which are laid out in Chapter 2, and we have tried to incorporate core components of biosocial, attachment and schema-focused models of personality disorder.

As with offending behaviour, discussed later in the chapter, the literature on personality disorder is dominated by research on negative or adverse features, rather than protective or resilience-based features. There is an assumption – probably reasonably correct – that the latter is simply the reverse of the former, although this is a more intuitively sensible approach with risk variables. Many of the features of assessment overlap, and they are divided rather artificially below; some relate to concrete experiences, others to core personality difficulties such as impulsivity, which can be manifest in a range of settings or situations such as schooling, relationships or offending behaviour.

Genetic/temperamental factors

There is evidence to suggest that schizotypal, paranoid and schizoid personality disorders are associated with increased rates of schizophrenia among first-degree relatives. Affective instability – a feature of borderline and histrionic personality disorders – has also been found in first-degree relatives, as have increased rates of affective disorder (such as panic attacks). There is evidence that impulsivity (a core component of borderline and antisocial personality disorder) is partially inherited; and finally, there seems to be an increased prevalence of anxious personality traits in the relatives of those with panic disorder and dependent personality disorder (all summarised in Dolan, 2003). There is also an established literature on the intergenerational pattern of substance misuse.

Offenders may not recall their infantile behaviour, or know their parents' perception of their temperament during the early months of life. They may be uncertain as to whether their behaviour was unusually challenging prior to attending primary school. Although family interviews are central to child and adolescent assessments, it is often forgotten that adult offenders may be very willing for parents or siblings to be interviewed in relation to these early – and less controversial – traits, and extended family histories. Offenders could be asked about criminality, substance misuse and psychiatric histories in the extended family; they may not recall exact diagnoses, but will know if someone was hospitalised or had a reputation for eccentricity or depression. Of course, care should be taken not to be over-inclusive, interpreting a maternal history of occasional tearfulness as a depressive illness, or mistaking the hospitalisation for longer-term care of a dementing relative for a severe (functional) mental illness.

Attachment

There is considerable evidence to suggest that personality disordered individuals – and offenders in particular – have been reared in dysfunctional families, and been subjected to abuse and neglect (see below). It seems that family stressors are linked to the interpersonal and affective aspects of psychopathy (and probably personality disorder more generally), while social stressors during childhood are more likely to be linked to the behavioural aspects of the disorders (Cooke and Hart, 2004).

Attachment begins with primary caregivers – usually parents – and this is where the assessment needs to start. Clearly, there is a difference between an offender's perception of his experiences in being parented, and external reality; some individuals (particularly those with emotional instability and high levels of personal distress) are likely to be highly sensitive to a perceived lack of consistent care and attention, whilst others (particularly those with emotionally detached, ego-syntonic behaviours) are more likely to be detached from, or to play down, such experiences. For example, Craissati et al. (2002) found that rapists were much more likely to report optimal bonding with both parents than a control group of non-offenders, whilst child molesters reported high levels of negative relationship with mothers, whom they experienced as affectionless but controlling. Rapists – and violent, non-sexual offenders – are more likely to idealise their parents or to minimise difficulties in their attachment experiences, reflecting their greater propensity for a dismissive and detached attachment style.

Initially, a broad open question can broach the subject of attachment, perhaps the request for a description of a parent and their relationship with the offender in childhood. However, many offenders are thrown by this, and find it difficult to generate a spontaneous qualitative account of the primary relationship. This may, of course, reflect an important feature of the individual's psychological functioning – his capacity to process and reflect on emotional experiences; it may reflect a lack of emotional memory for the early years as a result of a well developed capacity for blotting out difficult experiences or experiences incompatible with a current self-image; or it may simply reflect impoverished cognitive functioning and difficulties with verbal expression. Further prompting questions could include:

> 'What are the five words which come to mind when I ask you to describe your mother to me?'
> 'Tell me about a happy memory that comes to mind (and an unhappy memory).'
> 'Tell me about the bedtime routine when you were a child.'
> 'If you hurt yourself, or if you were upset, who did you use to turn to?'

The assessor will want to gain an impression of good enough parenting, rather than perfect parenting, in which the child was in receipt of reasonably consistent nurturing and validating experiences; and where intense emotional states – of distress or anger – could be tolerated and managed. These features are explored in a similar fashion in the Adult Attachment Interview (George et al., 1987), which is an intensive and detailed instrument designed to be administered as a semi-structured interview. There are quite specific experiences which can also shed light on attachments, notably the prolonged absence of a parent (usually an absent father) or separation due to illness or placement in care. No matter how impoverished the attachments to parents might be, there can be highly significant protective figures in an individual's life – often the presence of a caring grandparent during the formative years, or the sustained and benign interest of a key role model, such as a teacher.

Adverse developmental experiences

Adverse developmental experiences are closely related to attachment issues, as insecurely attached children are significantly more likely to be the target of abuse (Robins, 1966; Morton and Browne, 1998). There are experiences which are apparently relatively random – chronic childhood illness or witnessing a deeply traumatic violent event – whereas emotional abuse, physical neglect, and physical and sexual abuse appear to be intertwined with intergenerational family difficulties. There are definitional problems with these experiences, particularly in attempting to decide whether someone suffered from emotional abuse; other problems relate to the offender's own habituation to abnormal experiences, which means that he becomes an unreliable informant on these matters.

In talking about sexual abuse, the offender can be asked about early or first sexual contacts, as well as unwanted sexual contact, so that distorted interpretations as to what constitutes sexual abuse can be avoided. Physical abuse needs to be differentiated from culturally accepted physical chastisement for misdemeanours, by its persistence, excess, or apparent unpredictability or irrationality (that is, imposed regardless of whether the child has done something wrong). The offender can be asked what would happen if he was naughty as a child, was he ever hit, was a stick used, was he ever hit when he had not been naughty, were the other children hit as much, was he hit by a drunk parent, and so on. The assessment of emotional abuse overlaps greatly with the assessment of attachment, but the interviewer needs also to be alert to any marked experiences of psychological control or excessive imposition of fear or public humiliation, perpetrated by a significant adult.

The key to exploring abuse experiences is not just to determine what may have happened, but more importantly, the meaning of the experience for the individual offender. For example, some sexually abused boys may develop homosexual anxieties as a result of their guilty interpretation of responsibility for the abuse because they became physically aroused; others may idealise the abuse as meaning that they are desired and cared for in an otherwise emotionally bleak world.

Educational and occupational experiences

The important features of educational experiences fall into academic and social functioning. Academic ability may be poor, with an associated impact on the development of self-esteem and feelings of self-efficacy, perhaps secondary to experiences of belittlement and humiliation; or academic achievement may be less than an estimate of cognitive functioning would have predicted, and this failure would suggest that emotional factors were interfering with the offender's ability to progress. Behavioural features – inattentiveness and disruptive behaviour – might indicate the beginnings of difficulties with impulsivity, or the burgeoning of a coping mechanism in the offender, to identify with a delinquent peer group, in order to achieve social status and overcome the lack of identification with a paternal role model. Failure to make friends at school, of course, is also a sign of possible problems, which will be exacerbated in adulthood in terms of the capacity to forge enduring intimate relationships.

Employment history can shed light on cognitive capacity, impulsivity, attention, problem solving, social skills and rule-breaking behaviour. It is always important to ask about their longest period of work with a single employer, and, if the offender has ever been sacked, what the circumstances were.

Generally speaking, the capacity to achieve academically or to integrate socially – at school and at work – are highly protective factors. They suggest that an individual has problem-solving skills, the capacity to express themselves, and/or a warmth of personality and 'likeability' which facilitates psychological health and motivates others to support them.

Psychosexual functioning

This area of assessment is not just pertinent to sex offenders, but as we have seen, dysfunctional sexual and intimate relationships are an important feature of psychopathy specifically, and personality disorder more generally. Sexual abuse has been thought to be linked to borderline personality disorder, particularly in women (Paris, 2000), but in fact only appears to be present in a subgroup of such individuals. It is commonly found in around 40 per cent of child molesters, and in fewer rapists – around 25 per cent (Craissati and Beech, 2004); yet the same profile of psychosexual disturbance is found in both abused groups of sex offender, which differentiates them from non-sexually abused sex offenders in terms of range and disturbance in sexual and relationship functioning. However, psychosexual development includes early experiences which are not necessarily illegal, and which highlight the way in which sexual functioning and interpersonal functioning begin to integrate – or, more problematically, to diverge. Early experiences might include access to pornography, witnessing sexualised behaviour, unusually early masturbatory experiences, early preoccupation with sexual experiences, often diverse experiences, or difficulty in tolerating homosexual inclinations or orientation. Adolescent dating experiences are often fraught with embarrassment and fears of rejection, but some offenders will have had experiences of catastrophic humiliations or, alternatively, sudden and compelling boosts to their self-esteem by their capacity to attract and seduce young women.

Relationship histories should track the development of the offender from adolescent dating through to adult enduring intimate relationships. Clearly, frequent uncommitted sexual encounters which serve to boost self-esteem and status with peers (as might be found in antisocial personality disorder) are as problematic as persistent efforts to avoid any adult sexually intimate encounters (as with schizoid and avoidant personality disorder). When relationships do form, it is important to know how long they persisted; whether there was any jealousy or violence within the relationship and, if so, why; whether the offender was faithful; and why each relationship failed, at least from the perspective of the offender.

Management of emotions and ability to reflect on affective experiences

In the course of an assessment, compiling the background details (as above), a picture will emerge of the offender's ability to express and manage his emotional state, and his insight into this aspect of his psychological functioning (also called 'reflective functioning' in the Adult Attachment Interview). As with attachment, some of this is influenced by cognitive ability which in turn influences 'psychological mindedness'. But much will be influenced by the nature of the personality development, and the core difficulties. Emotional awareness can range from the superficial (psychopathic) and detached (schizoid) to the intense (borderline); overt emotional expression can range from long-term manifestations of anxiety or need (cluster C) to the fleeting manifestation of such states (borderline, antisocial, psychopathic). Emotional difficulties can be in both the positive (love) and the negative (hate) domains, with experiences that are excessive or forbidden. The feeling that control over his emotional life has been lost is an important feature of the offender's assessment, as are the identifiable situations in which such loss of control can be triggered. These styles of emotional sensitivity are ingrained from early life, influenced by both genetic and environmental factors, and will have become habitual. The capacity of the offender to identify their emotional processes and to reflect on their experiences is central to an assessment of their ability to make good use of psychologically driven treatments which rely on insight and reflection in order to achieve change (see Chapter 4).

Comorbidity

By now the reader will be familiar with the problem of comorbidity, most commonly the presence of substance misuse problems or dependency, and/or the problem of mental illness symptomatology (Axis I). The former can be approached in numerous ways, depending on the setting and the competencies of the assessor; the aim is to track the history of substance use in terms of onset, duration, quantity, style of use, capacity to desist, physiological versus psychological dependency, and relationship to offending behaviour.

Determining the presence of problems with mental illness requires an appropriately trained and experienced practitioner; as previously stated, disentangling the co-existence and interactions of mental illness and personality disorder is a complicated task. However, there are simple approaches – very much a screening approach – to identifying the possibility of mental health problems. Questions should cover: past episodes of self-harm and/or suicidal thoughts; contact with health practitioners for problems with depression or anxiety, and/or taking medication for such problems; having read a diagnosis in previous reports about himself; and experiences of being hospitalised. Some individuals would not consider themselves to have had a mental illness, but would recognise the terms 'nerves', 'nervous breakdown', 'reaction to stress', 'feeling very low or panicky'. Answering these in the affirmative can prompt more probing questions.

OFFFENDING AND RISK

Psychometric measurement of offending risk

Actuarially based measures of reoffending risk have become increasingly available in recent years. Many overlap in terms of the important variables incorporated into the measure, but they differ in terms of the populations from which they were derived, and the extent to which they have been validated and have established generalisability across settings and countries. As with all psychometrics, it is important to bear in mind the basic properties of the scales and the correct scoring procedure; with risk prediction in particular, the reader should take note of the base rate for violence on which the scales were based, whether the validation studies have been reliant on secure hospital populations, incarcerated criminal justice populations, or community populations, and whether the scales are reliable in predicting general recidivism or violent recidivism in particular, and over what time scale.

The question of a base rate for offending is often overlooked in risk assessment. Even with assessment procedures which perform to a very high level, the accuracy of risk prediction is greatly impaired if base rates are low; and a high rate of false positives – where offending is predicted but does not in fact occur – can have significant ethical consequences (for further discussion see Craissati, 2004 and Buchanan and Leese, 2001). Essentially, the base rate for offending needs to rise to over 50 per cent likelihood before predictions can be accurate for the majority (rather than the minority) of the time.

Statistical analyses with more recent prediction studies utilise Receiver Operating Characteristics (ROC). The area under the ROC is used as a measure of predictive accuracy. This can range from 0.50 to 1.0, with 1.0 indicating perfect prediction and 0.5 indicating prediction no better than chance. The area under the ROC can be interpreted as the probability that a randomly selected recidivist would have a more deviant score than a randomly selected non-recidivist. The area under the ROC has the advantage over other commonly used measures of predictive accuracy that it is not constrained by base rates or selection ratios (Thornton *et al.*, 2003).

Nevertheless, whatever the statistical methods used, the core dilemma with psychometric tools is the extrapolation from the group risk prediction (as determined by published data on the scales) to the individual risk prediction, as it is well known that the margin of error for the group is smaller than for the individual; or as Sir Arthur Conan Doyle said, 'while the individual man is an insoluble puzzle, in the aggregate he becomes a mathematical certainty'. If, for example, we look at the predictive certainty of the Risk Matrix 2000 (see below), then it becomes clear that a reasonably strong predictive scale for sexual reoffending has an enormous potential range of error for any one individual (see Table 3.2).

Table 3.2 Risk Matrix 2000 and confidence intervals

Category	Risk estimate	Group confidence intervals	Individual confidence intervals
Low	7 per cent	3–14 per cent	0–82 per cent
Medium	19 per cent	14–26 per cent	0–86 per cent
High	36 per cent	28–45 per cent	3–91 per cent
Very high	59 per cent	46–71 per cent	8–96 per cent

Generally, psychometric measures for violence contain both static (fixed or historical factors) and dynamic (changeable) variables; however, sex offender scales have tended to separate out these two domains. The static items allow one to place an individual in a risk category *relative* to others; the dynamic items allow one to consider whether an individual is likely to fall into the offending cluster of that category.

There is an extremely competent and comprehensive review of risk management tools available from the Risk Management Authority in Scotland (2006, also available online at www.rmascotland.gov.uk), which contains a summary of all tools currently in use, in terms of the use of their scores and type of judgement required, applicability and current published validation studies.

Violence scales

The PCL-R has been described above, as it is primarily a measure of personality. However, there has been extensive research published on its ability to predict recidivism, particularly violent and sexual recidivism. Some of these findings are summarised below.

In terms of sex offenders, the prevalence of psychopathy (a score of 30 plus) appears to be relatively high among convicted rapists, and those identified as sexually dangerous. Forth and Kroner (1995) found that 26.1 per cent of incarcerated rapists, 18.3 per cent of mixed rapist/child molester offenders, and 5.4 per cent of incest offenders were psychopaths. Of those rapists who were serial offenders or killed their victims, 35 per cent were psychopaths. These findings were supported by the work of Porter *et al.* (2000) who found that 39 per cent of their ninety-five psychopathic sex offenders had raped only adult victims, 17 per cent had offended against both children and adults, 4 per cent had committed only incest, 3 per cent had molested children outside the family, and 1 per cent had molested children both in and out of the family. They suggested that psychopathy may add little to the prediction of sexual recidivism in child molesters, given that psychopathy is considerably less common in molesters than in the general prison population. However, those who crossed over from child to adult victims were nearly all psychopaths and also had the highest factor 1 scores, indicating a ruthless and callous personality. Quinsey *et al.* (1995) followed up treated rapists and child molesters and found that within six years of release, more than 80 per cent of psychopaths but only about 20 per cent of non-psychopaths violently recidivated. Rice and Harris (1997) reported that sexual recidivism was strongly predicted by a combination of a high PCL-R score and physiological (penile plethysmograph) evidence of deviant sexual arousal.

The relationship between psychopathy and general/violent recidivism has always been strong (Hemphill *et al.*, 1998), with a correlation between PCL-R scores and recidivism of .27; relative risk statistics at one year indicated that psychopaths were four times more likely to recidivate than non-psychopaths. The contribution made by the PCL-R to predicting recidivism was significantly greater than that of criminal history or a personality disorder diagnosis. Grann *et al.* (1999) followed up personality disordered offenders in Sweden for an average of 3.7 years, and measured violent reconviction; with a base rate for violence of 34 per cent, they found that both factor 1 and factor 2 scores predicted recidivism at the two-year point (area under the ROC curve .72).

OASys – the probation system in England and Wales (Home Office, 2002)

OASys is an assessment system – designed to be administered on the basis of file information and interview – developed jointly by the prison and probation services. It is based on the latest research evidence, has been piloted extensively by prison and probation staff, and is subject to ongoing validation against reconviction and other data. It is an assessment of needs and risks, and is structured to help probation practitioners assess how likely an offender is to reoffend and the likely seriousness of any offences they are likely to commit. It assesses the risk of harm offenders pose to themselves and/or others, and has the capacity to measure how an offender changes during the period of supervision. OASys is designed to flag up problems, which indicate the need for further – possibly specialist – assessment. OASys is only available to prison and probation practitioners, albeit requiring little training to administer.

A preliminary evaluation study of the first three pilot areas to implement OASys (Howard *et al.*, 2006) covered 3,080 offenders: 26 per cent of offenders scored as 'low risk' were reconvicted within two years, and 80 per cent scored as 'high risk' were reconvicted over that period. Howard *et al.* (2006) reported that the OASys was effective but less accurate than the OGRS score which is embedded within OASys. OGRS – and OGRS2 – is a brief static scale used extensively within the England and Wales criminal justice system. The original scale provides an estimate of the probability that offenders will be reconvicted of a standard list offence within two years of release, and the revised OGRS2 provides an additional estimate of the probability that offenders will be reconvicted of a violent or sexual offence within two years of release (Copas and Marshall, 1998; Taylor, 1999). The scale has also been found to be useful with mentally disordered offenders discharged from medium secure units (Maden *et al.*, 2005). The scale provides five bands of risk. An OGRS2 score of:

- 0 per cent results in a risk estimator of 'none'
- 1–10 per cent results in a risk estimator of 'some'
- 11–16 per cent results in a risk estimator of 'moderate'
- 17–25 per cent results in a risk estimator of 'raised'
- 25 per cent results in a risk estimator of 'high'

OASys – Dangerous and Severe Personality Disorder (DSPD) comprises eleven items, some of which are scored as absent/present, and some of which can be scored on a three-point scale. Seven of the items require relatively subjective judgement, and are reminiscent of the psychopathy checklist. A score of either 1 or 2 on all or most of the items should trigger a DSPD assessment. Items include criminogenic factors (number of early court appearances, supervisory breaches, violence), attitudinal factors (recognition of the impact and consequences of offending), and behaviours (impulsivity, aggression and childhood problems). Howard *et al.* (2006) found that 34 per cent of prisoners and 11 per cent of probation clients scored on at least eight concerns; offenders with a principal violent or sexual offence had an average of five concerns, while burglary and robbery offenders had an average of six concerns. Craissati *et al.* (2006) found that OASys DSPD (as defined by at least eight items being endorsed) was triggered in 18 per cent of a London-wide community group of sex offenders; scores were closely associated with a range of other risk measures; and it was significantly associated with a greater risk of general recidivism in the short-term follow-up period.

The *HCR-20* (Webster *et al.*, 1997) is a framework or structure for the assessment of risk in mentally disordered offenders, which is based on empirical and theoretical findings in the field. It comprises three scales: ten historical items of a largely static nature; five clinical items referring to current mental, emotional and psychiatric states; and five risk management items which are concerned with forecasting the future social, living and treatment circumstances of an individual, and with attempting to anticipate the person's reactions to those conditions (see Table 3.3 for a list of the items).

The HCR-20 has good inter-rater reliability (for example, r = .80; Douglas and Webster, 1999), and established construct validity. It has been validated on a range of populations, including mentally and personality disordered offenders in forensic mental health and correctional settings, across North America, Scandinavia and the UK. It has reasonably strong predictive ability in terms of future physical violence (AUC .76, Douglas *et al.*, 1999; AUC .80, Strand *et al.*, 1999); and appears to perform as well if not better than the VRAG and PCL-R, producing larger effects with measures of violence (Douglas and Webster, 1999; Douglas *et al.*, 2005). The scale has been validated for use with women; it is slightly more robust in predicting community violence than institutional violence. There are no recommended cut-off scores for the HCR-20; various studies have compared high scorers versus low scorers, or those who score above the median. There is a useful review of the empirical literature relating to the use of the HCR-20 which can be found at www.fnrh.freeserve.co.uk/hcr20.html.

The HCR-20 can be purchased from the authors (Webster *et al.*, 1997) at very low cost, and can be used by all practitioners with access to the relatively short manual. Inter-rater reliability is improved with some limited training, and a working knowledge of the PCL-R or PCL:SV is required. The tool is based on file information, and does not require an interview; it probably requires between one and two hours to complete.

The *Violence Risk Scale* (VRS; Wong and Gordon, 2000) is a quantitative measure of the risk of violence of forensic clients, in particular those who are to be released into the community. It assesses risk and change in risk based on six static factors (past criminal behaviour or conditions) and twenty dynamic factors (lifestyle, antisocial attitudes/behaviours, personality and social support network) which are empirically or theoretically linked to violence (see Table 3.3 for a list of factors). Unlike other risk assessment tools, it is primarily targeted at a group of men who are being assessed in terms of treatment need, and it therefore has additional items which assess the offender's readiness for treatment, and provide a quantitative measure of treatment change and pre- and post-treatment risk. Any dynamic item which scores 2 or 3 is considered to be a potential treatment target.

The VRS has good inter-rater reliability (.91, Wong and Gordon, 2000) and construct validity (Wong and Gordon, 1996). There is limited research on the predictive validity of the scale; currently it is suggested that a cut-off score of > 45 denotes higher risk, 30–45 medium risk and < 30 low risk. Wong and Gordon (2000) found that VRS pre-treatment scores predicted pre-treatment but not post-treatment violent recidivism, and that VRS post-treatment scores predicted post-treatment violent recidivsm; the correlation between VRS scores and violent recidivism was r = 0.25, and with general recidivism, r = 0.36.

The HCR-20 and the VRS are the scales of choice in the UK at the present time, although the VRS is not generally available for a wider group of practitioners, requires a fairly long period of time to complete, and can only be obtained in conjunction with lengthy and infrequent training

Table 3.3 A comparison of the VRS and HCR-20

Violence Risk Scale (Wong and Gordon, 2000)	HCR-20 (Webster et al., 1997)
Scoring: 0,1,2,3 0 – no relationship with violence 3 – consistent and significant relationship with violence	Scoring: 0,1,2 0 – not present 1 – presence suggested/mild 2 – definitely present
Historical/static items Current age Age at first violent conviction No. of juvenile convictions Violence throughout life span Prior release failure/escapes Stability of family upbringing	*Historical items* Previous violence Young age at first violent incident Psychopathy Prior supervision failure Early maladjustment Employment problems Relationship instability
Dynamic items Work ethic Stability of relationships Criminal personality Mental disorder Substance misuse Criminal peers Insight into violence Criminal attitudes Cognitive distortions Impulsivity Violent lifestyle Emotional control Released to high risk situations Interpersonal aggression Community support Compliance with supervision Violence cycle Weapon use Violence during institutionalisation Security level of release institution	Personality disorder Major mental illness Substance use *Clinical items* Lack of insight Negative attitudes Active symptoms of major mental illness Impulsivity Unresponsive to treatment *Risk management items* Plans lack feasibility Exposure to destabilisers Lack of personal support Non-compliance with remediation attempts Stress

programmes. Readers may also wish to consider the Violence Risk Appraisal Guide (VRAG; Quinsey *et al.*, 1998), which is a scale with twelve weighted items, in which final scores are banded and these bands are associated with probability ratings for violent recidivism over a seven- and ten-year period at risk. The VRAG has very strong predictive ability for the population from which it was originally derived – a maximum security hospital population of seriously violent mentally disordered offenders – but has not always demonstrated such good results in studies with other related populations, restricting its generalisability.

Measures of sexual recidivism risk

The following static risk measures are recommended.

The *Static 99/02* (Hanson and Thornton, 1999) is an amalgamation of two earlier risk prediction tools: the Structured Anchored Clinical Judgement Scale (SACJ-min; Grubin, 1998) and the RRASOR (Hanson, 1997). The development of the tool was based on four samples (three Canadian and one from the UK), with an average follow-up period ranging from four to twenty-three years; the offenders were from both mental health and criminal justice settings, and there was a sexual recidivism base rate of between 15 and 35 per cent.

The predictive accuracy of the scales was relatively consistent across the samples, the variability being no greater than would be expected by chance. The results for the combined sample (n = 1,208), for whom the Static 99/02, RRASOR and SACJ-min were administered, were as follows. The Static 99/02 performed best; its correlation with sexual recidivism status was .33 (ROC .71), and this was comparable for rapists and child molesters. The Static 99/02 also performed quite well in predicting violent recidivism (r = .32, ROC .69), with comparable results for rapists and child molesters. Survival analyses allowed for differential recidivism rates to be calculated for five, ten and fifteen years.

The Static 99/02 is intended for use with adult, male, convicted sex offenders. It comprises ten static/fixed variables which can be derived from file information. An individual's score can range from 0 to a maximum of 12. The tool is useful for predicting violence recidivism in sex offenders, although the PCL-R, VRS and VRAG are likely to be superior tools.

Beech *et al.* (2002) used the Static 99/02 to assess sexual reconviction rates after six years at risk, in a group of fifty-three convicted sex offenders treated in probation sex offender treatment programmes (Beckett *et al.*, 1994). The sexual recidivism base rate was 15 per cent (8 out of 53 men). The Static 99/02 was a good predictor of risk, with high or medium-high risk men (33 per cent) being over six times more likely to be convicted of a serious sexual assault than low or medium-low risk men (5 per cent). Craissati and Beech (2005), in a UK urban population of sex offenders, found that the Static 99/02 was significantly associated with reoffending (defined broadly), but the sexual reconviction rate itself was so low – 2 per cent after four years at risk in the community – as to preclude any meaningful statistical analysis.

Information regarding the Static 99/02 can be obtained from the Solicitor General of Canada website: http://www.sgc.gc.ca/epub/corr/e199902/e199902.htm. This includes advice on scoring, the scale itself, and the sexual and violent reoffending probability estimates. The tool requires a limited amount of file information relating to criminal variables, and can be completed within a few minutes if the information is available.

The *Risk Matrix 2000* (Thornton *et al.*, 2003) is an improved and updated version of the Structured Anchored Clinical Judgement Scale – min (Grubin, 1998) which has been widely used in the UK. The revised system contains a section – Risk Matrix 2000/S – which is concerned with sexual reconviction, and a second dimension – Risk Matrix 2000/V – which is designed to predict future non-sexual violent reconviction of sex offenders. The development, and cross-validation, of the tool was based on two samples of male sex offenders released from prison in England and Wales, and followed up for between two and sixteen years. The scale has subsequently been cross-validated (Craig *et al.*, 2006), and it performed well in comparison to other risk prediction measures.

The four Risk Matrix/S risk categories showed a monotonic trend with sexual reconviction rates rising in the expected way. The area under the ROC curve was .75 to .77. Thornton does not provide comparable rates for child molesters and rapists.

The Risk Matrix 2000 is intended for use with adult, male, convicted sex offenders. It has not been validated on child, juvenile or female sex offenders. It comprises three steps, and all the data can be derived from file information: step one consists of three static variables which result in an individual score ranging from 0 to 6, and an associated risk category. Step two relates to four aggravating factors – if two are present, the risk category is raised one level; if all four are present, the risk category is raised two levels. The final category denotes the risk of sexual reconviction. Step three relates to the prediction of non-sexual violence: it comprises three static variables which result in an individual score ranging from 0 to 8, and an associated risk category. This category denotes the risk of future violent reconviction.

Risk Matrix 2000/V was designed as a simple predictor of violent reconviction, and has been cross-validated on three samples, including both sex offender and violent offender populations. It should be noted that this scale was designed to predict non-sexual violence only. Again, a monotonic trend was apparent with higher rates of violent reconviction being observed for higher risk categories. The area under the ROC curve was .80. This compares favourably with the results of the VRAG, and it may be that the Risk Matrix 2000/V is the violence tool of choice with sex offenders.

The results overall compare favourably with the Static 99/02. Craissati and Beech (2005) used both tools on a community sex offender population, and again on a separate community population (Craissati *et al.*, 2006). The former study found the Risk Matrix was significantly associated with general reoffending, but could not be tested on sexual recidivism (see above). Both tools classified sex offenders similarly, although there was some suggestion that the Static 99 was a marginally more powerful predictive measure (and slightly more complicated to complete), and tended to allocate offenders more evenly across the four risk categories.

Dynamic risk in sex offenders

This area of recent work is reviewed by Craissati and Beech (2003) and Craissati (2004). The approaches tend to rely either on self-report questionnaires (for example, Beech, 1998; Thornton, 2002) or on practitioner-observed assessments derived from file information and offender interviews (Hanson and Harris, 2000). Dynamic risk assessments have been found to significantly enhance risk assessment predictions in sex offenders, independently of static risk assessments, and a combination of the two approaches provides the optimum prediction. The approaches are organised differently, but tend to focus on either pro-offending attitudes or levels of social competency. High risk 'deviant' offenders (Beech, 1998) demonstrate dynamic factors which are relatively intensive and pervasive; low 'deviancy' offenders have dynamic risk factors which are relatively low in intensity and circumscribed.

The *Sex Offender Needs Assessment Rating* (SONAR; Hanson and Harris, 2000, 2001) – incorporating stable dynamic and acute dynamic factors – provides a standardised method for measuring change in sex offender risk levels over time. It was developed from Hanson and Harris's (1998) work with both child molesters and rapists (excluding incest offenders), in which they identified groups of recidivists and non-recidivists, matched on key static variables, and then interviewed their supervising officers in the community, using a structured interview schedule, and examined the offenders' files. The strength of the tool lies in its reliance on observable variables; it can be completed relatively easily, from a combination of file information and/or an interview (one to two hours); it does require an understanding of the features of sex offending characteristics but this can be acquired with relatively brief training.

The SONAR – now amended to the Stable 2000 and Acute 2000 – is based on six stable dynamic categories (expected to persist for months or years), with the addition of seven acute factors (the 'worry now' features which may persist for minutes or days). Overall the scale has shown adequate internal consistency and moderate ability to differentiate between recidivists and non-recidivists ($r = .43$; ROC area of .74). The tool is currently being validated on a large Canadian population of sex offenders who are being assessed prospectively and followed up. In the UK, Craissati *et al.* (2006) have utilised the SONAR on a community population of sex offenders, comparing child molesters and internet sex offenders; they found that it was relatively easy to administer, and that the final SONAR score for stable dynamic variables was associated with other risk measures, and with general reoffending and risky behaviours. The acute dynamic variables were also examined in relation to child molesters and rapists, and found to be associated with failure. A longer-term follow-up study is underway.

The stable factors comprise six domains:

- Significant social influences
  the balance of pro-social versus antisocial influences amongst the offender's family members and social peers
- Intimacy deficits
  the presence of intimate partners, emotional identification with children, hostility toward women, general social rejection/loneliness, lack of concern for others
- Sexual self-regulation
  degree of sex drive and preoccupation, sex as coping, deviant sexual interests
- Attitudes supportive of sexual assault
  sexual entitlement, rape attitudes and child molester attitudes
- Co-operation with supervision
- General self-regulation
  impulsive acts, poor cognitive problem-solving skills, negative emotionality/hostility

The acute factors comprise:

- Opportunities for victim access
- Emotional collapse
- Collapse of social supports
- Hostility
- Substance abuse
- Sexual preoccupations
- Rejection of supervision

There are other tools of interest. The Minnesota Sex Offender Screening Tool – Revised (MnSOST-R) (Epperson *et al.*, 1999; www.//psych-server. iastate.edu/faculty/epperson/mnsost_download.htm) is a sixteen-item measure comprising twelve static variables and four institutional/dynamic variables. The MnSOST-R has been validated and results are promising. It is relatively easy to complete with access to detailed file information, and does not require additional training. The Sex Offender Risk Appraisal Guide (SORAG) (Quinsey *et al.*, 1998) is an amended version of the VRAG, designed to measure risk in sex offenders drawn from the same population as the VRAG; it comprises fourteen variables which are predominantly static in nature, although it does include phallometric assessment results as a dynamic measure of deviant sexual interest. Unfortunately this limits its applicability to general sex offender populations as the physiological measures of sexual arousal are not widely available; however, the scale is detailed in Quinsey *et al.* (1998) with a helpful – albeit slightly out of date – summary of the sexual recidivism literature. The VRS also has a sex offender version (VRS:SO; Olver, 2003), which follows the same format as the VRS, with seven static and seventeen dynamic variables; however, it includes sexually deviant lifestyle, sexual compulsivity, offence planning, deviant sexual preference and intimacy deficits. As with the VRS, the VRS:SO is closely related to detailed treatment goals, with a clear and accessible manual; however, there are no published validation studies and the manual is not available without completion of an intensive training course.

Within the new services for personality disordered offenders, the Structured Assessment of Risk and Need (SARN) (HM Prison Service, 2005) is being used. This has a scoring system which has not yet been fully validated, but is a comprehensive framework to guide dynamic risk assessment in sex offenders. The main body of the dynamic assessment process comprises four domains:

- Sexual interests (sexual preoccupation, sexual preference for children, sexualised violence, other offence-related sexual interest)
- Offence-related attitudes (adversarial sexual attitudes, sexual entitlement, child abuse supportive beliefs, rape supportive beliefs, beliefs that women are deceitful)
- Relationships (feeling inadequate, emotional congruence with children, grievance stance, no emotionally intimate relationship with an adult)
- Self-management (lifestyle impulsiveness, poor problem solving, poor emotional control)

Clearly, the SARN is very similar in its focus to the SONAR, except that it omits social influences (the least validated and most uncertain aspect of the SONAR), and it does not have an empirical evidence-base in terms of predictive validity. There is some evidence of robust inter-rater reliability and utility (reported in Risk Management Authority, 2006). The SARN manual is enormous and comprehensive, which makes it instructive but also prohibitive in terms of ease of use. The SARN requires some training to administer, but essentially relies on a good level of understanding of the characteristics of sex offenders in order to complete it reliably. As with so many dynamic measures, it is dependent to a great extent on the skills of the practitioner. Although this tool has great potential, it is unfortunately not generally available for use.

Social factors

Social factors are generally downplayed by psychologists, who have been instrumental in the development of risk prediction tools. Yet social variables have repeatedly been shown to have a very significant bearing on general and violent recidivism, and have a complicated and interwoven relationship with psychological variables such as personality disorder and locus of control. Demographics (age, gender and social class) are implicated in psychometric variables to some extent; culture is not specified in any of the tools – either as a mitigating or an aggravating feature. Social deprivation, and micro-cultures of nihilistic attitudes, antisocial and macho attitudes and poverty and unemployment, are at the root of many problems with illicit drug use and gang aggression. Some of these features underpin risk variables such as criminal peers and attitudes, or violent lifestyles. Farrall (2004) is one of the few authors to approach the question of risk assessment and social factors from the point of view of desistance from offending, and he summarises the literature, with support from May's (1999) work and his own: for example, leaving criminal environments or cohabitation with a woman from mid-twenties onwards were factors associated with a good outcome. In his own research, Farrall found that motivation not to reoffend, when combined with improvements in the social context (mending damaged family relationships, making new relationships, moving home and finding employment), was highly significant in identifying those offenders able to overcome obstacles to desistance; and that these were the object of change as well as the medium of change.

Specific offender populations

There is a potentially enormous range of specific offender populations to consider. For ease and clarity, we have chosen to focus on arson, domestic violence, and stalking, as these are reasonably common offending behaviours which have been associated with psychological motivations and personality difficulties.

Arson

There are no widely available validated tools for assessing future firesetting risk in arsonists. Motives for arson differ greatly, and are detailed in Chapter 2. Powis (2002) briefly reviews the risk literature in this area, and concludes that risk in arsonists is associated with youth, male gender, and poor work records, and that those who have previously set fires are at higher risk for setting fires in the future (although the majority of arsonists do not become repeat firesetters). In Palmer et al.'s (2005) review, they highlight the research on the role of dementia and learning disability in arson. There are high levels of personality disorder found among firesetters, particularly recidivists, including features of hostility and impulsivity; a minority of firesetters have a diagnosis of schizophrenia; and arsonists are at increased risk of self-harm. It is possible that up to 50 per cent of firesetters have mental health problems. Recidivism is also associated with lower levels of intelligence, and a family history of conflict and abuse in childhood. Alcohol use and alcohol dependency are found in almost 50 per cent of firesetters, and those who act alone are more likely to recidivate.

In the absence of empirically validated tools for a UK population, in terms of risk prediction with this group, a framework for the assessment of risk in cases of arson should relate to the typologies from the literature. The features cited above should always be considered. In addition, features to pursue would be the presence of a persistent interest in firesetting from childhood, including interest in legal activities such as relevant television programmes and observing local fire stations (although it must be emphasised that these factors are not repeatedly encountered in the risk literature), as well as the interest shown by the offender in the emergency services called out to contain the fire. The clinical items on attachment and history of abuse are also very important.

It is important to differentiate the risk associated with firesetting *per se* – including the use of inflammatory materials and the efforts made to control or limit the fire's impact – from the likelihood that the offender will reoffend. A schedule – such as the Fire Assessment Interview (Murphy, 1990) – can assist. This tool is an interview schedule containing sixteen statements relating to the frequency with which eight cognitions are self-reported by the arsonist as being their motives before and after the firesetting, and include excitement, anxiety, attention, social approval from peers, responding to internal voices, sadness, anger, and the avoidance of undesired situations.

Domestic violence

There is an enormous literature on domestic violence, which cannot be done justice here. The risk literature in this area focuses on two issues: persistent domestic violence, and escalation to domestic homicide. There are a number of typologies of male domestic violence perpetrators (again summarised in Powis, 2002), who tend to fall into three categories: the family-only batterers (the least severely violent, abusing in the home only, and the most conforming and compliant group); the emotionally volatile batterers (the most angry, jealous, suicidal and psychologically abusive men); and the generally violent batterer (the most severely violent, with substance misuse problems and violence outside the home).

A general framework for assessing risk in domestic violence perpetrators is detailed in the Spousal Assault Risk Assessment Guide (SARA – 2nd edition; Kropp et al., 1994). This tool – similar to the HCR-20 – is a clinical checklist of risk factors for spousal assault, drawn together from a review of the empirical literature and published clinical judgement. It comprises twenty items, divided into four sections:

- Criminal history (previous assaults, violations of statutory supervision)
- Psychosocial adjustment (relationship problems, employment problems, childhood abuse, substance abuse, suicidal/homicidal ideation, symptoms of mental illness and personality disorder)

- Spousal assault (past physical/sexual assaults, weapon use, death threats, escalation, violation of 'no contact' orders, cognitive distortions)
- Current offence (severity of assaults, weapon use, death threats, violation of orders)

The SARA can be obtained from Multi-Health Systems, to be used in a wide variety of situations, and without restrictions as to the user qualifications or training. Practitioners are expected to be experienced in the area of assessments and spousal assault. In approaching a risk assessment interview, the assessor should have access to collateral information in terms of records but also in relation to the victim of the spousal assault or other family members.

There has been some research on the psychometric properties of the SARA (Kropp and Hart, 2000), with findings of moderate levels of internal consistency, high inter-rater reliability, and good convergent and discriminant validity with respect to other measures related to risk for general and violent criminality.

Stalking

There is a burgeoning literature on stalking, and both Meloy (2001) and Mullen (Mullen et al., 2000) have written comprehensively on the subject. Victims and perpetrators tend to be of both sexes, and work on typologies tends to emphasise whether or not the victim has or has had an intimate relationship, a non-intimate relationship, or no relationship at all with the perpetrator. Stalkers tend to be mentally disordered and deluded into believing that there is greater significance to their relationship with the victim than is in fact the case (becoming more dangerous when 'rejected'); or more commonly, stalkers pursue their partner or ex-partner, trying to control them by using fear of violence.

The risk of violence appears to be associated with a greater number of previous stalking incidents, a previous relationship with the victim and/or a history of domestic violence offences in that relationship. Delusional (mentally ill) stalkers also pose a greater risk of serious harm to their victims. At present, there is no widely available validated tool with which to reliably assess relative risk in stalkers.

Clinical approaches to the measurement of risk

There are three broad areas where clinical approaches to risk assessment are of paramount importance. First, a clinical approach is implicit in many of the psychometric measures detailed above: a thorough assessment of psychopathic functioning involves an interview process with the offender which explores patterns of thinking, feeling and behaviour; and the dynamic domains in other tools – for example, sexual preoccupations or the cycle of violence – require the collaborative clinical involvement of practitioner and offender. Thus clinical judgement is informed by and anchored within actuarially driven approaches to risk assessment.

The second aim of clinical approaches is to move from the general to the specific; to create an individualised account of offending which pays attention to the minutiae as well as the patterns of behaviour. Whether based on cognitive-behavioural or psychoanalytic models, the practitioner will seek to understand the situations which trigger problematic behaviours, and the cognitions and affects which mediate. This involves an understanding of the meaning of the offence for the individual offender, and the way in which it regulates his sense of self in relation to the world around him. However, achieving this understanding may well require a good deal of exploration, and indeed is a goal of treatment rather than assessment alone. Perhaps the majority of offenders will struggle to identify the thoughts and feelings which intervene between a triggering situation (the impulse) and an offence (the action). Others will be able to articulate the outer layer of explanation ('I hit her to stop her nagging'). The practitioner may hypothesise that the act of violence represented something much more fundamentally threatening to the offender, but it may require considerable introspection before the offender can understand that he hit her 'because her nagging made me feel belittled and helpless, and then I felt weak, and I wanted to get rid of this feeling'. This approach is described by Glasser (1996) in his discussion of the two fundamental types of violence: 'self-preservative' and 'malicious' or 'sadistic'. Self-preservative violence is triggered instinctively as a response to perceived danger; malicious violence has as its aim the infliction of physical or mental pain which affords the perpetrator some gratification. Understanding the meaning of the violent act in terms of the perpetrator's internal world is therefore more important than understanding the act itself. Glasser points out that there are risk and treatment implications for this model. For example, self-preservative violence is less likely to re-occur as long as the offender does not come into contact with the trigger to their violence; understanding the meaning of this trigger, and reducing the offender's vulnerability to perceive such a trigger as highly threatening, are the targets of treatment. The maliciously violent offender poses more of a problem in terms of risk, but may respond in treatment to the development of a therapeutic relationship. This helps us to understand how a catastrophically violent and shocking murder can be associated with low future violence, whilst repeated domestic violence can be so intractable a behaviour.

It is worth pausing here to consider the particular issues posed by fantasies – whether sexually deviant or violent – which are sometimes touched on by the more comprehensive dynamic risk assessment tools. The presence of such fantasies within the context of individuals who have already committed violent acts would appear to be straightforward, but in fact this direct relationship is weakened when personality disorder is considered. That is, careful clinical consideration is needed, to determine the function of fantasies as 'rehearsal' or as 'compensation'. Rehearsal fantasies are closely related to the known offending behaviour, and often involve ruminating on further offending, with associated feelings of arousal (sexual or otherwise); such fantasies form part of the planning process for a further offence, desensitise the offender to further offending, and are almost always considered to aggravate risk. Examples of rehearsal fantasies include paedophiles masturbating to memories of previous offences, or a man seeking out his partner who he believes to have been unfaithful, anticipating in vivid detail how he will humiliate her.

Compensation fantasies represent a coping mechanism for individuals who use their imagination to regulate self-esteem, overcoming perceived humiliation by soothing fantasies of domination and vengeance. For some personality disordered offenders – often those with dramatic traits, particularly within the borderline spectrum – the disclosure of fantasies to others becomes a substitute for self-directed behaviours such as self-harm, with similar effects of drawing others into their internal world, avoiding the terrifying possibility of neglect and rejection by portraying a sense of self to others which is powerful and dangerous. Examples of compensatory fantasies include individuals spontaneously disclosing violent fantasies which seem more extreme than their actual offence history (or out of keeping with it), and which escalate as others show an interest in them.

The third role for clinical approaches is to broach risk issues in those individuals who have committed offences outside the norm – that is, offences with unusual features, or rare offences which are not captured by the broad sweep of actuarially based risk assessments. We have already highlighted the need for a specialised approach to domestic violence, arson and stalking. Other features might include homicide offences (where the risk prediction data are sparse), the presence of sexual sadism (which has a particularly close relationship with offence escalation and potential homicide – see Craissati, 2004, for a broader review of this area), or mock-terrorist hoaxes (offences which may not cause direct harm to others but are disruptive and likely to be closely linked to personality difficulties).

Denial is often a preoccupation within the assessment, and the feature of an offender's presentation most likely to cause an impasse. The subject is covered fully in Chapter 4 on treatment. The relationship between denial and risk is often misunderstood: essentially, total denial of the offence – either claiming that nothing illegal took place, or that someone else committed the crime – has not been shown to be related to an enhanced risk of recidivism (Craissati, 2004). This is because denial is so often related to conscious and deliberate attempts to avoid responsibility, or to more complex feelings of shame in relation to offending, and not related to fundamental and entrenched psychological difficulties. Denial of the offence overlaps with refusal to enter treatment, and again, this does not have a direct relationship to enhanced risk (Hanson *et al.*, 2002). Partial denial – as in cognitive distortions which minimise and justify offending behaviour – is integral to many of the dynamic measures of risk.

The relationship between personality disorder, offending behaviour and risk

It will be absolutely clear to the reader by now that there must be a reasonably strong relationship between personality disorder and offending behaviour and risk. First, the PCL-R is both a measure of personality disorder and a powerful risk prediction tool in its own right. Second, a range of psychometric measures include the presence of psychopathy (graded according to score) and personality disorder (simply present or absent) within their measures. Third, dynamic features of psychometric tools – such as general self-management, intimacy deficits, emotional control and cognitive distortions – overlap with core components of personality disorder diagnoses.

There have been empirical attempts to relate personality traits or clusters to criminal and violent offending. Blackburn and Coid (1999) found that violent mentally disordered offenders were clustered into six personality disordered groups:

1 Antisocial–narcissistic
2 Paranoid–antisocial
3 Borderline–antisocial–passive-aggressive
4 Borderline
5 Compulsive–borderline
6 Schizoid

They found that offenders in the first three groups had more extensive criminal careers and higher psychopathy scores; almost two-thirds of group 2 had a history of psychotic disorder. Offenders in the last three groups were more likely to manifest violence within the context of more situationally specific interpersonal problems. An earlier study (Coid, 1992) found that borderline, antisocial and narcissistic disorders were the most prevalent in male and female violent offenders. An MCMI narcissistic–antisocial–histrionic profile has been found to be consistent with high psychopathy scores (Blackburn, 1996), whilst secondary psychopaths were found to be passive-aggressive, avoidant, schizoid, paranoid, antisocial, dependent and borderline; controlled personalities were compulsive and dependent, and inhibited personalities were avoidant, schizoid, dependent and schizotypal. Of course, the relationship between antisocial personality disorder and violence is well established, but Hiscoke *et al.* (2003) also found that this relationship diminished with age; whilst there was also a significant relationship between schizoid personality traits and violence, which remained even when age was controlled for. It seems quite likely that impoverished interpersonal functioning and callousness/flat affect – features of both schizoid and psychopathic personality – may be important features mediating between personality type and violence.

It may be over-simplistic, but perhaps the central component shared by personality disorder and violence (sexual or physical) is the interpersonal focus: just as personality disorder cannot exist in isolation from other people, offending always requires a victim, either symbolic or actual, who has meaning for the offender. This raises the importance of arriving at a formulation of the offender's risk which not only details the likelihood of him reoffending, but places experiences and difficulties in a contextual and explanatory framework which generates a working model and a linked set of hypotheses and treatment needs.

In summary, this chapter outlines the broad areas of investigation involved in an assessment of personality disorder and offending risk. Good practice dictates that judgement should be linked to an evidence-base, and that every effort should be made to endeavour to meet the needs of the offender and the public. The pilot services which have been developed for personality disordered offenders have adopted a common database of personality disorder and risk prediction instruments. These include the IPDE and SCID-I, the PCL-R, HCR-20, VRS, Static 99 and Risk Matrix 2000, and the SARN. The overlap between measures reflects the relative lack of evidence-base for measures in a UK population, and it is hoped that, in time, the evidence-base will enable the teams to reduce the psychometric package to a minimum. However, there is still considerable room for individualised approaches to the problem, which might depend on the setting, the practitioner competencies, the task to be achieved and the resources available. The tools should operate in the service of the practitioners; the practitioners should not be slaves to the tools.

Two case studies

Brian

Brian was a 36-year-old-man, presenting to services as he was about to be released from prison having served a prison sentence for grievous bodily harm on a female care worker. He had perpetrated a vicious assault when intoxicated, having become enraged when she berated him for returning late to the hostel, kicking and beating her around the head. His childhood had been extremely disturbed – he had been placed in care at the age of 5 following a period of neglect and physical abuse at the hands of his parents. They occasionally visited, but were unreliable, and reneged on promises that he could return home. He was disruptive in care and failed in three foster placements. There were some allegations of inappropriate sexual activity with his female peers which were not detailed in the file. It was known that his mother worked as a prostitute and that he had been exposed at an early age to sexual activity, whilst his father was in and out of prison. As an adolescent, he lived on the streets and worked intermittently as a rent boy, justifying this behaviour as a necessity at the time, and denying that he had any uncertainties or anxieties about his sexual orientation. In adulthood, he had had a number of brief and turbulent intimate heterosexual relationships, he had been unable to sustain work, he self-harmed repeatedly, and he drank heavily, often binge drinking. On two occasions he had been admitted to psychiatric hospital, and an initial diagnosis of psychosis was amended to personality disorder, after his auditory hallucinations quickly settled and he brought quantities of alcohol on to the ward. His offending history included an arson attack on a foster carer's car in childhood for which he was not convicted, delinquent acts from the age of 15 (taking cars, breaking into non-dwelling premises, possession of cannabis), and adult convictions for criminal damage, assault and burglary.

In interview, Brian was willing to talk about his difficulties, but rather guarded when asked to describe his early life, saying that such conversations tended to upset him as his mother was a 'slut' and his father a 'violent monster' of whom he had very vivid memories. He was angry about social services' attempts to care for him, emphasising the extent to which they had replicated his earlier experiences of abuse. He spoke in an agitated tone of his fights in prison, and his capacity to kill someone when he lost control of his temper. He completed the MCMI, presenting a valid profile but one characterised by excessively high levels of self-disclosure and a tendency to present himself as overwhelmed with difficulties; there were significant elevations on the antisocial, negativistic and borderline scales, with high levels of anxiety and depressive mood as well as post-traumatic difficulties. An exploration of core beliefs (or schemas) suggested that he predominantly felt the world to be a hostile and persecutory place in which he was very vulnerable, and that his strategy was to vacillate between a rather acquiescent, passive and dependent style and a verbally abusive and emotionally explosive state which allowed him to mask his feelings of fragility and control – by intimidation of those around him. Clearly, in terms of his offending behaviour, alcohol played a central role in disinhibiting him, such that he lost control of his habitual strategies. Although Brian was unable to account for why he had attacked the care worker with such ferocity, acknowledging that she was generally well thought of and her reprimand was entirely justifiable, he was ashamed. It seemed probable that it was just those elements – her role as carer, her kindness and her justifiable accusations – which induced in his fragile and intoxicated state a sense of both acute guilt and also betrayal, and with a feeling that he could not survive this encounter he became enraged and attacked her as though his own life depended on it.

The clinical interview and psychometric measure suggested that Brian met DSM criteria for borderline and antisocial personality disorder (the primary presentation being borderline), with traits from avoidant and dependent personality disorders. In terms of psychometric approaches to risk, he achieved moderate-high scores on static measures. That is, he had previous convictions for violence but was not particularly young when these convictions first appeared, although he was young at the time of the arson and subsequent driving offences; he had had marked problems with relationship instability, employment problems, alcohol use and early maladjust- ment, as well as the presence of personality disorder. However, on the PCL-R, he scored only moderately, with elevations on the antisocial factor but a total score of just less than 20. On more dynamic items, there was a range of concerns including continuing problems with unstable relationships, emotional control and interper- sonal aggression; criminogenic attitudes, peers and lifestyle were present but only mildly so, and he had no history of weapon use. There were difficulties with his level of impulsivity and his lack of insight into the triggers for his violence; he also had some problems with an unstable mental state, ambivalent attitudes towards his alcohol use, and a likely inability to cope with stress and instability in his environ- ment in the future. Additional specific concerns were raised regarding his sexuality, and the fact that the victims of his violence had always been women.

Clive

It seemed at first that Clive was very similar to Brian, in terms of his personality classification and his level of risk. However, there were subtle but important differences between them. Clive was a 28-year-old man, living in a probation hostel, on bail, and charged with gross indecency and affray. This related to an offence with a 12-year-old girl who lived on his estate, and who had previously been abused by her stepfather and somewhat neglected. Clive befriended her one day and offered her a can of coke and some cigarettes; she spent some time in his flat, and he put on a pornographic video and invited her to perform oral sex on him, subsequently masturbating. Later that day she told her male cousin about what had occurred, and he came round to the flat, and a fight ensued. The police were called, and Clive refused to calm down, shouting and resisting arrest.

Clive's childhood history was that he was one of a number of siblings, cared for by his mother; his father was unknown to him. His mother was an alcoholic and when sober could be warm and caring towards him. However, these times were limited, and more often she was aggressive and unpredictable when intoxicated.

Clive had to take on something of the parenting role as he was the eldest sibling, and he could recall taking his mother to the toilet and having to pull up her underpants because she was incapable of managing it herself. He frequently ran away from home, and these were remembered as happy carefree moments. He tended to thieve to survive, but was usually caught by the police or social services and returned to his mother's care. At school – from which he habitually truanted – he was thought to be bright although he never achieved anything academically. He left home at 15, and lived a very itinerant lifestyle, sometimes on the streets, sometimes in hostels or in his own accommodation. He seemed to have a remarkable ability to obtain money, and liked to dress well, go out to clubs and dabble in gambling. He had accumulated a long string of convictions for theft, burglary, handling stolen goods, deception and fraud; however, he had only once had a custodial sentence, and otherwise had received community penalties, some of which he had breached by reoffending. There were no previous sexual convictions, and only one previous violent conviction for common assault some years ago. He had had a number of brief relationships, none of which were long-lasting. He tended to surround himself with other individuals who were antisocial or offenders, but had no strong friendships. He was a frequent drug user, usually cannabis but sometimes class A drugs, but said that he could 'take it or leave it'. He had lost contact with his siblings for many years, but thought that they had been more compliant as children (although less close to their mother), and that there was no forensic history in the wider family.

Clive had a reputation for being difficult, but in fact could choose to be quite charming and amenable as long as he was not unduly agitated or frustrated by matters which were out of his control; at such times he had a hot temper and could be verbally abusive and threatening. There were some relatively minor difficulties at the hostel when it emerged that he was gossiping about some staff to others, praising and denigrating individuals as it suited him, and causing rumours and rifts to emerge in the staff group. In interview he was quite willing to discuss his past, and provided vivid anecdotes of distressing events in his childhood about which he showed very little emotion. However, he did sometimes feel very depressed, and was annoyed when his distress was not taken seriously. His attitude towards the sexual offence was less open and frank, and he tried to justify his behaviour in terms of denigrating the victim and placing much – but not all – of the responsibility at her feet.

The IPDE was completed, and Clive was interested and involved in the process, enquiring and commenting on the scoring system. The results suggested that he had a diagnosis of personality disorder not otherwise specified, that is, marked features of a number of disorders, including antisocial, borderline, paranoid and narcissistic traits. He scored very high on the Brief Symptom Inventory, with problems of anxiety and depression, although there were few symptoms of clinical depression apparent in interview. The PCL-R score was high – 29 – because in addition to antisocial features (proneness to boredom, poor behavioural controls, early behavioural problems, lack of realistic long-term goals, impulsivity, irresponsibility, juvenile delinquency and revocation of conditional release), he had marked personality features, including glibness, a grandiose sense of self-worth, conning, lack of remorse and empathy, shallow affect and a failure to accept responsibility for his own actions. The risk scales were equivocal: static scores were elevated in terms of psychopathy, personality disorder generally, early maladjustment, substance use, prior supervision failure, employment and relationship instability. However, dynamic factors suggested that there were problems with impulsivity, criminal attitudes and peers, with a lack of insight into violence and cognitive distortions; however, there was no weapon use, no violent lifestyle, limited interpersonal aggression and no institutional violence. He was apparently compliant, accepted support, and had some resources to cope with stress. Specific sex offender scales placed Clive in the second highest category of risk, on the basis of his general offending history, age, choice of acquaintance victim, and lack of cohabiting relationships. Dynamic features for sexual risk emphasised his significant intimacy difficulties – frequent uncommitted sexual encounters; some relatively minor pro-offending attitudes in terms of justifying and minimising his behaviour; no real problems with sexual self-regulation and preoccupations, but marked problems with general self-regulation, as described above.

Chapter 4

Treatment models

Introduction

The evidence-based literature on treatments for people with a personality disorder has tended to focus on psychological or mental health need, with little reference to offending behaviour (Bateman and Tyrer, 2002). Indeed, traditionally in mental health services, there has been a lack of confidence that treatment can have an impact on offending behaviour. In contrast, the 'what works' literature on offenders has almost exclusively addressed offending behaviour and the diminuation of risk to others.

In compiling this review, we have aimed to complement the review on personality disorder treatments compiled by Bateman and Tyrer (2002). Our selection criteria were simple: widely used and standardised treatment programmes, with a published evidence-base for offenders in England and Wales. We have therefore excluded a body of evaluated – and potentially effective – work which is derived from small sample sizes or has not been replicated.

As with the Bateman and Tyrer (2002) review, we have attempted to categorise the programmes in terms of *efficacy* (0 = ineffective, 1 = unknown efficacy, 2 = efficacy demonstrated in small studies (< 50 patients) only, 3 = efficacy demonstrated in large studies); and *generalisability* (0 = highly selective and not generalisable, 1 = selective and generalisability uncertain, 2 = some limited selection precluding full generalisability, and 3 = typical offenders with condition who are representative). These ratings were made on the basis of criminogenic evidence, not on efficacy in relation to personality disordered offenders specifically.

Review of Treatments for Dangerous and Severe Personality Disorder (Warren et al., 2001)

The aim of this review was to update the work of Dolan and Coid (1993) in their book, *Psychopathic and Antisocial Personality Disorders: Treatment and Research Issues*. The authors reviewed studies of any design, evaluating

regime for people identified as having any personality
~d as psychopathic – using the PCL-R – or detained
f the Mental Health Act (1983).
,, and associated research, focused on a variety of out-
..cluded targeting:

..ending behaviour to reduce the risk of reoffending
Symptoms associated with personality disorder (aggression, self-harm
or substance misuse)
- Core personality structure and functioning

With particular reference to antisocial personality disorder and psychopathic disorder, the authors found that the outcome variables most commonly studied were substance misuse and psychological changes such as
mood or cognitive functioning. They conclude that cognitive-behavioural
therapy may produce some decrease in substance abuse, and pharmacological treatment can effect a decrease in anxiety. Long-term therapeutic
community treatment in high secure settings seems promising, although
therapeutic communities are subject to criticisms that they are highly
selective.

Key treatment models from the mental health literature

Cognitive therapy (efficacy = 1; generalisability = 2)

Cognitive therapy is a goal-directed problem-solving therapy which focuses
on teaching specific cognitive and behavioural skills to improve current
functioning. With personality disorders, more emphasis is placed on
changing core beliefs than dysfunctional thoughts, and on maintaining a
collaborative therapeutic alliance. Schema-focused therapy (Young *et al.*,
2003) is an integrative approach which includes some psychoanalytic
approaches in addition to conventional cognitive-behavioural therapy: it
places more emphasis on the therapeutic relationship, affective experience
and the discussion of early life experiences.

Davidson (1996) used brief (ten-session) cognitive therapy for the treatment of antisocial and borderline personality disorders, with improvement
in target problems; this is now being evaluated in a randomised controlled
trial. Another small trial, using a mixed cognitive therapy and dialectical
behaviour therapy protocol for treating cluster B personality difficulties,
involved the random allocation of self-harm repeaters to 'manual assisted
cognitive behaviour therapy' (MACT) or to 'treatment as usual'. The rate
of suicide acts and self-rated depressive symptoms was lower with MACT;

furthermore the observed average cost of care was almost half in the MACT group (Evans *et al.*, 1999).

Dialectic behaviour therapy (efficacy = 2; generalisability = 1)

Dialectic behaviour therapy (DBT) is a manualised therapy (Linehan, 1993) which includes individual therapy, group skills training, telephone contact and therapist consultation. It involves behavioural techniques, cognitions and support. The skills group addresses core mindfulness skills, interpersonal effectiveness skills, emotional modulation skills and distress tolerance skills; there is a hierarchy of targets for individual therapy which start with decreasing suicidal behaviours, progressing through to other therapy interfering behaviours, increasing self-esteem and negotiating individual targets with the patient.

DBT was originally developed as a treatment for parasuicidal women with borderline personality disorder. Initial research (Linehan *et al.*, 1993) demonstrated that the DBT group (compared to a control group) demonstrated significantly greater improvement in the number of suicide attempts, spent shorter periods of time as inpatients over the year of treatment, and were less likely to drop out of the therapies that they were assigned to; at a one-year follow-up there were no between-group differences.

A more recent Dutch study (Verheul *et al.*, 2002) randomly assigned women with borderline personality disorder to one year of DBT or to treatment as usual. DBT resulted in better retention rates and greater reductions of self-harm. It has been difficult to determine whether the efficacy of DBT in reducing self-harming and self-destructive impulsive behaviours has been due to the treatment model *per se*, or to factors such as allegiance to the treatment model, staff training and ongoing supervision (Robins and Chapman, 2004).

The efficacy of DBT has been examined in relation to borderline personality disorder and substance misuse (Linehan *et al.*, 1999, 2002). DBT patients demonstrated greater reductions in drug use than a 'treatment as usual' group. Attempts to establish the efficacy of group DBT skills training (provided in conjunction with non-DBT individual therapy), as compared to individual therapy only, found that outcomes were no better than for individuals who received non-DBT individual therapy only. This would suggest that DBT individual therapy may be an essential component of the model, particularly for those patients with borderline personality disorder and/or self-harming behaviour (Linehan, 1993).

Dynamic psychotherapy (efficacy = 2; generalisability = 2)

Much of the work on psychodynamic psychotherapy has focused on borderline personality disorder, probably because of its characteristics of help-seeking behaviour and wish to change. The model assumes that behaviours and actions have a personal meaning to the individual as a result of their thought processes and emotional states; the treatment of a patient takes place in the context of a therapeutic relationship in which the emotional involvement of a trained therapist is a central factor. The model pays particular attention to unconscious and partially conscious, as well as conscious, mental states.

Bateman and Fonagy (1999) undertook a randomised study examining the effectiveness of psychoanalytically oriented partial hospitalisation compared with standard psychiatric care for patients with borderline personality disorder. Treatment included individual and group therapy and lasted for eighteen months. The partial hospitalisation group demonstrated significantly greater improvement on all outcome measures, including the frequency of self-harm, duration of inpatient admissions, the use of psychotropic medication and a variety of self-report measures. Chiesa *et al.* (2002) compared the relative effectiveness of three treatment models for a mixed group of personality disorders: long-term residential therapeutic community treatment; briefer inpatient treatment followed by community-based dynamic therapy; and general community psychiatric treatment. Brief inpatient therapeutic community treatment followed by outpatient dynamic therapy was more effective than the other two treatment modes on most measures, including self-harm and readmission rates to general psychiatric wards, and was more cost-effective.

Mentalisation (efficacy = 1; generalisabilty = 2)

Mentalisation-based approaches to therapy are developments of the psychodynamic and attachment traditions. They postulate that a key deficit in personality disorders is the lack of a fully or securely developed 'reflective function', i.e. the capacity to understand the subjective states of oneself or other people. Bateman and Fonagy (2004) propose that therapeutic techniques which are adapted to this deficit and enable mentalising capacities to develop are a key common factor in many successful treatments, which can be enhanced by therapists and programme designers being conscious of this process. The aim is to promote curiosity and engagement with different subjective perspectives on emotional and interpersonal experience and to maintain affective arousal and cognitive complexity at an optimal level in order to sustain this enquiry.

Mentalisation is a new approach to treatment and is as yet not tested in published trials. However evaluations are underway in the UK, the Netherlands and Norway. Preliminary results are reported to be strong. The programme evaluated by Bateman and Fonagy (1999), referred to above, has been progressively reconceptualised in the light of this theoretical approach and results of current trials are expected to at least match or improve upon those of the previous regime. Trials of an outpatient adaptation of this programme, consisting of once-weekly individual and group sessions conducted on mentalisation principles, are close to publication at the time of going to press.

Cognitive analytical therapy (efficacy = 1; generalisability = 2)

Cognitive analytical therapy (CAT) postulates that a set of partially dissociated 'self-states' account for the clinical features of borderline personality disorder (Ryle, 1997). Such patients typically experience rapid switching from one state of mind to another, and in the process undergo intense uncontrollable emotions alternating between feeling muddled and emotionally cut off. There are some indications that this treatment method may be of help in some patients (Ryle and Golynkina, 2000), although there have been no controlled trials to date.

Therapeutic community treatments (efficacy = 2; generalisability = 1)

A therapeutic community treatment is an intensive form of treatment in which the environmental setting becomes the core therapy in which behaviour can be challenged and modified, essentially through group pressure. This is a long-standing model of treatment – existing in the UK for over fifty years – but it has only recently been subjected to direct controlled evaluation.

Much recent research has been based on the work of the Henderson Hospital. The consensus has been generally favourable (Lees *et al.*, 1999) but poor methodology and heterogeneity between the treatment conditions have undermined attempts to establish efficacy. Patients have shown symptomatic improvement (Dolan and Evans, 1992), a reduction in core features of personality disorder (Dolan *et al.*, 1997), and a reduction in health service usage (Dolan *et al.*, 1996; Krawitz, 1997).

Drug treatment

There are difficulties in establishing the efficacy of drug treatments with personality disorders. Antipsychotic drugs (efficacy = 1; generalisability = 2): recent studies suggest the utility of atypical antipsychotic medication (such as olanzapine or risperidone), although there is a high dropout rate of around 50 per cent from the studies. Antidepressant drugs (efficacy = 2; generalisability = 2) have been studied – both tricyclic antidepressants and selective serotonin reuptake inhibitors (SSRIs) – but largely in borderline personality disordered patients. SSRIs do appear to reduce impulsiveness and anger, and may also reduce self-harm. Finally, mood stabilisers (efficacy = 1; generalisability = 1) have been used, again predominantly with borderline personality disordered patients. Results have been inconsistent, although sodium valproate does appear to reduce agitation and impulsive aggression and improve level of functioning.

Summary

Bateman and Tyrer (2002) conclude that a combination of psychological treatments reinforced by drug therapy at critical times seems to be the consensus for treatment in personality disorder. This is supported by the review of Perry *et al.* (1999). Successful treatments include a focus on clear structures, enhancing compliance, clearly differentiating between a focus on problem behaviours and interpersonal relationship patterns, being theoretically highly coherent to both therapist and patient, being relatively long-term, and being well integrated with other services available to the patient – that is, there may be little to be gained from seeking to establish the superiority of any particular model over another (specificity); rather non-specific factors relating to the coherence and application of any treatment model may be more salient to treatment success.

Key treatment models from the criminal justice literature (what works)

The criminal justice literature essentially focuses on offending behaviour and criminogenic need. Personality disorder has not generally been evaluated and has not been a criteria for inclusion or exclusion from programmes. Where personality disorder has been considered, this is detailed in the summaries below.

Thinking skills (efficacy = 3; generalisability = 2)

A review by Vennard *et al.* (1997) concluded that cognitive-behavioural methods combined with training in social skills and problem solving give the most positive results with both juvenile and adult offenders, in terms of recidivism. However, even these approaches do not achieve large reductions in reoffending with mixed groups of offenders – on average, reconvictions are 10–15 per cent lower than for matched comparison groups.

The range of theoretical and practical training for cognitive-behavioural approaches varies enormously across professions and agencies. Currently the main thrust in relation to offender programmes is an emphasis on brief focused training of multi-professional groups in order to ensure treatment integrity and consistent programme delivery.

Cognitive skills programmes have been developed and accredited for use in prison, in the community and with probation clients. Reasoning and

Rehabilitation (R&R) is a general offending behaviour programme, originally developed in Canada and later revised for use in the English and Welsh Prison and Probation Service. It comprises thirty-eight two-hour sessions, and targets high risk offenders. Enhanced Thinking Skills (ETS) was developed by the English and Welsh Prison Service as a shorter alternative to the R&R programme; it comprises twenty two-hour sessions and is targeted at medium risk offenders. Think First was developed as a general offending behaviour programme for group work with offenders, and comprises twenty-two two-hour sessions, again targeting medium risk offenders. All three programmes target related goals, including enhanced self-control, interpersonal problem-solving skills, social perspective taking, critical reasoning skills, cognitive style, and an understanding of the values which govern behaviour.

An evaluation study (Friendship *et al.*, 2002) compared 670 adult male offenders serving a custodial sentence of two years or more who had voluntarily participated in one of two cognitive skills programmes run by the prison service between 1992 and 1996, with 1,801 matched offenders who had not participated in a programme. Two-year reconviction rates fell considerably after cognitive skills treatment, particularly in those who were deemed to pose a medium risk – up to 14 per cent reduction. Furthermore, both ETS and R&R packages produced a unique effect in significantly reducing the probability of reconviction, whilst controlling for other related variables. However, a more recent evaluation of ETS and R&R by Cann *et al.* (2003) found more equivocal results: they followed up 2,195 adult male and 1,534 young offenders who had participated in either of the programmes and compared them to a matched group of offenders for one- and two-year reconviction rates. Risk was assessed using the revised Offender Group Reconviction Scale (OGRS). There was no difference in the one-year reconviction rates (18.1 per cent for programme participants versus 19.5 per cent for the comparison group), although when programme non-completers were excluded from the analysis (9 per cent of the adult sample), there was a significant improvement in the reconviction rate for programme completers (17 per cent versus 19.5 per cent in the comparison group). This improvement was greatest in the high risk group, where there was a 7 per cent reduction in reconviction. The programme dropouts had the highest reconviction rate at one year (28.7 per cent), and dropouts comprised a large proportion of high risk offenders. However, this lower rate of reconviction for programme completers at one year was not maintained at two years for either the adult or young offender groups. When the programmes were examined independently, it was found that there were no significantly improved results for the R&R programme.

A retrospective analysis of pathfinder programmes in the probation service (Hollin *et al.*, 2004) compared 2,230 offenders sentenced to a probation order with a requirement to attend one of five offending behaviour programmes (Think First, ETS, R&R, Priestley One-to-One and Addressing Substance-Related Offending), with a comparison group of 2,645 offenders sentenced to a probation order without any additional requirement. The two groups were matched for gender, age, OGRS2 score and offence history. There was no significant difference in reconviction rates between the two groups (69.87 per cent for programme participants versus 57.92 per cent for the comparison group). However, when programme non-completers were examined separately, it was found that while 54.55 per cent of programme completers were reconvicted, 77.60 per cent of non-completers and 57.92 per cent of the comparison group were reconvicted. The data were again analysed in terms of appropriateness of risk band (medium as compared to too low or too high, on the basis of OGRS2 score): programme completion had very little effect on reconviction in the 'too low' group, but the non-completers in this group were reconvicted at a high level (52.48 per cent); there was a treatment effect for completers in the appropriate and 'too high' risk bands, with the non-completers continuing to perform worse than both the completers and the comparison group. The authors conclude that the treatment results are promising for those who complete the programme, but non-completers – two-thirds of the treatment sample – pose particular concern in the community.

Dialectical behaviour therapy (Linehan, 1993) with offenders (efficacy = 1; generalisability = 2)

DBT is currently being evaluated for use with women in three prisons in England and Wales. A small-scale study in a high secure hospital which provided one year of DBT for ten female patients with a diagnosis of BPD found that there was a significant reduction in self-harming behaviour following treatment (Low et al., 2001). A modified version of DBT, for use with men with a diagnosis of antisocial personality disorder, has been evaluated in a secure forensic service in Colorado, USA, and is currently being adapted for use by the Personality Disorder service at Rampton High Secure Hospital. McCann et al. (2000) adapted DBT for use in forensic settings, including behavioural targets related to interpersonal violence, attention to the reinforcement of honest recording of maladaptive behaviours, testing skills acquisition with exams and role-play quizzes, and emotional insensitivity of antisocial patients. They proposed a biosocial theory in which offenders with antisocial personality disorder – as with their counterparts with borderline personality disorder – experience an invalidating environment, but one which is characterised by harsh and inconsistent discipline, little positive parental involvement and inadequate supervision. Consequently, individuals with ASPD appear emotionally insensitive, in sharp contrast to those with BPD who are remarkably sensitive emotionally. Berzins and Trestman (2004) reviewed the DBT adapted programmes at seven forensic sites within North America: unfortunately there are no published results available regarding efficacy, although one correctional centre (Twin Rivers) did find that emotional regulation skills were effective in reducing irritability, particularly in high risk inmates.

Anger/violence and management of challenging behaviours (efficacy = 2; generalisability = 1)

There is a wide range of programmes for the management of anger and violence, largely cognitive-behavioural in orientation. For example, Saunders (1996) treated 136 male domestic violence offenders in an out-patient department, comparing feminist-driven cognitive-behavioural therapy with process-oriented psychodynamic treatment, for 16–20 sessions. Although there was no difference in recidivism rates (of between 45 and 50 per cent at between 2.0 and 4.6 years post-treatment), the researchers found that those men with antisocial personality disorder fared better in the feminist CBT trial, and those men with dependent personality disorder fared better in psychodynamic treatment (according to women partners' reports of behaviour).

Recent evaluated programmes for personality disordered offenders in secure health settings include social problem solving (McMurran et al., 2001). McMurran and colleagues were able to demonstrate greatly improved scores on psychometric testing before and after treatment for a small group of personality disordered offenders, both in terms of a social problem-solving intervention and a 'controlling angry aggression' intervention.

Wong and Gordon's (2000) Violence Risk Programme is being evaluated in the UK at Rampton High Secure Hospital, and within the Forensic Intensive Psychological Treatment Service in South East London. The aim of the programme is to decrease the frequency and intensity of aggressive behaviours, to decrease or eliminate the antisocial beliefs and attitudes that support the use of aggression and violence, and to teach appropriate interpersonal skills that are effective in reducing the risk of future recidivism. The model is closely allied to the VRS assessment and incorporates a Stages of Change Model to guide the selection of strategies. Phase 1 focuses on enhancing the understanding of aggressive behaviours, developing a treatment alliance and identifying treatment targets; phase 2 focuses on the acquisition of relevant skills; and phase 3 focuses on relapse prevention and the generalisation of skills across contexts and situations. This is an intensive programme, run on a daily basis over a period of four to six months.

The RAID ('Reinforce Appropriate, Ignore Difficult and Disruptive'; Davies, 2001) approach to working with extreme behaviour is based on a positive philosophy. As personality disorders are characterised by inter-personal difficulties, and RAID focuses upon improving and strengthening interpersonal relationships, it is expected that the model would have benefits for such patients. The Personality Disorder Service at Ashworth Hospital has secured funding to introduce RAID training to staff, and to evaluate the outcome of this approach, as applied to a complete service for offenders detained under the Mental Health Act and held in conditions of high security. RAID is primarily a management strategy which can be applied to institutional settings, and therefore has limited applicability to community treatment services.

Substance misuse (efficacy = 2; generalisability = 1)

Treatment approaches to personality disordered substance misusers have been summarised by Welsh (NIMHE, 2003). She concluded that although people with personality disorder may have greater pre- and post-treatment problem severity, the amount of improvement achieved in drug and alcohol treatment does not differ significantly from that achieved in those without personality disorder. However, there is evidence to suggest that alcohol users with personality disorder do relapse earlier following treatment, even after controlling for pre-treatment severity of problems. DBT (see above) has been shown to be useful with women with BPD and comorbid drug dependency, with improvement in a number of areas including drug abstinence. Ball (1998) described a treatment approach to individuals with personality disorder and substance use disorders which combined relapse prevention work with identification of, education about, and techniques for changing maladaptive schemas and coping styles.

Drug Treatment and Testing Orders (DTTOs) were introduced as a new community sentence under the Crime and Disorder Act 1998, and designed as a response to the growing evidence of links between problem drug use and persistent acquisitive offending. DTTOs involve regular drug testing and reports to the court during a period of fairly intensive treatment involving contact with the offender several days a week. Treatment models vary, but tend to include individual and group work, motivational inter-viewing and relapse prevention. Hough et al. (2003) evaluated three pilot sites, following up 174 offenders over a two-year period. They found that the reconviction rate was 80 per cent; however, completion rates for DTTOs were low, and only one-third finished the treatment successfully. The reconviction rate for those who completed their order was 53 per cent, whilst 91 per cent of those whose orders were revoked were reconvicted, and completion was the best predictor of reconviction. Furthermore, for those who completed, their annual conviction rate reduced to well below the rates of the previous five years. Again, as with the pathfinder programmes, the researchers advise that considerable attention be paid to improving retention rates. However, no data were available to assist in understanding the characteristics of those whose orders were revoked.

Sex offender treatment programmes (efficacy = 3; generalisability = 2)

Accredited sex offender treatment programmes (SOTP) were developed in the 1990s as part of a national prison strategy for the integrated assessment and treatment of sexual offenders. These programmes are now delivered in high secure hospitals. Community-based programmes – largely run by the probation service – have adopted recently accredited programmes such as the West Midlands programme, and are currently standardising their treatment approach. The only community residential unit for adult male sex offenders – the Wolvercote Unit – has been run by the Lucy Faithful Foundation, and is also accredited. This is currently closed. Other remaining standardised programmes are based on similar principles and models, and may be designed to meet the needs of adolescents (for example, G-MAP), or as a partnership between health and probation (for example, the Challenge Project). Treatment, having been predominantly designed for child molesters, now incorporates the treatment needs of all sex offenders, largely utilising group treatment as the preferred model.

All the above programmes are based on a cognitive-behavioural model of treatment. This involves recognising the patterns of distorted thinking which allow the contemplation of illegal sexual acts, understanding the impact which sexually abusive behaviour has on its victims, and identifying key triggers to offending as an aid to relapse prevention. Support for the efficacy of cognitive-behavioural treatments for sex offenders has been established by Hanson *et al.*'s meta-analytic review (2002), which found that there was an overall treatment effect – in terms of a reduction in sexual recidivism – of around 5 per cent.

The STEP (sex offender treatment evaluation programme) team have evaluated both community and prison SOTP programmes since 1994, on behalf of the Home Office. The team (Beech *et al.*, 1999) evaluated twelve treatment groups in six prisons, comprising eighty-two child molesters. They used a range of psychometric tests pre- and post-treatment, designed to measure four areas: denial of deviant sexual interests and offending behaviours, pro-offending attitudes, predisposing personality factors, and relapse prevention skills. Overall the programmes were successful in achieving change in a positive direction, and 67 per cent of the sample were judged to have shown a treatment effect. Longer-term treatment (of about 160 hours) was more successful in achieving results which were maintained after release than shorter-term therapy (of about 80 hours).

A STEP evaluation of community programmes (Beech *et al.*, 2001) examined the reconviction data for fifty-three child molesters, who had undergone treatment and had been at risk in the community for six years. They distinguished low deviancy child molesters from high deviancy child molesters on the basis of their psychometric profile (Beech, 1998). A clear treatment effect was found, in that only 10 per cent of the men who were classified as 'benefiting from treatment' were reconvicted in the six-year follow-up, compared with 23 per cent of men who were classified as 'not having responded to treatment'. However, again, a brief dose of treatment was not found to be as effective with men measured at the pre-treatment stage as being high deviancy, compared with those who were low deviancy.

A community treatment programme for personality disordered sex offenders – the Challenge Project – has published a preliminary evaluation of the programme, in terms of offence-related outcomes: if those in treatment were simply compared to those not in the community treatment programme, then they appeared to fare worse in terms of failure on community supervision and sexually inappropriate behaviours (17 per cent versus 9 per cent); however, if the comparison groups were controlled for risk level and a history of developmental trauma (both being higher in the Challenge Project subjects), then there was a marked trend for the specialist programme to show better results (18 per cent versus 33 per cent). Interestingly, low risk offenders showed no benefit from the specialist programme.

Deviant sexual interest – identified as a key dynamic variable associated with risk – has attracted pharmacological interventions (American Psychiatric Association, 1999). These include anti-libidinal hormonal treatments, which can be effective in conjunction with cognitive-behavioural approaches, but which have a range of significant side effects. They are best considered for those offenders who pose a high risk of sexual recidivism associated with marked impulsivity. Recent interest in selective serotonergic reuptake inhibitors suggests that SSRIs may be the drug treatment of choice for those offenders who seek to maintain legal, consenting intimate relationships, or whose deviant sexual interests are closely allied to anxiety and depressive disorders. See Craissati (2004) for a more detailed review of pharmacological approaches.

Therapeutic communities (efficacy = 2; generalisability = 1)

Until recently there were two therapeutic facilities in the UK designed specifically for offenders: HMP Grendon Underwood and the Max Glatt centre at HMP Wormwood Scrubs. The latter facility is now closed. HMP Grendon is a specialist prison for males, designed to run on the lines of a therapeutic community for those with a personality disorder. This is therefore the only offender treatment model which specifically targets personality disorder. No one is transferred against their will; motivation to change and a willingness to participate in group work are important selection criteria. Prisoners can return to the general prison system if they wish, or can be sent back without consent.

HMP Grendon was originally evaluated by Marshall (1997) and this study has been replicated by Taylor (2000). The sample comprised 700 prisoners who had been admitted to Grendon between 1984 and 1989. There were two comparison groups: the waiting list control group consisted of 142 prisoners selected for Grendon during the same period but who did not actually go there; the general prison group consisted of 1,800 male offenders released in 1987 and with similar characteristics to those admitted to Grendon. The findings suggested that prisoners selected for Grendon tended to be high risk; lower rates of conviction were found for those admitted than for those on the waiting list. Reconviction rates were lower for prisoners who stayed for at least eighteen months, and this was particularly the case for life sentence prisoners in Grendon; there appeared to be some reduction in the reconviction rate for violent offences among the treatment group, and for sexual and violent offences among repeat sexual offenders.

Forensic psychoanalytic psychotherapy (efficacy = 1; generalisability = 1)

The centre of assessment, treatment, consultation and training for forensic psychotherapy is located at the Portman Clinic in North West London. It accepts referrals from anywhere in the UK. The Portman Clinic is an outpatient National Health Service psychotherapy clinic for people who suffer from problems with criminal or violent behaviour, or from disturbing sexual behaviour or experiences. The aim of treatment is to help free patients from the more self-destructive ways of feeling, thinking and behaving and so enable them to live and function more easily in the community. Treatment can include individual or group psychotherapy, or family or couple psychotherapy. The staff are multi-disciplinary, but all have undertaken further training as psychoanalytic psychotherapists or psychoanalysts. An extensive training programme includes the Diploma in Forensic Psychotherapeutic Studies, which is a two-year day-release course for all disciplines, and a five-year full-time training in forensic psychotherapy for psychiatrists, integrated with the Three Bridges Regional Secure Unit at Ealing Hospital.

Although staff at the Portman Clinic have published widely in terms of theoretical perspectives and case studies, there are unfortunately no outcome studies which evaluate the efficacy of treatment in terms of psychological need or criminogenic behaviour. The model has enormous potential (and experience) in its application to staff and institutional dynamics, and it may be that future research will demonstrate efficacy in this area of work.

Psychopathy

High scoring psychopaths – as measured by the Psychopathy Checklist (PCL-R; Hare, 1991) – have been thought to perform poorly in therapeutic programmes. As summarised by Losel (1998), they reveal less motivation and improvement on various behavioural measures, they frequently drop out of programmes and recidivate more quickly after being released. Scepticism is supported by general characteristics of research into psychotherapy, which include contra-indications for treatability related to factor 1 features of PCL-R high scorers, and the lack of affective intimacy, openness, engagement and therapeutic co-operation. They score particularly badly on measures which tap into moral reasoning, interpersonal awareness, socialisation, empathy and social convention understanding.

Rice *et al.* (1992) studied the outcome of psychopaths and non-psychopaths (as measured by the PCL-R) who had spent over two years on a Social Therapy Unit; whilst non-psychopaths recidivated violently less often if they had been in treatment (22 per cent versus 45 per cent), the psychopaths recidivated violently more often if they had been in treatment (77 per cent versus 55 per cent). More recent prison-based research in the UK (Clark, 2000) found that 13 per cent of a representative sample of prisoners scored over the cut-off point of 25. A subsection of those individuals who had been discharged from prison for at least two years were examined for the impact of short offending behaviour programmes run by the prison service. The most common forms of programmes were social skills training and anger management. High PCL-R scorers reoffended at a higher rate (85 per cent) if they had been in a programme than those high scorers who had not (58 per cent). Seto and Barbaree (1999) examined the relationship between psychopathy, behaviour in treatment and subsequent recidivism of imprisoned sex offenders treated with a relapse prevention model. Higher scoring psychopaths dropped out of treatment and tended to score worse on treatment behaviour; those with a high PCL-R score and an apparently good treatment response were almost three times more likely to offend again than those with a poor treatment response and/or low PCL-R scores. However, in a long-term follow-up study on the sample, treatment behaviour was found not to be related to outcome, although PCL-R score was. Other studies have found similar results (reviewed in D'Silva *et al.*, 2004). Nevertheless, these studies have been criticised for poor methodology, idiosyncratic treatment regimes, or insufficiently intensive treatment programmes. In particular, D'Silva and colleagues point out that if high scoring psychopaths in treatment are compared with other high scoring psychopaths, and if treatment completion is taken into account, then there is little evidence for entrenched pessimism.

A study, similar in design to that of Seto and Barbaree (Looman *et al.*, 2004) found that although higher PCL-R scorers reoffended at a higher rate, those who were rated as being lower risk at post-treatment in fact reoffended at a lower rate than those whose risk was rated as unchanged (50 per cent versus 70 per cent); this finding was irrespective of whether the high PCL-R scorers demonstrated good treatment behaviour. The authors concluded that there may be some psychopaths who are responsive to a

highly structured intensive cognitive-behavioural interventio'
is not necessarily associated with good treatment behaviou
suggest 'going through the motions' rather than a more h
but argumentative and resistant group of psychopaths).
more optimistic view is a meta-analytic review (Salekin, 2'
treatment studies on psychopathy which, despite methoaving
tions, suggested a hopeful way forward, as significant treatment effects were
found for this group of patients. Specifically, eclectic approaches, such as
group and individual therapy, psychoanalytic and cognitive-behavioural
therapies, and the inclusion of family members in treatment programmes,
were found to be most effective. Furthermore, effective treatments were
intensive and long-term (at least one year). Therapeutic communities were
found to have the lowest success rate (25 per cent), in contrast to combined
cognitive-behavioural therapy and insight-oriented approaches which had
the highest success rate of 86 per cent. Interestingly, those studies which
utilised Cleckley's criteria had a success rate of .81, compared to .57 with
those defined using the PCL-R. However, Salekin's findings should be
interpreted cautiously as not all the studies applied the same criteria for
selection, and outcomes were not always measured in terms of offending
behaviour as well as psychological change.

Summary

There is an impressive body of evidence, compiled over the past ten years,
which lends support to the premise that programmes addressing criminogenic need in offenders do contribute to the management and reduction of
risk (see Table 4.1). Such programmes undoubtedly include offenders with a
personality disorder, particularly with antisocial features, and this is evi-
dently so with prison-based therapeutic communities. However, a number
of questions remain unanswered, and are a priority for future research and
programme development.

Developments in treatment approaches probably need to marry components of mainstream treatment provision for people with a personality
disorder (Bateman and Tyrer, 2002) with the effective criminogenic literature, to provide a holistic framework for interventions which address a
range of needs.

General treatment issues

Attrition

Individuals dropping out of treatment, for any reason, is a feature of all
psychological therapies, but there are reasons to consider attrition with

Table 4.1 Summary of treatment efficacy and generalisability

	Efficacy[1]	Generalisability[2]
Mental health literature		
Cognitive therapy	1	2
Dialectical behaviour therapy	2	1
Dynamic psychotherapy	2	2
Mentalisation	1	2
Cognitive analytic therapy	1	2
Therapeutic community treatments	2	1
Drugs:		
Antipsychotic	1	2
Antidepressant	2	2
Mood stabilisers	1	1
Criminal justice literature		
Thinking skills	3	2
Dialectical behaviour therapy (offenders)	1	2
Anger/violence management	2	1
Substance misuse	2	1
Sex offender treatment programmes	3	2
Therapeutic communities (offenders)	2	1
Forensic psychoanalytic psychotherapy	1	1

[1] 0 = ineffective, 1 = unknown efficacy, 2 = efficacy demonstrated in small studies (< 50 patients), 3 = efficacy demonstrated in large studies

[2] 0 = highly selective and not generalisable, 1 = selective and generalisability uncertain, 2 = some limited selection precluding full generalisability, 3 = typical offenders with condition who are representative

personality disordered offenders to be a particularly important problem. First, non-compliance – with treatment, statutory supervision, conditional release on restriction orders under the Mental Health Act, and so on – is a feature of many risk prediction measures (see Chapter 3); that is, attrition increases an individual's risk rating. This was also evident in the review on cognitive skills programmes for offenders, where failure to complete treatment was clearly associated with a significantly greater risk of recidivism, both in terms of following up treated prisoners in the community, and in terms of community-based programmes.

Second, attrition has been shown to be predicted by the presence of personality disorder, particularly with sexual offenders (Abel *et al.*, 1988; Chaffin, 1992). Craissati and Beech (2001) found that although low to medium risk status on the basis of a static measure of risk prediction was associated with treatment compliance in child molesters, attrition from treatment was predicted by the presence of psychological disturbance and childhood trauma rather than offence-specific measures. This finding was replicated in a more recent study (Craissati *et al.*, 2006) evaluating child molesters and rapists across the London area.

Third, it is sexual and violent offenders, who are high risk in the first instance, who are more likely to fail to complete treatment (Cann *et al.*, 2003; Craissati and Beech, 2001). Thus, there is a circular and interrelated pattern involving high risk status, personality disorder and likelihood to drop out of treatment. This problem is particularly acute in the community, where there is no physical or institutional containment of individuals which might help maximise the possibility of treatment completion. Practitioners have often observed that offenders who have been compliant and motivated for treatment in prison, change upon their release into the community, where the behavioural features of their personality difficulties become more apparent, including emerging chaotic lifestyles and impulsivity.

The problem of attrition poses a dilemma for the community treatment provider. To what extent should such programmes adopt flexible and adaptable approaches in order to maximise adherence, perhaps, in doing so, masking the underlying risk which would normally be evidenced by non-compliance? Poor time-keeping, missed sessions, failure to complete homework, verbally aggressive outbursts in treatment, refusal to comply with treatment tasks, argumentative resistance in response to key treatment targets such as victim empathy, disruptive social environments, increased substance misuse, and psychological crises should all be anticipated by programme providers. General guidance on these issues might include consideration of the following:

- Preparation for the treatment, which could include giving practical information, desensitisation tasks (such as rehearsing an offence disclosure in individual sessions prior to group work), and developing an empathic and collaborative working relationship. This relates closely to motivational interviewing approaches – detailed later in the chapter – and to much of the personality disorder literature (see Livesley, 2003).
- Treatment rules should be clear but kept to a minimum, with some flexibility which is transparent (rather than opaque) and negotiated with the offender. Managing the treatment contract in such a way mirrors the rules of 'good enough' parenting which includes a combination of clear boundaries tempered by the modelling of mutually respectful negotiation.
- Rigorous and active follow-up – concerned rather than critical – of all missed sessions, with strenuous efforts made to ensure the offender comes to treatment. This might include enlisting the help of the referrer, paying transport costs, telephone reminders and so on.
- Identifying key risk areas for individual offenders, even when standardised treatments are deployed; this allows the treatment providers to 'roll with resistance', by prioritising only those treatment goals within the programme which are either acknowledged by the offender as being

problematic for him, and/or identified by the treatment providers as those most closely related to risk.

- Very active positive social reinforcement when treatment tasks and homework are attended to – initially, regardless of the quality – and an associated strategy of non-reinforcement (rather than punishment) of failure to comply with such tasks.

- Anticipating features of the offender's behaviour which might interfere with his capacity to attend treatment (such as self-harm, substance misuse or chaotic living situations) and proactively ensuring that there are strategies and agencies in place to manage these in parallel with the treatment process (see below).

Case examples

These examples illustrate the tensions in managing attendance at a group treatment programme for high risk personality disordered offenders who had a history of community failure. Every effort was made to ensure that overall consistency of therapist attitude was tempered by an individualised approach. There were two group rules regarding attendance: first, that all sessions should be attended, and absences accounted for by a medical note; and second, that anyone arriving more than fifteen minutes after the start would be excluded, and this would count as an 'unacceptable absence'.

John arrived thirty minutes late to his first group session, agitated and annoyed, complaining of a complicated travel route to the venue. He was considered to be highly motivated for treatment generally, and was attending on a voluntary basis; it was thought his significant learning difficulties may have contributed to his lateness. The group was consulted, and it was agreed to allow him to join the group late as a silent member, observing only.

Gary was late for a session, ten weeks into the programme, having left too little time to travel and not taking into account possible transport delays; he was an offender with a high psychopathy score, but having previously participated well in the group. He was refused entry, but it was evident that he had rushed to try to arrive on time, and he was treated sympathetically; staff external to the group discussed his propensity to 'take risks' with him, and they went through the transport timetable together, agreeing a better time frame for travel in the future.

Finally, George missed three sessions out of six in the first group module, all of which were supported by a sick note from the GP; he was considered to be anxious and prone to somatising distress, partly as a way of avoiding the themes of the group programme. He was discharged from the group, but following a number of individual sessions with one of the group leaders, encouraged to re-start the programme with additional support from a psychologist on a monthly basis.

All of these decisions were discussed in a transparent manner with the group members, although their views were only solicited in relation to John. This enabled the group leaders to adhere to the rules, whilst resorting to individualised responses; the transparency of approach was driven by a wish to engage with the group in a mature and reciprocal fashion, modelling reflective boundary-setting.

Risk–needs–responsivity (Andrews et al., 1990)

The risk principle states that treatment should be provided to those at highest risk of recidivism, violence or other forms of antisocial behaviour. It is based on the premise that the greatest treatment effect is for high risk offenders, and as such they warrant the investment of resources; treatment for low risk offenders may be ineffective – largely due to a floor effect – or may even lead to more adverse outcomes in terms of recidivism. Yet programmes are often drawn inadvertently to select lower risk offenders, because they may be more motivated and compliant, less likely to be threatening or anti-authoritarian, or less likely to drop out of treatment.

The needs principle states that treatment should target the offender's criminogenic needs, using an appropriate intervention, and that as wide a range of criminogenic factors as is possible should be targeted for greatest efficacy. These are the dynamic factors identified in some risk prediction scales, which directly cause an offender to commit crimes or other antisocial acts.

The responsivity principle states that intervention must be sensitive and tailored to the offender's individual abilities and capabilities. This includes consideration of levels of cognitive functioning and different personality characteristics. Clearly, the literature review above suggests that failure to adequately consider responsivity issues with personality disordered offenders is likely to be central to problems with treatment attrition. Other factors, such as transient psychotic states or paranoid thinking, may need to be addressed in order to improve responses to treatment, or they may have a direct association with violent or criminal behaviours, and would need to be targeted as a risk factor.

Whilst the risk–needs–responsivity approach is widely accepted within the criminogenic literature, it does not take into account the issue of psychological distress which, for mental health services, may be a legitimate focus of treatment in its own right. Furthermore, the model does not take into account the differentiation in personality disordered offenders between core traits (or basic tendencies) which are largely stable over time (and may be resistant to treatment), and behavioural characteristics which are an expression of the core traits, and much more likely to be subject to instability over time.

What to do about psychopathy

Given the shift in approach to psychopathy, from regarding it as an untreatable nihilism to a more optimistic but inconclusive view about possible treatment efficacy (see above), it may be helpful to return to Cooke *et al.*'s (2004) revision of the concept, as a three-factor presentation: an arrogant and deceitful interpersonal style, deficient affective experience, and an impulsive and irresponsible behavioural style. This work is broadly supported by the epidemiological study of Verheul *et al.* (1998) which showed that although there was high temporal stability for 'no regard for the truth' and moderate stability for 'recklessness', there was consistently low stability for 'inconsistent work behaviour', 'failure to meet financial obligations', 'failure to plan ahead' and 'parental irresponsibility', as measured by DSM-III criteria for antisocial personality disorder. Murphy and Vess (2003) proposed that there are four subtypes of psychopathy, as measured by the PCL-R:

- Narcissistic (clinical presentation includes primarily narcissistic features of a pathological degree, including grandiosity, entitlement and callous disregard for the feelings of others)
- Borderline (affective instability and self-destruction are the most evident features)
- Sadistic (prominent evidence of deriving pleasure from the suffering of others)
- Antisocial (the most purely criminal of the four, with behavioural manifestations of psychopathy reflecting criminality or conformity problems)

They suggest that consideration of these four subtypes has implications for treatment, as do the three factors proposed by Cooke *et al.* For example, detailed disclosure of offending behaviour, with the sadistic psychopath, should be avoided, as it might reinforce the pleasure derived from committing these crimes and increase risk. The narcissistic psychopath is likely to be very argumentative and to fail to recognise the need for treatment such as relapse prevention, so that treatment needs to be presented in such a way as to circumvent his sense of entitlement and contempt for others if he is not to be a disruptive force within a therapy group.

There may be moderating variables which intervene with the core psychopathic traits, rendering the offender more amenable to treatment. First, low IQ in psychopaths is associated with greatly increased frequency of violence and poor impulse control, and may therefore be a contraindication for treatment. Anxious and depressive symptoms in psychopaths (borderline type) have been thought to assist in their amenability to treatment, in that an individual who is able to experience anxiety may be more likely to respond to traditional treatment approaches and be slightly more sensitive to the typical consequences of inappropriate behaviour. Externally driven moderating variables might also include the realistic appraisal of receiving a life sentence if an individual were to reoffend, or strong pro-social influences, such as (narcissistic) pride in having a son over whom the offender wishes to have some influence.

Wong and Hare (2001) have outlined programme guidelines for the institutional treatment of violent psychopathic offenders, much of which replicates good practice in general cognitive-behavioural programmes (such as the violence risk programme (VRP)). However, they do highlight some helpful features which are directly relevant to treating psychopaths. They clearly state that treatment targets should be impulsive, irresponsible, violent and antisocial behaviours, and that it is futile to target affective and moral features. They emphasise the need for an individualised approach to the analysis of the offence cycle and the importance of learning self-management skills – both features catering to the narcissistic personality features of the psychopath – with a focus on those issues which are seen to be in the offender's best interests (encouraging enlightened self-interest). They suggest that not too many participants with high factor 1 scores should be put in a group together, and recommend – perhaps optimistically – that a ratio of 1:1 psychopath and non-psychopath could be in a group. Therapy material should be personally relevant, delivered in an engaging and stimulating way (catering for a low boredom threshold), and positive rewards should be highly visible and responsive to any evidence of pro-social behaviour. Within an institutional setting, treatment should be intensive (occupying 50–75 per cent of the offender's time) and of 18–24 months' duration; clearly this is much more difficult to achieve in the community. Finally, whilst pro-social modelling in the group should be encouraged, the participants should not be allowed to take a position of authority.

Summarising broadly, it seems likely that psychopaths can change if they decide that it is in their best interest to do so; that is, they need to be helped to see how their behaviour, while ego-syntonic, can result in consequences that do not satisfy their needs. Enabling staff to free themselves up from having to focus on amoral and unpleasant core personality traits in the psychopath, in favour of a focus on modifying violent and self-destructive behaviours, will also assist in the therapeutic alliance and avoid staff burnout. This approach does not confront the psychopath's inflated sense of self-esteem head on, but circumvents it, resulting in less resistance. Thus, when assessing a psychopathic offender's capacity for treatment change, it is important to consider the type of psychopath they appear to be, the nature and range of their behavioural difficulties, their level of intellectual ability and capacity for self-control, and whether or not there are Axis I features such as anxiety and depression which may assist engagement in the treatment process.

Specific programmes for incarcerated psychopathic offenders are currently being piloted within the DSPD prison services. 'Chromis' is an intensive intervention which aims to provide participants with the skills to reduce and manage their risk; that is, not to change offenders' life goals but the way that they achieve them. It places emphasis on motivation and engagement, and comprises five core components which combine individual and group work, requiring approximately two years to complete. The five components include:

- Motivation and engagement
- Creative thinking
- Problem solving
- Conflict resolution
- Cognitive self-change

The programme is in its infancy. Although it is strongly anchored within an evidence-base, and undoubtedly of clinical utility, it will be many years before its efficacy can really be determined.

Determining treatability

Approaches to this question of treatability can range enormously. Criminal justice programmes may require no more than a risk score, a relevant offence, and an offender's willingness to enter the room and sit down. At the other end of the spectrum, psychoanalytic psychotherapists devote time and theory to the question of treatability. For example, in a classic paper, Coltart (1987) detailed nine factors necessary in the patient for psycho-therapy. These included: a capacity to take a distance from his own emotional experience; self-reflection as a result of being listened to; quality of affect; a capacity to recognise and tolerate internal reality; a lively curiosity and concern about this internal reality; some capacity for the use of the imagination; a capacity to recognise the existence of an unconscious mental life; signs of success in some limited area of life, and proper self-esteem in relation to this. Forensic practitioners may reject these factors as ludicrously out of touch with the real world of personality disordered offenders, but such criteria should not be summarily dismissed; it may be that they serve a useful benchmark by which to measure an offender's progress in treatment.

More concrete considerations of treatability are described below.

Cognitive functioning: generally treatment programmes tend to exclude offenders whose IQ falls below 80, largely because cognitive-behavioural programmes expect a certain capacity for verbal reasoning, abstract thinking, perspective taking and problem solving. However, a measure of IQ alone can be misleading. Some offenders may mask low intellectual ability with reasonably good verbal skills and high social functioning; others may appear much more intellectually disabled than they actually are. If an offender is verbally fluent, he may keep up in a group situation, but require additional individual sessions to consolidate his learning; another offender might achieve little in a group, largely because he appears to be impaired in his functioning and therefore avoids being challenged. Some programmes are adapted to meet the needs of less intellectually able offenders, and these adaptations include a much greater amount of visual material, less emphasis on written homework, a slower pace, and simpler, more concrete cognitive skills tasks.

Denial is a multi-faceted phenomenon. Total denial, however, clearly poses a challenge in terms of treatability. Just as with treatment refusal, total denial is not in itself a significant risk variable (Hanson *et al.*, 2002), merely an obstacle – rather an exasperating one. It is important to remember that treatment should match risk–needs–responsivity, and that this is not synonymous with offence-focused treatment. For example, an offender might deny the index conviction of rape, but will accept that he has problems with substance misuse, being adversely influenced by delinquent peers, and a quick temper when under stress; these features all indicate clear treatment need which could be addressed whilst circumventing the area of resistance. This does, however, require the practitioner to have a cool confidence and reliance on the evidence-base, in order to sustain such an approach.

Understanding denial

Psychodynamic theories classically understood denial as a primitive mechanism of defence: an attempt to disavow a present existence of reality (Stevenson *et al.*, 1989), in which determinants of motivation are primarily unconscious and therefore inaccessible to the individual (Rogers and Dickey, 1991). Such motivations may symbolise impending psychotic disintegration or be used to ward off overwhelming anxiety. Examples of such defence structures might be found in those fixated paedophiles who insist that their 'love' for the victim has been misrepresented and distorted, and whose denial allows them to maintain in fantasy a relationship with an idealised object, an identification with themselves as a child. However, as Stevenson *et al.* (1989) point out, the offence is often fully present in the mind of the denying sexual offender and may not involve a primitive unconscious set of internal defences. Suppression may offer a more apt alternative definition, which refers to the conscious inhibition of an impulse or a feeling, as in the deliberate attempt to forget something and put it to the back of one's mind. For example, it may be that some father figures, who minimise the abusive behaviour and project the blame for the offence onto the victim, are attempting to deny their own sexualised feelings towards the child which are unacceptable to them given their parallel desire to be a 'good and loving parent'.

If unconscious denial and suppression lie on a continuum, then the next stage prior to admittance may be Rogers and Dickey's (1991) adaptational model, derived from Rogers's work on malingering: the adaptational approach is based on decision theory which postulates that the choice of malingering (or denial) is based on expected utility. The sexual offender, when confronted, almost always perceives himself to be in an adversarial setting in which he will lose by self-disclosure and gain by denying; feigning or denying in these instances may be perceived as a more effective (or the only alternative) strategy for achieving his goal. In support for this strategy-decision, Craissati and McClurg (1994) found that in South East London, it was always advantageous to a perpetrator to plead not guilty to charges of rape or buggery against a child; even if found guilty at trial, they received shorter sentences than perpetrators who made full admissions of penetration from the outset. Further research (McClurg and Craissati, 1997) revealed that judges were increasingly inclined to ignore recommendations for community treatment and impose custodial sentences for offences of indecent assault against children, even when other pertinent variables were controlled for.

Whether unconscious, semi-conscious or a deliberate strategy, the primary function of denial is self-protection: it enables the perpetrator to preserve an acceptable self-image which is not contaminated by negative perceptions such as 'pervert' or 'child batterer'; it protects him from uncomfortable feelings of guilt and self-denigration; it may help to deflect violent reprisals away from himself, and spare him and his family the wider shame which follows admission. Specifically and crucially, the perpetrator may fear the disintegration of key personal relationships if denial is not maintained. This is supported by anecdotal evidence that death of or abandonment by a key emotional figure – usually wife or mother – often leads to a breakdown of denial in the perpetrator. In this sense, denial in the early stages of abuse disclosure may have a positive function for the perpetrator in that it allows for a period of adjustment for the individual (and perhaps his partner), so that in time other less radical defences may be mobilised.

Motivational interviewing (MI) is an approach originally developed in work with problem drinkers (Miller, 1983). It is an interviewing style which can be used to help clients identify, explore, and possibly resolve ambivalence about a problem behaviour. The aim is to activate and consolidate motivation to decide to change. The emphasis must always be on the client – not the worker – expressing concerns about the problem behaviour and arguments for change. A key text for further reading is Miller and Rollnick (1991).

More recently, the MI model has been applied to sexual offenders whose behaviour has been likened to other 'addictions' (that is, repetitive, self-reinforcing behaviours), and a detailed exposition of this work is usefully outlined in the NOTA publication, *Motivational Interviewing with Sex Offenders* (Mann, 1996), and in Craissati (1998). There are no comparable texts for motivational interviewing work with violent offenders. It is important to emphasise at this point that many of the interviewing methods recommended by motivational interviewing authors reflect standard, high quality therapeutic skills which many experienced practitioners will intuitively deploy with perpetrators. For example, the use of open questions and reflective listening will be familiar to many, although all too often the skills required are underestimated. With offenders, reflective listening can be used to selectively ignore or emphasise aspects of a perpetrator's response to an open question; to reinforce certain elements of what has been said; or to reframe or summarise the answer and, in doing so, alter its meaning slightly. At all times, the interviewer is concerned to elicit and reinforce self-motivating statements which approach some recognition that there is a problem, some expression of concern, and any intention to change or optimism about change.

Undoubtedly, punitive impulses on the part of the interviewer when faced with an irresponsible, unrepentant, evasive perpetrator can be overwhelming. It may be difficult to identify – outside of supervision – when a challenging remark has entered the domain of a punitive remark, or when the necessary exploration of offending behaviour in a group setting has become persecutory.

The goals of MI can be summarised as (Beckett, 1994):

- Anticipating offender resistance
- Maximising offender co-operation
- Establishing a non-collusive, collaborative relationship

Beckett outlines two basic assumptions of the adapted model:

- Denial is constructed by the perpetrator during the course of the offence to help minimise guilt and anxiety.
- Interview strategies which moderate fear and anxiety lessen the need for such a defence and increase the likelihood of engaging the offender in constructive dialogue.

There are five principles of motivational interviewing (Miller and Rollnick, 1991; Mann, 1996), which have been adapted here to demonstrate positive and negative examples with personality disordered offenders:

1 *Express empathy*, which is communicated through the skill of reflective listening, with the firm understanding that ambivalence is normal:

'. . . he was more concerned with feeling persecuted by the Courts than with the impact his behaviour may have had on the victim.' (problematic)

If the traumatic experiences of the victim are put to one side momentarily, there can be few experiences more humiliating for a hitherto 'law-abiding' citizen than to be convicted of a sexual offence against a child: his behaviour is detailed in Court; his family, friends, local community and employer are all likely to know something of what has occurred; and he faces the unknown fear of custody as a 'nonce'. Few strategies are more effective in setting a constructive tone to an interview than responding empathically to the perpetrator's current situation.

2   *Avoid argumentation*, and even direct persuasion, in order to evade being trapped in a confrontation–denial discussion:

> '. . . she says you attacked her out of the blue, that you picked up a kitchen knife and threatened to kill her . . . there's no reason for her to lie . . .' (problematic)

> '. . . yes, can I interrupt you there? I do understand that you don't agree with everything he's said in the witness statement, but I know you pleaded guilty to at least one of the charges, and you do admit that there were some problems, so perhaps we can set the differences to one side for now, and focus on the aspects of the offence that you are happy to discuss.'

There are two difficulties with challenging the assertion that victims lie; first, although victims rarely lie, they may be confused, have poor recall or exaggerate (particularly if they are frightened of the perpetrator), and such a debate with an offender can take the interview down an unconstructive dead-end path; second – and more importantly – the perpetrator is, in essence, being called a liar, and such an approach is likely to activate his most defensive stance. Approaches which encourage offenders to provide their own narrative of the offence are more successful, as it then provides the opportunity to explore key ideas – for example, 'you felt she was being unreasonable? . . . Let me know a little more about what you mean by unreasonable'.

3   *Roll with resistance*: resistance is an expression of ambivalence, not a personality characteristic:

> '. . . he denies any planning, he denies responsibility for the offence, he blames the victim and has no insight . . . therefore I would not consider him to be suitable for the accredited programmes, and he's probably not treatable.' (problematic)

Here, denial has been mistakenly labelled as a stable personality trait, rather than a strategic manoeuvre, consciously or unconsciously designed to protect the perpetrator from the anxiety engendered by feelings of shame and guilt. Again, honest reflection and insight are the goals of treatment not of assessment.

4   *Deploy discrepancy*, where ambivalence is characterised by a lack of discrepancy between what the individual is doing and what he wants to do; motivation develops as a sense of discrepancy between present behaviour and important goals is created:

> '. . . how can you possibly call yourself a loving father when you abused your son?' (problematic)

> '. . . I can see that you have wanted to love a woman and care for her, yet here you are, alone and rejected all over again.'

> 'You clearly experience thieving as lucrative and easy, and yet you also recognise that it has been difficult to enjoy a really good quality of life as you have been in and out of custody so much.'

In responding with indignation to a perpetrator's claims to have cared for his victim, the interviewer has lost a prime opportunity to emphasise the discrepancy between the perpetrator's caring feelings and his abusive behaviour, which could have enhanced his perception of concern or risk. The subsequent statements are careful to avoid sanctioning the offender's behaviour, but do empathise with the dilemma, and the use of vivid vocabulary or a slight exaggeration of the dilemma helps to highlight the discrepancy.

5   *Support self-efficacy*, demonstrating belief in the possibility of change, and eliciting and reinforcing clients' own problem-solving strengths:

> '. . . once a sex offender, always a sex offender . . .' (problematic)

> '. . . and that is why you are labelled high risk . . . but certainly it is true that not all high risk sex offenders reoffend. The problem for you is how you might persuade everyone around that you are able to persist with your very good intentions.'

The first statement, implicitly or explicitly stated, demonstrates the interviewer's pessimism regarding the intentions of and potential for change in the perpetrator; and there can be few greater barriers to engagement in treatment than a sense of inevitability regarding reoffending. The second example models a non-defensive honest approach which emphasises the worthy intentions of the offender and invites him to strive to achieve his goals, perhaps by means of entering a treatment programme.

The treatment process – general principles

For a detailed account of treatment models, the reader must go to the original source. However, there are general themes which emerge from a comparison of the main treatment models, and these are encapsulated by Livesley (2003). Essentially, there is a hierarchy of change, which Livesley translates into five phases of intervention.

Crisis management is always a priority, possibly requiring inpatient treatment for a very brief period, with the aim of returning the patient to the previous level of functioning with symptomatic improvement and containment of affects/impulses. *Shorter-term therapies and early stages of longer-term treatment* initially focus on those aspects of psychopathology that directly underpin symptoms and crises – self-regulation of affects and impulses – and identifying triggering events; then move on to include maladaptive interpersonal patterns, maladaptive expressions of dispositional traits and dysfunctional cognitive styles. The final phase, *longer-term therapy*, holds as its goal the development of a more adaptive self-structure and integrated representations of others.

The phases of intervention mirror the above:

I   *Safety* requires interventions which ensure the safety of patients and others; in the community they are likely to include proactive plans to manage crises, be they psychological, social or criminal. With offenders, it should include an agreement about the limits of confidentiality and anticipation of offending behaviours.

II   *Containment* has the goal of settling crisis behaviour, and containing impulses, affects and behaviour. General therapeutic strategies are required, such as support, empathic understanding and validation. This phase has otherwise been described as dealing with Axis I symptoms, and it is the time when medication could be considered.

III   *Control and regulation* is the phase when the patient is helped to acquire the skills needed to manage and control affects and impulses. More structured strategies are used – behavioural and cognitive – which are effective in reducing self-harm and promoting emotional regulation. Less emphasis is placed on exploration than in later phases of treatment, to avoid intense emotional arousal which can destabilise the patient.

IV   *Exploration and change* involves the greater exploration of psychopathology, where maladaptive schemas and negative cognitions are addressed. Treatment models might include cognitive, interpersonal or psychodynamic approaches. This stage involves collaboration regarding the focus on particular problematic patterns of behaviour. Both this phase and phase IV involve the more traditional use of therapy to identify, understand and change maladaptive behaviours, developing and practising adaptive alternatives.

V *Integration and synthesis*, as the final phase, integrates the fragmented components of personality, developing a more adaptive self and interpersonal system, with a capacity for self-directedness.

Although Livesley's language is that of a cognitively oriented theorist, the phases do capture the essence of other models. A purely criminogenic approach would focus on phases III and IV, with its emphasis on identifying triggering cognitions, affects and behaviours, challenging cognitive distortions and improving impoverished problem-solving skills. Psychoanalytically oriented therapists would tend to rely on others to achieve the patient's stability and capacity to manage emotional dysregulation, before embarking on a treatment process which would focus on phases IV and V.

It is also important to note that a number of existing models do not require the successful completion of all five phases. There are a number of interventions which are closely tied to crisis management, involving brief periods of psychological and pharmacological intervention to contain the extremes of cognitive, affective and behavioural disturbance (phases I and II). Clearly criminogenic approaches do not focus on crisis management, nor do they attempt to target core personality structure as a treatment goal. This flexibility in relation to the phases of treatment is particularly important with personality disordered offenders, where core traits may be resistant to change.

Treatment modality

Generally speaking, there has been an emphasis on individual treatment for personality disordered patients within mental health services, and an exclusive focus on group treatment within criminal justice services. There is, however, remarkably little research which aims to evaluate which modality is superior and for whom; the sparse findings would generally point to there being important components of treatment but not necessarily important modalities.

The primary advantage of individual treatment over group treatment is the capacity of the therapist to focus on the minutiae of maladaptive behaviour and the details of psychopathology, which is central to the ability of the patient to develop impulse regulation and gain control over suicidal behaviours. Furthermore, patients with a developmental experience of long-term institutional care or large neglectful families may require the personal attention of an individual therapist in order to effect change. However, group treatment provides considerable advantages over individual treatment in terms of the identification of maladaptive inter-personal patterns and the development of interpersonal skills. For those patients who experienced enmeshed relationships with a parent or who are prone to excessive dependency or regressed behaviour, the group forum provides a safer space – less intrusive – in which they can explore their difficulties.

With offenders, there are additional considerations. Some offences are simply too terrible for other offenders to contemplate, and indeed some offenders are too threatening and antagonistic to manage in a group. But the group process does allow for the therapist to take a more distant role, enabling offence-related challenges to be made by peers. Groups can be resource-efficient, and save the therapist from endless hours of individual therapy with offenders who are passive and avoidant, or hostile and anti-authoritarian.

Therapeutic models, such as DBT, utilise mixed modalities; others, such as therapeutic communities, utilise only group therapies on a very intensive basis. Some approaches are symptom- or offence-specific (self-harm groups or sex offender groups), and thus homogeneous, whilst others are fully heterogeneous. There are, of course, difficulties in combining sexual and violent offenders in the same group. Too many paedophiles in a group could create a ring; too many markedly antisocial violent men would provoke a riot; too many self-harming women with borderline personality disorder in a group might trigger an escalation in distress and acting out. Perhaps it would be fair to say that an ideal treatment package would include both individual and group work, and that the latter should include consideration of a mixed homogeneous group – offenders with shared behavioural or offence features who have a range of maladaptive person-ality traits and life experiences.

Team structure and delivery of treatment

The range of possible team structures is enormous, including generic roles, uni-professional roles, multi-agency, single agencies, rotating keyworkers, shared keyworking, parallel teams and integrated teams. Bateman and Tyrer (2002) refer to three service models: sole practitioner, divided func-tions and specialist team. All have advantages and disadvantages, the key elements being the three 'C's – communication, consistency and constancy.

For less disturbed clients, the sole practitioner has the advantage of managing a shared model of treatment with the client, and consistency of approach; he/she can provide an integrated model – if sufficiently experi-enced – which attends to all relevant aspects of the client's functioning.

The divided functions model adheres closely to professional identities and roles, but may mirror the fragmentation in the client, as each need is addressed separately; and there can be difficulties in communication between professionals, including the acting out of rivalries, and some loss of consistency. However, there is less dependence upon the availability of a single professional than in the former model, and it can be appealing when reflecting diverse agency responsibilities, such as a psychiatrist providing treatment and probation providing public protection.

The specialist team model appears attractive, although initially it may seem to be resource-intensive. It fosters good communication, and inconsistency between team members and the client can be minimised. Inconstancy – the absence of keyworkers – can be attended to, as the client has been encouraged to foster an attachment to two or more team members. Specialist teams may work generically, sharing skills, or they may specialise in the light of their professional identities or key competencies.

Case example

Brian's background and risk profile are discussed fully in Chapter 3 (see pp. 84–86). To summarise, he was being released from prison on licence, having served a sentence for grievous bodily harm. His risk profile included moderate levels of violence risk, with a limited history of firesetting and inappropriate sexual behaviour. In terms of mental health functioning, he presented with a moderate level of psychopathic traits, largely of an antisocial nature, with marked personality disorder in terms of borderline and antisocial traits, and a significant problem with alcohol use. His early life was characterised by extremes of neglect and abuse – both physical and sexual – and he had been placed in care, living both in children's homes and in foster placements.

The management plan for Brian was fraught initially, because of a dispute between criminal justice and mental health services as to whether he should be placed on CPA (see p. 124). The probation services highlighted – quite understandably – Brian's level of distress, his abusive childhood, and his range of treatment needs, including a request for long-term psychotherapy to resolve early trauma, and participation in group treatment for anger management. A joint meeting resolved the dispute, with an agreement for an integrated approach in which probation would manage the case under licence conditions, and forensic mental health would provide support to probation, and specialist treatment as deemed appropriate.

An assessment of treatment need quickly identified that Brian would be unable to make use of mainstream outpatient therapy in the first instance; his propensity to self-harm and abuse alcohol, and his history of chaotic presentation to services suggested that these features would interfere with the take-up of services. It was anticipated that he was high risk to fail in a probation hostel because of intense mood swings and a propensity to be frustrated and aggressive, or indeed violent when intoxicated. The hostel also felt anxious about managing his self-harm. Brian himself – when visited in prison just before his release – reported difficulties in sleeping, high levels of anxiety, and distress in response to occasional 'pseudo-hallucinations'.

A crisis plan was put in place, which included three features: first, it was negotiated that Brian could voluntarily present himself for admission to the local psychiatric unit for a period of 24–72 hours, at any time that he felt the need to do so, and this was made clear at the front of his hospital file. Second, the hostel staff provided him with a bag of ice, kept in the fridge near his room, into which he could plunge his arm should he feel the need to cut himself. Brian, who found it difficult to reflect and express his emotions, felt contained by the idea of self-management with the bag of ice, which provided a sense of symbolic containment (as it did for the staff who felt reassured that they had a clear strategy for managing his distress). Third, it was anticipated that Brian would respond to stringent rules with an increase in his rather persecutory thinking style, and therefore only one additional rule was applied: that if he returned to the hostel intoxicated, he should make his way to his room without any violent incident.

The second intervention phase was to address his agitation, sleeplessness and hallucinatory experiences (Axis I problems). The medical staff in the prison were asked to prescribe antipsychotic medication to Brian, and a quick follow-up in the community was arranged in order to ensure continuity. The medication reduced his emotional lability, improved his sleep pattern, and improved his engagement with services as he felt his primary concerns were being addressed.

The third intervention phase was to provide some psychological therapy. Interestingly, with the cessation of self-harming behaviour, a new problem was emerging: Brian was spending long periods of time, at odd hours of the day, confiding in hostel staff; during these meetings he alternated between expressions of tearful distress and a rather excitable discussion of his fantasy life, which included sexual offence fantasies. In response to the evident concern and interest of staff, these fantasies were becoming elaborated over time, and included violent and sadistic rape fantasies, sometimes associated with claims that he feared 'I might end up killing a woman'. There was no evidence of any behavioural enactment of these fantasies, and they seemed to represent compensatory ideas which served to maintain his self-esteem, and to garner the attention of others, for fear that he might otherwise be abandoned and neglected as he was in his childhood. Nevertheless, they raised the concern of agencies and threatened to scupper his community rehabilitation.

The focus of psychological support was shifted to regular outpatient appointments with a psychologist, and the hostel staff were encouraged to provide regular but limited supportive input to Brian which avoided exploration of trauma and fantasy. A psychiatrist reviewed his psychotropic medication which was slightly increased, and reduced a few weeks later. He was accepted onto a specialist work project for personality disordered offenders which structured two days of his week, in addition to the appointments.

The outpatient sessions initially focused on a supportive psychotherapeutic approach, complemented by an exploration of emotional self-management and cognitive skills, which seemed to be central to Brian's ability to manage the everyday demands of life in the community, particularly the management of interpersonal situations. He was not deemed suitable for group approaches, largely because of his resistance and his rather persecutory cognitive style which would have been exacerbated by the group situation. However, his attendance at individual sessions was reasonably good, and bolstered by intermittent reminders for appointments and telephone contact when he felt unable to attend. His mental state and personality structure were felt to be too fragile for any further exploration into core schemas and resolution of trauma.

The management approach and treatment package were surprisingly successful, and although he has required long-term support and has had occasional crises, five years later he is living independently, with a reasonable quality of life, in the community. It could not be said that he ever engaged in a more insight-oriented approach to his history of traumatisation, but he dipped in and out of psychological therapy sessions with a positive attitude, and also continued to visit the hostel for a couple of years. He is caught for shoplifting from time to time – to fund his occasional drinking binges – and he has bouts of depression and agitation. Occasionally the police are called out to the flat because of a domestic disturbance, the result of a fight between him and his girlfriend (an affectionate and assertive woman with her own history of mental health difficulties). However, this loving but turbulent relationship has also provided warmth and meaning to his life, and is the kind of 'luck' that every community mental health team should hope for.

Summary

The criminal justice system has developed a highly credible set of pro-grammes, many of which are entirely suitable for personality disordered offenders, particularly those with antisocial traits. However, there is no doubt that delivering treatment in secure settings is, by and large, much easier than in the community. It is true that the community provides real examples of risky situations, and activates core schemas in a way that is rarely possible in prison; however, it can be a real struggle to keep the offender motivated in treatment, sufficiently organised to be able to attend treatment, and sufficiently skilled and supported to avoid the temptations to lapse between sessions. It seems likely that practitioners in the community will need to draw on models from the mental health literature to complement the offence-focused approach. Treatment models vary, but successful programmes tend to have in common: a core philosophy of approach, shared by team and offender; a multi-modal and multi-disciplinary set of interventions; and a range of priorities which include attention to resistance and denial, management of crises and mental health symptoms, focused interventions, and support.

Chapter 5

Management approaches

Introduction

All too often, management has been seen as having a separate function from assessment and from treatment. Yet is this really the case? As we saw in Chapter 3, assessment needs to be considered as an intervention in its own right, and it would be true to say that management, also, is a form of intervention. This raises the question of what is therapy and what is management; indeed, Chapter 4 identified that the majority of therapeutic models for personality disordered offenders include management – usually for crises – as an integral component of the approach. Perhaps one difference is the central importance of a coherent theoretical framework for treatment (Bateman and Fonagy, 2004), whilst management approaches have traditionally been viewed as a pragmatic constellation of decisions and actions.

Management structures for personality disordered offenders do often consider treatment as one component of an overall package, and although recent directives ('Duty to Co-operate', Department of Health, 2004) expect collaboration between treatment providers and risk management structures (or between the health service and the criminal justice system), the nature of this relationship is rarely spelt out in detail. For other offenders, treatment may not be an option, either because the individual refuses treatment – perhaps because he maintains total denial of the offence – or because he is deemed to be untreatable (see previous chapters).

Essentially management structures are put in place to regulate the relationship between the offender and society. A simplistic and rather glib goal of management is to survive! That is, survival for the offender in the community, survival in terms of the public avoiding harm, and survival of the practitioners and institutions who have responsibility for the offender's management. A less defensive and more client-centred aim for management approaches would be *to enable the personality disordered offender to integrate successfully into the community, enabling them to maintain an improved quality of life, with the appropriate level of support, the least possible restrictions, and minimising potential harm to the public.* Clearly changes in the social and political climate, as well as differing institutional priorities, will have an influence on which aspects of this goal are emphasised. The stated aim of the public protection agencies might be *to ensure the personality disordered offender's risk of reoffending is minimised, thereby protecting the public and contributing to a safer community, with concern for the prevention of harm for future victims, and the successful rehabilitation of the offender into the community.*

This chapter aims to consider some of the psychological principles which may underpin commonly encountered management issues. Some of the core characteristics of the different types of personality disorder diagnoses, with their implications for management strategies, are discussed in Chapter 6. We explore two central structural approaches to management, and then review the management tools available as resources, particularly, in the light of recent policy developments, the role of the Multi-Agency Public Protection Arrangements (MAPPA).

Structural bases for management models

Traditionally, health and criminal justice services have been driven by apparently disparate motives: meeting mental health need versus public protection. Whilst health service approaches to offender rehabilitation may aim to demonstrate clinical change, offending behaviour may not change, undermining confidence in the health service's capacity to protect the public with treatment alone. The criminal justice literature concentrates on those who pose greatest risk of reoffending, focusing on criminogenic need, whilst psychological well-being remains peripheral (Thomas-Peter, 2002). We have now seen how the emphasis on programme delivery may – for the personality disordered offender – come at a cost: high attrition rates (Chaffin, 1992; Craissati and Beech, 2001), paradoxical effects on risk (Clark, 2000; Seto and Barbaree, 1999), or raising anxieties and leading to impasse. This separation of roles is mirrored in the disparate management systems: mental health services have traditionally relied on the Care Programme Approach (CPA), designed primarily to deal with those individuals presenting with severe mental illness, which provides a structure in which to co-ordinate care and address need; the probation service has relied on risk management structures which identify the level of risk to others and potential victim impact of reoffending, and then impose conditions within the criminal justice structure which aim to manage risk and protect victims.

Parallel management structures

Broadly speaking, personality disordered offenders have such disparate needs and raise such anxieties, that they have inevitably drawn the services into a greater level of communication and co-operation with each other. It is rare that a single agency would have sole knowledge of such an offender: for example, the probation service might refer an individual to health services for help with depressive episodes or anger management; the health service might feel unable to provide treatment to an offender but might ask the local authority to assist with housing, or the community drug service to tackle the problem of crack cocaine use. This structure is outlined in Figure 5.1 (overleaf), which demonstrates the range of services that might be thought to be appropriate for personality disordered offenders. At the centre of this model now lies the MAPPA (for a detailed discussion of MAPPA, see the section below), representing the core agencies and co-ordinating the public protection issues. With a management structure of parallel models of care, each presenting problem can be matched to its corresponding agency/professional/intervention. The advantage of this system – the one with which we are traditionally most comfortable – is that each agency or practitioner can hold to a clear service specification, with criteria for entry designed to mirror fairly narrow bands of competence and resource availability within that service; each agency or practitioner can then take full responsibility for those competencies and for the service that they provide.

In many instances this appears to be an entirely efficient system. But the peculiar challenges in meeting the needs of personality disordered offenders – particularly those who cause the most anxiety – tend to cause cracks in the model to appear. The fundamental difficulty lies in the fragmentation of services which mirrors the fragmentation in the offender's own psychological functioning; this feeds the habitual defences of the offender and allows for a holistic view of him to be lost. Readers will be familiar with the ease with which such offenders are refused access to services on the grounds that they do not meet the criteria or have not behaved well enough to access help; and the frequency with which they are referred on to or back to other services which might best meet their needs. Faced with challenging demands, it is all too easy to see the problem as someone else's responsibility. Indeed, accepting an offender into a service carries with it the full assumption of the burden of responsibility, with all the public interest and agency anxiety that accompanies such a move.

Integrated management structures

Implementing a psychologically informed strategy for personality disordered offenders within the current legislative framework requires a more integrated or holistic approach which avoids the fragmentation of the individual. Figure 5.2 (on page 127) illustrates the core components of an atheoretical model, in which assessment, treatment and management must all address three problem domains: mental health difficulties, offending behaviour and social functioning. These domains can be thought about at the individual

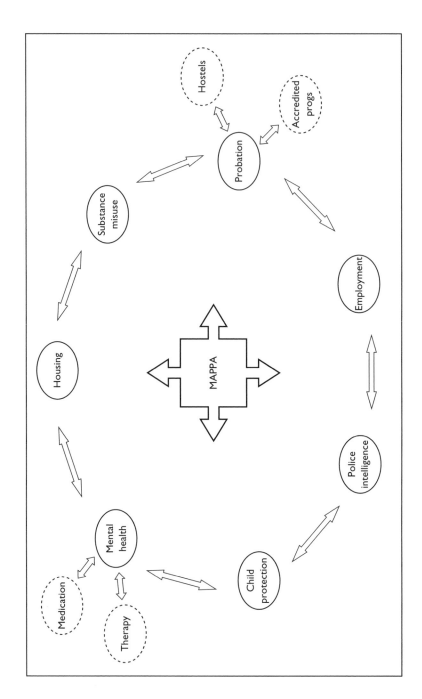

Figure 5.1 Parallel risk management structure

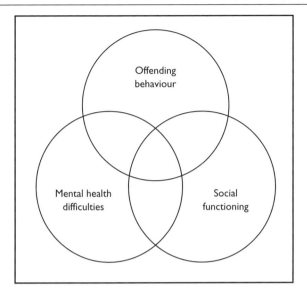

Figure 5.2

psychological level – where mental health might represent core schemas, their relationship to the individual's offending behaviour (perhaps domestic violence), and the way in which the personality difficulties lead to marked interpersonal problems, particularly in the realms of intimacy. The domains can also be thought of in terms of therapeutic need: how medication and individual psychotherapy could be complemented by offence-focused cognitive group therapy, which in turn could work on some of the difficult interpersonal issues which are being highlighted in the probation hostel environment. Essentially, this structure implies that a formulation of any individual personality disordered offender is central to management, and must integrate risk and offending behaviour with an understanding of the offender's psychological functioning and his interpersonal strategies for managing the world around him.

The model also suggests that there are practical needs – for support and medication, monitoring and supervision, and access to the usual structures of daily life, employment and housing. This last aspect reflects both a core difficulty with interpersonal behaviour in personality disordered individuals and their exclusion from meaningful community living as a result of anti-social behaviour. It should be clear that it is most unlikely that any one agency – including health – could appropriately and adequately address all three areas. Without necessitating adherence to one theoretical approach, any one of the three spheres of functioning could be addressed in multiple ways.

An integrated model of care would suggest services that are also integrated – partnerships between stakeholders which are committed to a single objective. This is the model suggested by MAPPPs but not traditionally the model of forensic mental health development (Thomas-Peter, 2002). Autonomous or parallel structures do allow for maximum flexibility in services developing local solutions, contracting in agencies as required. Integrated models intuitively appear to hold the solution to the fragmentation found in parallel services, but associated with this, there is inevitably a significant impact on the autonomy of each member of the partnership, which is restricted as a result of multi-agency collaboration. This loss of control needs to be weighed up against possibly the single most important advantage of an integrated model of care with this group of individuals: that is, the risk-sharing element for the critical few where no single agency is burdened with perceived responsibility for an individual's behaviour.

Multi-Agency Public Protection Arrangements (MAPPA): an example of a parallel or integrative management structure?

Currently, both police and probation can be held 'responsible' for virtually any offender who has the potential to cause harm to others. This has far-reaching consequences and is one of the legislative responses to the sad death of Sarah Payne, a young girl murdered by a convicted sex offender in the summer of 2000. Sections 67 and 68 of the Act extend the brief of the probation service beyond that of offenders currently in custody or on supervision or licence, to include anyone in the community who poses a danger. It poses a considerable test to the organisation at a time when it has to target its resources very carefully.

There has been vigorous activity between the National Probation Service and the corresponding Police Areas. Each area has to have a panel meeting to discuss the highest risk offenders – the 'critical few'. There then needs to be a host of supporting measures to ensure this statutory duty is fulfilled. The Act was clear in its expectations that the public are better protected from these types of offenders by agencies acting on their behalf to manage these individuals and take action when necessary.

The involvement of other agencies – social services, health, education, prison colleagues and housing – has not been without some difficulties, and agencies inevitably vary in their practice and values around the UK. Initial guidance was issued and launched in March 2001 – and updated in 2003 – defining the seven minimum requirements that the 'Responsible Authorities' had to make sure were up and running. Currently, MAPPA protocols are in place in each area, endorsed by senior representatives of each agency. These protocols cover the terms of reference and, crucially, policy and procedure in relation to confidentiality and the disclosure of information.

New guidance (National Probation Service, 2003) has now been written which aims to standardise much of the current variety of MAPPP arrangements. Each area's Strategic Group overseeing the work is likely to expand the membership to providers from the electronic monitoring field. Various agencies will have a 'duty to co-operate', and although this falls short of the statutory obligations (this remains with the police and probation services) all other agencies listed, such as the prison service, social services and health, will be expected to attend at a sufficient level of management oversight and authority.

MAPPA is responsible for the risk management of the following offenders:

- Registered sex offenders
- Violent offenders and those sexual offenders who are not required to register
- Any other offender who, because of the offence(s) committed by them, is considered to pose a risk of serious harm to the public

The largest proportion of MAPPA offenders are managed at Level 1, where the risks posed by the offender can be managed by one agency alone. These are usually low to medium risk offenders. Level 2 local inter-agency risk management is used where the active involvement of more than one agency is required, which agencies being determined by the characteristics of any particular case. This usually involves a monthly meeting to determine plans, and permanent representation from core agencies. Level 3 MAPPP meetings deal solely with offenders who present a high or very high risk of causing serious harm – the critical few – and who require a management plan involving close co-operation at a senior level. This may be due to the complexity of the case or the unusual demands it creates, or because of the likelihood of media interest or public scrutiny.

MAPPP reports are published annually, and state the number of offenders, in each category, that the panels are dealing with. This information is for the first time now in the public domain and the media are inevitably focusing on how this work is carried out and to what degree it satisfies the public's demands to know more about sex offenders in their area (see Table 5.1 for examples of the 2003/4 figures).

The random selection of four areas of the country in Table 5.1 highlights some disparities, including the use of Sex Offender Orders, and the number of offenders being discussed at Level 3 MAPPP meetings. In terms of this latter, very high risk, group, some of the areas record the outcome during the year in question: Norfolk returned fourteen Level 3 offenders to custody for a breach of licence, one for breach of a Sex Offender Order, but none were charged with serious new offences; Northumbria returned seven to custody for breach of licence only; Warwickshire returned only one

Table 5.1 Annual MAPPA figures (2003/4)

	London	Warwickshire	Norfolk	Northumbria
Category 1: RSOs				
No. living in community	2,272	183	484	750
No. per 100,000 of population	31	36	60	53
Sex Offender Register breaches	99	3	23	68
Sex Offender Orders				
• Applied for	18	0	9	6
• Imposed by the Court	10	0	9	5
Category 2: Violent and other sex offenders				
No. living in the community	1,422	53	237	73
Category 3: other offenders				
No. living in the community	400	37	27	64
No. of Restraining Orders imposed	0	0	0	0
Category 4: MAPPP cases				
RSOs	19	2	35	15
Violent offenders	7	1	62	10
Other offenders	4	0	3	12

offender for breach of licence; and London breached four offenders. This suggests that Level 3 MAPPA is reasonably successful in its aim. However, broader figures for the recall of any offender considered under the MAPPA (including lower levels of risk and concern), or new charges relating to sexual and violent offences, are unfortunately not provided.

An evidence-base for MAPPA is not yet established. However, Plotnikoff and Woolfson (2000) reported on some preliminary data on sex offender registration, from the police perspective. In 1998, only 4 per cent of sex offenders released into the community, and required to register, were committing an offence by failing to register within fourteen days. The compliance rate varied from 85 to 100 per cent across individual forces, averaging 95 per cent. Police forces reported a significant increase in their workload, but less than 50 per cent had provided additional manpower. There was a high level of police visits to offenders, to record further details about the offender and his/her circumstances, or simply to verify the address. All forces had a community notification policy, but only five had invoked this in respect of a specific sex offender. Only one-third of police forces thought that the monitoring activity had contributed to crime prevention, and one-quarter reported using register intelligence in investigations.

Maguire *et al.* (2001) reported on one of the early pieces of research to examine the workings and effectiveness of Public Protection Panels. The team observed fifty-nine risk assessment/management panels and inter- viewed 147 practitioners, ranging from senior managers to front-line staff (police, probation, social services, housing, psychiatrists and prison staff). Maguire *et al.* (2001) highlighted three areas which needed attention:

- Standardisation and consistency in the structure of panels, tighter gate- keeping in risk assessment, and improved recording of decisions
- Resourcing, which needed to be more clearly designated, with dedi- cated co-ordinators to service preparatory work for panels
- Monitoring, managerial oversight and accountability of the public protection system

Their subsequent evaluation of the MAPPA process (Kemshall *et al.*, 2005) involved a survey of the forty-two MAPPA areas in England and Wales, and case studies in six areas. They found that there was evidence of greater effectiveness and consistency across MAPPAs, with formalisation of the three-tier public protection structure; the naming of HM Prison Service as an additional Responsible Authority was a positive step; and the role of other agencies was much more active, as a result of the 'duty to co-operate' through the Criminal Justice Act 2003.

Two further publications – *MAPPA – The First Five Years* (Home Office, 2006) and a Joint Thematic Inspection Report, *Putting Risk of Harm in Context* (National Probation Service, 2006) – set the current scene. By 2005/ 6, 1,278 offenders were being managed in England and Wales at Level 3, the 'critical few', and a further 12,505 were being managed at Level 2. There was also an encouraging reduction in the number of serious new offences (sexual or violent) for MAPPA cases, from 79 (0.6 per cent) in 2004/5 to 61 (0.44 per cent) in 2005/6. However the Inspection Report echoed the findings of Kemshall *et al.* (2005), recommending that there should continue to be a focus on ensuring consistency of practice, and of risk assessment standards (both likelihood of offending and risk of harm), and that there should be increased priority given to early sentence planning and follow-through.

Knock (2002) reported, from the police perspective, on the use of Sex Offender Orders (SOOs). Between December 1998 and March 2001, ninety- two had been awarded in England and Wales, nearly one-half of these being applied for by just six forces. Forty-six per cent of offenders under these orders had been prosecuted for a subsequent breach due to non-compliance, sentencing ranging from fairly lengthy custodial sentences to small fines. Fears that press coverage would be problematic were not founded, in that only 40 per cent of SOOs had received written press coverage, mostly in relation to the breach aspect. Only 14 per cent of articles gave precise details of where the offender lived. In 2005/6, 933 SOOs were granted, and 104 orders were breached. This demonstrates the increasing use – and utility – of the new range of civil orders.

Lay members are now being considered for membership of the Strategic Groups. Members are being recruited in five pilot areas, and their training in the area of sexual abuse is being carefully planned. Again this is a response to the increasing demands for much more open access to the Sex Offenders Register and is seen as a step to try to better involve the communities where these offenders are predominantly based. Crucially, a serious offence case review (SOCR) is to be set up to examine MAPPP cases who reoffend. There is some debate around the role of the chair. Currently the chairing is shared between police and probation, but ideally this should be an independent person. The controversial matter of offender representation at MAPPPs and/or legal representation remains to be addressed under the Human Rights Act; this is likely to be played out in the courtroom as increasingly individuals expect to be party to discussions involving their management.

Integrated models are implied in multi-agency and multi-professional structures, such as the MAPPA. Yet is this really the case? Their primary role is to protect the public, and this objective is directly shared with the police and probation services who have a statutory duty to co-ordinate MAPPA, and supported by the Youth Offending teams and Child Protection social services departments. However, housing bodies have a different set of priorities, as does the health service whose primary aim is to serve the needs of their patients. This raises some questions and concerns (Craissati, 2003) – not apparently answered by current policy guidance (NIMHE, 2003) – which are detailed in the dilemmas (as discussed by clinicians involved in local MAPPPs) outlined below:

- *Can multi-agency liaison sometimes mean little more than the transfer of information – and therefore anxiety – without effective action?*
  Agencies and professionals often deploy enormous energy in the relatively easy task of risk assessment, yet show little interest in the creative resourcing of the far more complex task of risk management. The transfer of information – usually confirming what each agency already knows – then provides a semblance of activity which falsely suggests that the problem has been managed. This phenomenon is central to many multi-agency fora, and may well be a defensive response to core anxieties raised by the client group (Menzies, 1988).
- *How visible should multi-agency partnerships be, if treatment is not to be 'contaminated' by risk management?*
  The overt partnership between probation and police in managing high risk offenders has undoubted benefits but, many would say, with the loss of a potentially important 'welfare' relationship between a probation officer and an offender. Questions of emotional containment and

therapeutic boundaries – balancing the personal against the public – are even more salient when treatment is provided. Offenders can be hypersensitive to feelings of betrayal and persecution which mirror their own childhood experiences and are replicated in their own offending behaviour. Thus, whilst all agencies may subscribe sincerely to a multi-agency model, it may be appropriate for certain aspects of the liaison to be muted, on a 'need-to-know' basis, or stronger in one direction than another; that is, a policy of information exchange which is 'semi-permeable', with more information being made available to treatment providers than treatment providers transmit to the world outside the therapeutic arena. This arrangement needs to be separated off from problems of disclosure in relation to enhanced risk, but in fact the two are often confused with each other, leading to the (usually) paranoid belief of other agencies that treatment providers are concealing valuable information related to risk.

- *Different agencies have different thresholds for managing risk, which can lead to tensions and contradictory goals.*
  Gross inconsistencies in the assessment of risk are diminishing, as agencies become practised in utilising simple actuarial measures (usually Risk Matrix 2000, sexual and violent versions; Thornton, 2003). However, it is easy to forget, for example, how low the base rate for sexual recidivism can be, particularly in the short term; this is in contrast to the intensity of immediate concerns that an individual might reoffend whilst under our care. Agencies such as the police and social services rarely see offenders who have done well in terms of offending, and tend to remember those who re-present. For example, intimacy difficulties and social exclusion mean that child molesters often befriend similar offenders; what is viewed by one agency as the only source of companionship is viewed by another as the beginnings of a paedophile network.

- *Agencies – such as health – are given access to police intelligence which they must keep secret from the client, and which will be used to aid criminal justice interventions rather than used therapeutically.*
  Nowhere is this more salient than when an offender has been subject to police surveillance, and has demonstrated risky behaviours – drinking alcohol, loitering in a shopping centre where children are present, or forging a relationship with a learning disabled woman. A therapeutic approach would involve a confrontation with the offender, withdrawal of certain liberties or privileges, prolonged discussion of the behaviour and, if collaboration is possible, the enhancement of relapse prevention strategies. Clearly this is not allowed when such a heavy investment of police resources can only be directed towards one end – recall or re-arrest.

- *Short-term risk management strategies (that is, managing a licence or seeking to exclude an offender from the locality) may directly contradict longer-term strategies (for example, engaging an offender in meaningful personal change within a therapeutic relationship).*

For example, a probation officer is likely to feel pressurised to recall a high risk offender on licence, for a risky behaviour, even though that individual will be released six months later without any statutory restrictions. The mental health professional providing care to that offender may be exasperated at the loss of a painstakingly developed rapport, for what appears to be behaviour that could be otherwise managed (or may even mask a modest reduction in overall risk).

- *How can different standards and consistency of views be managed within one agency, let alone across several agencies?*

  It is, perhaps, self-evident that agencies struggle to achieve consistency of practice. However, well-intentioned strategies to ensure evidence-based practice and rigid standards may ultimately stifle innovation and creativity. Finding a balance between adherence to consistent guidelines, and individual autonomy and responsibility, is something of a tightrope, and professional practice is often reflected in the message conveyed to the individual offender – that is, the extent to which the offender is encouraged to pursue or to refrain from individualised decision-making and self-management of risky situations and behaviours.

- *Should the health service try to play a direct role with all offenders with an antisocial personality disorder, even those who refuse to see mental health practitioners and experience little or no distress at their condition?*

  Attendance at a single MAPPP will make it abundantly clear that a significant proportion of high risk violent offenders with substance misuse problems have marked personality difficulties and resolutely refuse offers of assistance and fail to engage with the probation service. The new Policy Guidance for People with a Personality Disorder does not confront this issue head on, although a new Mental Health Act – if along the lines proposed – will raise uncomfortable dilemmas: such offenders may technically meet the criteria for assessment under a new Mental Health Act; indeed a proportion may meet the criteria for DSPD. Yet surely it was not envisaged that hospitals would detain armed robbers on the grounds of their marked antisocial traits.

Whether or not an integrated model should be centred around the MAPPP is unclear. These examples of dilemmas that arise in such a management structure suggest that MAPPA is not a fully integrative model, largely because the multi-agency group do not subscribe to and share a fundamental philosophical and theoretical approach to the management of personality disordered offenders. The MAPPA suggest a mixed model which allows for integration and parallel care, providing a compromise which is mostly acceptable to agencies. Figure 5.3 mirrors aspects of the personality

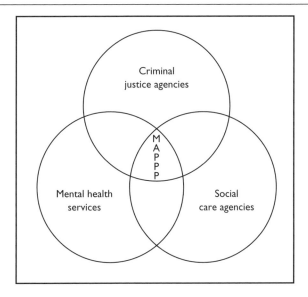

Figure 5.3

disordered offender's functioning (Figure 5.2), allowing the MAPPP a central strategic role and capacity for managing the 'crucial few', whilst health, criminal justice and social care agencies (including local authority and voluntary sector roles) have capacity for independent roles and collaborative projects.

The tools of risk management

Risk assessment and information sharing appear to be relatively straightforward procedures, governed by protocols, research and a methodical examination of the 'facts'. By contrast, risk management involves a great deal more individual judgement, negotiation and creativity, if it is to walk the fine line between over- and under-control. Negotiation, specifically, needs to take place between professionals, between agencies, and with the offender himself. Risk management plans involve an intelligent interpretation of the assessment, transforming static and dynamic concerns into a coherent and individualised strategy which complements the psychological formulation.

The tools at hand can range from legislative safeguards to the offender's own areas of strength. This range of externally to internally driven controls is shown diagrammatically in Figure 5.4.

Internal controls relate to the offender's capacity to refrain from further offending as a result of his own abilities and motivation. These could be features of his personality, such as compliant and dependent traits which

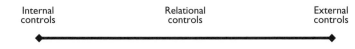

| Internal
controls | Relational
controls | External
controls |

Figure 5.4

are associated with a willingness to seek and follow helpful advice. Therapeutic work may have helped an individual to improve his problem-solving ability, to regulate his emotional state and reduce impulsive behaviours, which are all features of improved psychological functioning. Insight, again perhaps as a result of treatment, creates a capacity to think and to effect choices as the time between the impulse to offend and action lengthens.

Motivation not to offend can be driven by many things, and sometimes practitioners are too quick to condemn a selfish motivation, whilst hoping for a morally superior motivation – such as victim empathy – as replacement. Yet the fear of a life sentence – however unlikely to occur in reality – can be a powerful force for good, as can the desire to avoid dying in prison. As all offenders age, they are less able to tolerate the regime and the frustrations of prison; for personality disordered offenders, repeated incarcerations or hospitalisations mean their usual defences against recognition or ownership of their problems begin to crumble with age, particularly narcissistic and paranoid mechanisms, and depression creeps in. Some individuals are able to associate a positive self-image and self-esteem with the idea of themselves as reformed offenders, in the same way as recovering alcoholics, and they invest emotionally in a future without offending. Others, who may still dismiss the impact of their behaviour on the victims, wish to protect close family members from future heartache and humiliation.

It is, however, the role of the management team to maximise the possibilities of these internally driven motivations and to harness them to a plan which increases the chance of successful rehabilitation. Motivational interviewing and the principles on which it rests (see Chapter 4) can guide the practitioner, enabling a truly collaborative approach to risk management to be developed. This feature of the offender/client–practitioner relationship is often forgotten in the effort to develop an exacting and rigorous risk management plan. Nevertheless it has to be recognised that very high risk offenders – no matter how well motivated or treated – cannot and should not be contained by a risk management plan which relies excessively on internally driven controls. There are also numerous offenders who have very impoverished internal controls, where the management strategy is forced to adopt external controls.

In terms of *external controls*, the probation and police service are central to the management plan for personality disordered offenders emerging into the community via the criminal justice system, as is the Responsible Medical Officer (RMO) for those moving through the hospital system.

Supervision and surveillance

Stringent reporting requirements, and conditions of treatment and residence attached to hospital restriction orders, licences or community rehabilitation orders, create firm boundaries for the offender with which he must comply. Conditions of residence, for example, at a probation hostel can provide necessary physical containment, and additional curfew restrictions may help to manage high risk times of day, albeit perhaps restricting and isolating the offender in his room.

Police measures – via the MAPPA – include regular visits, carried out informally and usually without antagonism. Perhaps more than any other recent development, this is the change which has had the most powerful impact on sex offenders' behaviour and attitudes. A curiously firm yet collaborative relationship can be forged, in which the offender is reminded of his risk, a 'paternal' eye is kept on him, and in return he is protected from potential community retaliation. In contrast, behind the scenes, police surveillance is used in cases of grave concern, where evidence is required for breach, recall proceedings, or new charges to be brought. The cost of surveillance is so prohibitive that an offence must be thought to be imminent, or an offender so impulsive and reckless that the necessary evidence will be obtained within a very few days.

Legislative measures (externally driven)

There is a range of legislative measures available, including standard Mental Health Act (1983) and sentencing procedures, as well as the development of statutory responsibility for the police and probation service to develop MAPPA. There are some additional recent legislative changes which are specific to dangerous offenders, and worth considering as one part of a package of external controls.

The Crime and Disorder Act 1998 (Section 20) introduced the Sex Offender Order (SOO), now known as the Sex Offences Prevention Order (SOPO). This is applied for in court by the police when they have reason to believe that a convicted sexual offender is behaving in a way that previously seemed to be a precursor to offending. It is a civil order requiring the civil standard of proof and preventing a convicted sex offender from doing a specified activity or going to a specified place. Evidence has to be gathered to support a SOPO application, both to show that risky behaviour has taken place and to inform the development of suitable prohibitions. A breach, however, constitutes a criminal offence, triable either way, and attracting a maximum penalty of five years' imprisonment. SOPOs are only sought for the most pernicious of sex offenders, and it is unclear, in practice, whether they are designed to ensure the risk free rehabilitation of the offender, or to ensure that he is caught breaching the order but before a sexual offence has occurred. There is a fairly persecutory and comprehensive quality to SOPOs – avoiding close proximity to schools, parks, children (supervised or not) and any other suspicious behaviours – which feeds the offender's view of himself as unwanted, unloved and excluded. Over time, statistical outcomes will be available, although high failure rates may simply serve to support the view of the offender as high risk.

The Crime and Disorder Act 1998 also introduced the potential for extended supervision, for periods of up to five years for a violent offence, and ten years for sexual offences. This seems like a good idea in terms of public protection, as risky behaviours can lead to enforcement in the form of recall. But extended supervision poses considerable dilemmas for the probation service, for it is often associated with the higher risk recidivist offenders; if the offender is an uncooperative, belligerent individual, with marked personality difficulties, then the officer is faced with years of tortuous supervision sessions, which in themselves may add little to the management plan.

Amendments under the Criminal Justice and Court Services Act 2000 require sex offenders to notify of foreign travel, and there are also increased penalties for non-registration (as well as a requirement to register within seventy-two hours). Sections 67 and 68 of the Criminal Justice and Court Services Act 2000 provided statutory provision for joint risk assessment and management by police and probation, officially creating the MAPPP.

Much more recent is the Criminal Justice Act 2003, which came into force in April 2005. The aim was to update the criminal justice system by making changes to the sentencing framework, targeting prison sentences for the more dangerous or persistent offenders. Of particular relevance to personality disordered offenders is the new IPP (Imprisonment for Public Protection), which is an indeterminate sentence which must be imposed on adult offenders convicted of sexual and violent offences where the court judges that there is 'significant risk to members of the public of serious harm' from further offences and where the offence carries a maximum penalty of ten years or more. The IPP is similar to a life sentence in that the court will set a tariff period, after which release is at the discretion of the Parole Board, and on release the offender will be subject to supervision on licence for at least ten years. The second important provision is that of an Extended Sentence for Public Protection (EPP) where the sexual or violent offence committed carries a maximum penalty of less than ten years; the court must set a custodial period and extended licence period, the latter being up to five years for violent offenders and eight years for sexual offenders.

Although extended periods of supervision carry enormous difficulties, there are very clear advantages to the increased use of life sentences for high risk personality disordered offenders. Not only do they serve as a future deterrent, but they place the role of management firmly within the criminal justice system, with its emphasis on socially acceptable behaviour, and they place responsibility on the offender for demonstrating change before he can access the community. Furthermore, there are reasonably clear guidelines for recall in response to behaviours which are clearly associated with risk. In contrast, the Mental Health Act – the use of hospital orders with restrictions – provides a much less clear strategy for management, with responsibility somehow shifted towards the professionals to treat the offender and ensure his progress, and difficulties in knowing when to recall an offender in relation to behaviours which may be more closely related to risk than to a deterioration in mental health. However, with an anticipated dramatic increase in the number of indeterminate sentenced prisoners – some of whom are likely to have very short tariff periods to serve – it remains unclear how the prison service will manage the potentially over-whelming demand for places on accredited programmes, these providing the main means for prisoners to demonstrate meaningful change and reduced risk.

Disclosure

The decision to disclose highly sensitive information to a third party has to be thoroughly justified, and integral to an individualised risk management process. Unlike the American experience (see below), England and Wales have almost no experience of community notification. From the criminal justice perspective (led by the local MAPPA), a proposed public disclosure has to be authorised by a senior police officer. Early rulings suggested that disclosure of details of the identity and whereabouts of an offender can only be authorised when, after all the relevant factors have been considered, it is deemed necessary for the protection of the public. However, in reality, decisions about disclosure to specific individuals or to organisations – rather than the public – take place more frequently: for example, informing the learning disabled girlfriend of a rapist of his history; or warning scouting or football associations of a particular offender who has recently assumed an alias in order to gain re-entry.

Good practice dictates that disclosure should not just involve the passing on of information, but also pragmatic advice as to what course of action to take. For example, telling the head of a school that there is a dangerous paedophile in the vicinity is not particularly helpful. Should that head inform parents, how much should he/she tell parents, should the teachers simply be more vigilant, or is general education about offenders required? If a man with a previous conviction for domestic violence and attempted murder of a girlfriend attends a college course where a number of young women are in contact with him, what should be done? The women are adults and may or may not be vulnerable. Should the college tutor or principal be told, or should a girlfriend be warned once a relationship is established? In many cases difficult decisions have to be made as to whether the offender is informed of the intention to disclose. Transparency may trigger the offender to take action which avoids the need for disclosure. However, there may be fears that he will be driven underground or otherwise seek to manipulate the situation.

From the health perspective, the duty of confidentiality weighs heavily, and any breaches thereof may have grave implications for the client–practitioner relationship. This is perhaps more so than for any other agency represented on the MAPPP, where duties lie primarily in protecting the public. There are guidelines, including professional standards (for example, the British Psychological Society and British Medical Association guidelines for good practice), and policies such as the Data Protection Act, Sharing Letters, and the role of the Caldicott Guardian (a senior health professional who oversees staff use of patient personal health information).

Case law in relation to health service breaches of confidentiality remains sparse, although there is a lead from North America which is rooted in the Tarasoff case in the 1970s. Although a complex case, briefly the circumstances were that a university student in therapy – clearly personality disordered – made threats to kill a young woman with whom he had wished to form a relationship; he subsequently discharged himself from therapy and, some time later, killed the woman. Her family were successful in suing the therapist for failure to warn the intended victim. This was the first successful case of its kind, and although subsequent similar lawsuits did not always uphold a 'duty to warn', the Tarasoff case sparked considerable interest and concern.

Much of the subsequent writing on disclosure and duty to warn potential victims has adhered to the key principles that the practitioner is responsible for:

- Exercising the care and skill of a reasonable professional in identifying those patients who pose a significant risk of physical harm to third persons
- Exercising reasonable professional care in protecting third parties from those patients identified as 'dangerous'
- Noting and evaluating the intensity and focus of the subject's hostility
- Noting threats that have been made and their seriousness and any violent past actions
- If necessary, obtaining another concurring professional opinion

Decisions to act could include changing the nature of the treatment, liaising with other agencies, arranging for hospitalisation, discussing the concerns with the offender or close family members, and so on. Breaching confidentiality without the offender's permission is only one of a range of options.

Taking into account the above guidelines, it is clear that, in the majority of instances, the mental health practitioner is faced with numerous decisions about confidentiality, only the most extreme – and most rare – of which involve a duty to warn potential victims.

The American experience

So far this chapter has outlined the legislative changes – and associated developments in practice – made in England and Wales over the last ten years or so. It is, however, worth pausing to compare such developments with practice in North America, whose lead England and Wales have followed to some extent. In the USA, sex offender registration laws have been in place since the late 1980s to early 1990s (Bedarf, 1995), based on the premise that there are high rates of recidivism among sex offenders and therefore they need to be kept under police surveillance. Registration requirements have been very similar to those currently in place in England and Wales. In 1990, Washington State was the first to take registration a step further, enacting a sex offender community notification law. Community notification statutes are currently in place in fifty states.

There are three basic types of notification statutes (Finn, 1997; Zevitz and Farkas, 2000a, 2000b):

1   Most identify an agency which is responsible for determining the level of risk an offender poses and then implementing a notification plan that reflects the level of risk.
2   Others provide for community groups and individuals to take the initiative to request information about whether a sex offender is living in their community, and to request details about the sex offender.
3   One state uses a self-identification procedure which requires offenders themselves to notify – under close supervision – the neighbourhood where they live.

Many local jurisdictions have used a three-tier system of determining risk. Low risk notification is likely to be limited to area law enforcement and correction officials; medium risk notification includes specific agencies or organisations which fall within the offender's identified pattern of behaviour. High risk notification may include additional procedures such as household visits, posting flyers, media releases or conducting community meetings (Zevitz and Farkas, 2000a, 2000b). For example, of all the flyers in Washington State which related to medium risk offenders, 49 per cent showed a photograph, and 21 per cent gave the exact address of the offender; flyers in relation to high risk offenders had a photograph 86 per cent of the time, with 53 per cent detailing the exact address (Finn, 1997).

It is unfortunate that, to date, the extensive American experience has not been well researched. It is clear that there are difficulties in maintaining compliance with sex offender registration, and some states have published their compliance rates. Bedarf (1995) reports that compliance with registration in California and Washington was said to be around 70 per cent. However, limited police resources meant that they were unable to keep track of offenders, as they moved around. In terms of the key question of protecting the public, there has been one research study comparing the recidivism rates of sex offenders subject to notification, with a matched group of sex offenders not subject to notification. The sexual recidivism rates were 19 per cent and 22 per cent respectively, with no statistical significance between the two groups (Schram and Milloy, 1995).

There has been concern that community notification would lead to vigilante attacks on the sex offenders. Commentators report that this has been surprisingly unproblematic: for example, less than 10 per cent of offenders in Oregon experienced some form of harassment. Wisconsin, Washington, Oregon and New Jersey all report that less than 1 per cent of their notification cases incurred physical assaults or property damage (Finn, 1997; Zevitz and Farkas, 2000a, 2000b). Zevitz and Farkas have also explored the impact of neighbourhood meetings. They found that attendees almost always found the amount of information provided to be sufficient. However, a positive attitude to the meeting was related to the following: being alerted to the meeting by a public official; the meeting being well planned and organised; and the purpose of the meeting being clearly explained before and during the meeting. A large minority of attendees remained angry and resentful: they had hoped to be able to prevent the placement of a sex offender locally; and they were more likely to leave the meeting feeling frightened and powerless.

Overall, commentators highlight the potential advantages of community notification in educating the public in general terms about sex offenders. It may assist with the rapid investigation of sex offences, and seems to improve the criminal justice system's involvement in the community. The *threat* of notification is seen as a motivating factor in sex offenders who are resistant to supervision or treatment. All commentators seem to agree that there is a problem with lack of resources to manage community notification, which is a burdensome process. Critics of the system point to the possible displacement effect when sex offenders move several times, often across states, and sometimes without re-registering. There is some evidence to suggest that social exclusion has increased as a result (Zevitz and Farkas, 2000a, 2000b), with sex offenders being sacked from their employment and refused housing, and their families and victims suffering as a result of the public exposure. The system may also lead to a false sense of security, insofar as residents conclude that they know who the sex offenders are in their community; alternatively, it may incite excessive community fear or anger.

These issues are highlighted in the recent NSPCC report (Fitch, 2006), which concluded that there was inadequate evidence to demonstrate any meaningful efficacy for community notification, and that it may provoke non-compliance in offenders and provide false reassurance to parents and potential victims, with no actual improvement in vigilance. Bedarf (1995) speaks eloquently of community notification as shame punishment. A true shame punishment would aim to shape the offender's moral character – to shame him into conforming to the community's moral code. However, Bedarf points out that advocates of community notification reject the notion of rehabilitation for sex offenders; thus shaming becomes merely an outlet for the community's rage. The sexual recidivism rates are often lower than the recidivism rates for other serious crimes of violence, and community notification is likely to exacerbate the already large discrepancy between the public's estimate of risk and actual risk. If community notification is an effective method of public protection, why would the public not wish to know about the wider group of personality disordered and violent individuals living close to them? Whether or not community notification is an effective method of public protection, this does appear to be a resource-intensive approach which devotes a level of attention not supported by the evidence thus far.

This section on tools of management has listed a number of measures – by no means exhaustive – which range from internally driven to externally driven controls. Another way of conceptualising management approaches would be to draw upon some of the psychosocial models already discussed in previous chapters. In this way, the tools can be reframed within three paradigms: the attachment, behavioural and environmental planning paradigms.

The *attachment* paradigm is based on the premise that personality disordered offenders require a secure base from which to make excursions into pro-social or optimal functioning, developing the capacity to explore possible cognitive and affective change. This is essentially a relational strategy – compatible with many of the internal controls – in which empathic listening, the provision of information in a non-threatening way, and consistency of approach can all help to reduce anxiety and anger and promote stability (Adshead, 1998). Behaviours can be understood as a struggle for control over powerful emotions or traumatic re-enactments of earlier rejection and abuse; changes in practitioner, or changes in the practitioner–offender contract (including discharge), can be seen as having the potential to provoke anxiety and behavioural disturbance; too little or too much attentiveness to the offender, or contradictory messages – particularly 'you must do exactly what we say . . . but you must take responsibility for your own behaviour' – may elicit hostile responses. Adoption of this approach will require some capacity in the offender to engage in a meaningful relationship with a practitioner, and will not be easy with antisocial offenders, and is positively contra-indicated with highly psychopathic offenders. Proactive attention paid to these attachment processes may well create an environment in which the offender can think about change. Achieving secure attachments within a multi-agency setting is a challenging process, and some of the issues are highlighted in the section on containment below.

The *behavioural* paradigm is based on the core principles of classical and operant conditioning; that is, that behaviour can be shaped and maintained by the linking of stimulus and response (act and consequences). Many of the external controls fall within this paradigm in which outcomes are contingent upon the offender's behaviour. Good practice would suggest that a behavioural paradigm should emphasise transparency in the drawing up of expected behaviours and outcomes, that sanctions should be explicit and proactively stated, and that responses to behaviour should be consistent. There is considerable research to demonstrate that positive reinforcement (rewards) – particularly social rather than physical/financial – is more powerful in shaping and maintaining behaviour than punishment systems. This requires a creative reframing of many of the external tools which are explicitly punishment driven. With personality disordered offenders, behaviourally driven approaches would involve a clear behavioural contract being drawn up in advance, with an emphasis on tangible rewards (for example, relaxation in reporting conditions, greater freedom at the hostel, lowering of risk status) which gradually move towards a greater degree of social reinforcement (less discussion of offending and more discussion of future plans, praise and being given greater responsibility). Clearly sanctions still have a role to play, but these should receive less prominence, and should be associated with consistent approaches to enforcement. The explicit aim of behavioural approaches would be to achieve compliance and desistance from offending, although the implicit aim would also be to protect the public. This approach is suited to all offenders, but is particularly helpful with antisocial and highly psychopathic offenders who tend to be guarded and suspicious of practitioners and frequently complain about agencies.

The third paradigm, *environmental planning*, pays attention to the situational dimension to behaviour, its primary aim being to focus on altering the environment and triggering stimuli. This is an approach advocated by disparate authors, including Farrall (2004) and Tyrer *et al.* (2003). Farrall emphasised the central role of the social context in promoting desistance, whilst Tyrer *et al.* proposed a model of 'nido therapy' – interventions which circumvented the personality disordered individual's core traits and difficulties, altering the environment to match their needs. Although from different theoretical backgrounds, both approaches promote interventions which aim to change the environment. For some offenders, this might entail consideration of specially designed work projects which understand difficulties in team working or managing boredom, but which promote personal responsibility and autonomous decision-making; for others, a housing move from a small urban estate to a quiet suburban street might overcome obstacles to success – allowing a paranoid individual – prone to fighting with his neighbours – to live next to a derelict building, and ensuring that he is never forced to wait in a busy probation office waiting area, and so on. Positively encouraging participation with certain religious groups who understand the issues of public protection might create immediate communities for offenders who feel isolated and who are prone to seeking out criminogenic peers. This is a model that is exemplified by the work on Circles of Support and Accountability (COSA; Correctional Services of Canada, 2003). COSA has been in existence in Canada for more than ten years, and emerged as an attempt to respond to high risk sexual offenders as the most abhorred and excluded group of offenders, whose resettlement needs were neglected. It is led by the Quakers, and the chaplaincy defines a 'Circle of Support and Accountability' as a group of four to seven primarily faith-based community volunteers, who are committed to enhancing public safety by supporting community re-entry, through covenanting, meeting and walking daily in friendship with a person who has been detained to the end of his sentence because of a sexual offence history. Quakers brought the idea to England and pilot projects are being carried out and evaluated by the Hampton Trust, Thames Valley and the Lucy Faithful Foundation hosted by Quakers and Secula respectively. Whilst the Canadian model is faith-based – very open and befriending – it will not be the same in the UK, due to tighter boundaries to ensure safety.

The aim with environmental planning is to provide a social context in which the triggers to an offender's destructive behaviours are minimised, and in so doing, to create a calm environment in which the offender can gain confidence in achieving desistance from offending. This approach is important for those antisocial offenders who are motivated to change, but liable to succumb to immediate environmental temptations, and for those personality disordered offenders with particularly rigid and intransigent cognitive styles – cluster A traits – which are difficult to address.

Case example

Clive's background and risk factors are detailed in Chapter 3 (see pp. 86–88). Charged with an offence of gross indecency (on a 12-year-old girl) and affray, he was remanded on bail to a probation hostel. He presented a medium risk of sexual and violent offending, and scored very high on the PCL-R, with additional borderline traits. The management plan at the hostel was well thought through, and a good example of multi-agency collaboration. It was decided to focus on a mixed model of external constraints with behavioural consequences, as well as on internally driven motivation, particularly in relation to his wish to avoid prison and willingness to consider sex offender treatment programmes. Given the psychopathic traits, it was understood that he needed as few rules as possible, but that these should be adhered to consistently, with obvious behavioural sanctions attached.

After an initial verbal and written warning about late returns, he settled into an apparently compliant – if sometimes challenging – pattern of behaviour. He could be anxious and depressed at times, albeit fleetingly, and consulted with the psychiatric team about managing these episodes with medication and support. The team were able to identify his tendency to split staff by confiding in some and gossiping about others, and took steps to contain this, by imposing limitations to the length and frequency of keywork sessions, and with quick intervention by the manager to resolve any emerging disputes. Enormous efforts were made to ensure that Clive received a consistent message that was empathic but firm.

Clive attended psychology assessment sessions, and initial features of defensiveness and minimisation around his offence were managed sensitively, and reduced over time. It was identified that resistance to joining the sex offender group programme was largely related to anxiety, and preparatory work in this regard was largely successful.

In the meantime, the police public protection team were involved in monitoring Clive, in terms of his movements, his contact with criminal associates, and ensuring that he kept away from the locality of the victim. The only remaining obstacle was the resolution of the court case, the proposal being that he receive a three-year community sentence with associated conditions. For a range of legal reasons outside the control of the multi-agency group, the court dates were repeatedly delayed, involving a change of courts, and of solicitors. Clive was clearly agitated about this, but was managing to keep his behaviour acceptable and within the rules.

It was an enormous surprise to everyone when Clive was discovered to have run away from the hostel, just after hearing that the court date had finally been set for six weeks hence. Not only had he run off with another resident's money, but it seemed that the literacy support worker who visited the hostel weekly had also run off with him (soon to be discarded). Clive was missing for two years, but was eventually found by the police and brought back to court, although interestingly, he did not appear to have offended in any way during his time on the run.

In reflecting on the case, and with the benefit of meeting with Clive some years later, it began to be clear that the management plan had not taken into account sufficiently the dynamics of the hostel environment, and the attachment issues for Clive. His primary attachment experience was with an alcoholic mother who provoked deeply ambivalent responses in Clive: one moment she could be loving, the next aggressive and unpredictable. His coping mechanism was to ignore social rules and run away, avoiding the need to tolerate unbearable anxiety. Clive's personal experience of the hostel – nurturing, rule-bound, observant of his needs – was seductive but suffocating, and compounded by the unpredictability of his impending court date. Running away was his best defence, and when he was unfettered by constraints and expectations, it is clear that he had little need to act out or offend.

Whether or not such insights at the time might have prevented the collapse of the plan is unclear. It certainly would have helped if the court hearing had been finalised quickly and without delays; and it may have helped if greater attention had been paid to Clive's relationship with the environment and the agencies. It is certainly true that whilst the more professionally qualified staff are given support in thinking about complex cases, it is often the least qualified who are the victims of the offender's psychopathology, and this is why including all staff in training and support is important with personality disorder services.

Containment: theoretical principles

The view is taken that professionals who deal with offenders are not free agents but potential actors who have been assigned roles in the individual offender's own re-enactment of their internal world drama. The professionals have the choice not to perform but they can only make this choice when they have a good idea of what the role is they are trying to avoid. Until they can work this out they are likely to be drawn into the play, unwittingly and therefore not unwillingly. Because of the latter, if the pressure to play is not anticipated then the professional will believe he is in a role of his choosing. Unfortunately, initially, only a preview of the plot is available in the somewhat cryptic form of the offence. . . . It is also important to comment that it is not only the offender's internal drama that professionals are called upon to enact but also those more explicit scripts of their own organizations and central government. They will also be under pressure from themselves to re-enact their own dramas.

(Davies, 1996, p. 133)

Although psychoanalytic ideas within treatment have become more marginalised with the development of an evidence-base for cognitive-behavioural treatments, there is no other theoretical model with such experience of considering the dynamic interplay between client (or offender) and practitioner. Davies puts the case simply and imaginatively: the details of the offence(s) provide a glimpse into the internal world of the offender, hinting at the unbearable emotional conflicts which cannot be processed and absorbed but have to be acted upon; as a violent offence is an interpersonal act, so the offender's emotional state is played out in his broader relationships with others. As has been readily recognised, the severely personality disordered offender relates to others within a world dominated by feelings, often unpleasant ones, which are likely to interfere – albeit outside conscious awareness – with the feelings of professionals involved in their care. 'We feel impelled to conform to a pattern imposed by the patient, so that we begin to feel provoked, hostile, persecuted and have to behave exactly as the patients need us to, becoming rejecting and hostile' (Pines, 1978, quoted in Hinshelwood, 1999). In mental health services, this means that the practitioner can no longer see the individual as his/her patient, as, within a climate of mutual abuse, the practitioner moves from diagnosis to moral evaluation: 'manipulative psychopath, untreatable, wasting time'. The result is an inability to contain the anxiety of relating to the patient, and, ultimately, rejection.

Within a team, or a multi-agency, multi-professional context, containment is threatened, quite commonly, by the phenomenon of 'splitting' and 'manipulation'. These are words in common parlance, and usually understood to account for all types of disagreement among practitioners regarding a patient or offender; with the identification of splitting, there is usually agreement that the offender is to blame. However, in Gabbard's excellent paper (1989), he points out that splitting is an unconscious process that the patient/offender uses automatically to maintain his emotional survival. That is, splitting first occurs within the individual as a means of separating good from bad, love from hate, in order to preserve positive experiences and emotions. The motivation behind this may be to gain a sense of mastery through repeated traumatic experiences with a primary carer, or a preference for a 'bad object' over no object at all, or perhaps a yearning for a more positive relationship with the object. These ideas relate closely to the work on object relations and attachment theory outlined in Chapter 3. Splitting is enhanced by projection, which involves unconsciously attributing the bad qualities to a person in the environment, whilst all good qualities remain within; this brings some order to chaotic internal experiences. However, it may be that the practitioner unconsciously identifies with that which is projected and begins to feel or behave accordingly. In doing so, and if unchecked, the patient/offender is able to achieve a fleeting sense of triumph at the illusion of having gained control over the unwanted and projected parts of the self.

As Gabbard points out, the task of the team or multi-agency structure is not to prevent splitting occurring, as it should be considered as a safety valve that protects the patient from what is perceived as overwhelming danger. Rather, splitting needs to be identified before it can destroy either treatment or the management plan, by means of appraising unusually intense feelings, shared discussion, and supervision.

These are complicated, but important ideas, which are central to the idea of management structures acting as a container of the offender's most destructive impulses. They can perhaps best be understood within the context of a case example.

Case example

Tony was considered by his probation officer to be a highly dangerous and manipulative offender, and he was subjected to a rigorous list of conditions attached to his licence in order to try to manage his behaviour. He responded with evasiveness, hostility and a tendency to resort to formal complaints, which resulted in him only being seen by two probation officers who recorded the sessions verbatim. His community psychiatric nurse (CPN), in an effort to avoid confrontation and wanting to establish some level of rapport, made strenuous efforts to empathise with the difficult aspects of Tony's circumstances, and focused sessions on his difficult early life. Tony was openly denigratory towards probation, extolling the supportive attitude of the CPN. This provoked irritation within probation who envied the CPN for her ability to avoid the onerous public protection issues; whilst the CPN found herself advocating for Tony in trying to persuade probation to reduce his curfew hours at the hostel, believing the attitude of the MAPPP to be overly persecutory and dismissive of Tony's psychological vulnerability.

The obvious hostilities between the agencies were enormously gratifying for Tony, mirroring as they did his own experiences as persecutor and victim which he had been unable to process and resolve, and absorbing on his behalf his intolerable anxieties about intimacy with others. Unable or unwilling to come together to reflect on their experiences, the agencies were ultimately defeated by these dynamics: Tony was triumphant in his success at reducing the length of his licence by a legal challenge due to a judicial error, thereby rendering the criminal justice agencies utterly impotent; and dropping out of treatment with the CPN as soon as his attendance became voluntary, it was only a matter of a few weeks before Tony was re-arrested for a serious violent assault on his new partner.

Manipulation can be confused with splitting, and with lying (which is a much more consciously exploitative and ruthless behaviour). Manipulation is particularly noticeable in some personality disordered offenders, and is viewed as a highly negative and pernicious trait. Yet it is often forgotten that manipulation is also a survival mechanism for those who live in constant dread of abandonment: such individuals often display an inordinate need to control the behaviour of others, thereby reassuring themselves that they are not as vulnerable to the whims of those around them; or they may also repetitively seek attention because they yearn for a particular response from others which might affirm or repair experiences with primary caregivers (Gabbard, 1989).

Case example

Barry was a high risk paedophile, with marked dependent, avoidant and borderline traits. He was highly demanding of staff time, presenting with a series of minor crises, and pleas for companionship to counter his loneliness and distress. A high support package was put in place, with input from a range of agencies in order to try to meet his evident need. Barry aggravated staff by confiding in them, only for them to find later that he had confided similarly in other staff; he double-booked appointments, letting staff down as a result, and forgot appointments at other times; it was discovered that he was claiming fares off more than one agency; and efforts to resource a 'treat' visit to the seaside were undermined by other arrangements to go to the cinema. Staff empathised with his distress and isolation, mindful of his dreadfully rejecting and emotionally barren childhood, but they found it difficult to develop any depth of empathic engagement with Barry who muddled up their names, was utterly absorbed in his own sense of deprivation, and although politely grateful, always conveyed a sense of disappointment. Offering more support made little meaningful difference, as though he were a sieve, fleetingly filled up only to be empty again within seconds. For this profoundly damaged man, it seemed that nothing could repair the emptiness within him; he was unable to replace the fleeting but intense gratification of sexual contact with a child with a more sustaining sense of emotional connection with others.

Such defences were explored by Menzies (1988) in her seminal paper on defensive techniques in the nursing service, many of which are helpful in considering the management of personality disordered offenders today. She highlighted organisational systems which protected staff from core anxieties, including:

- Splitting up contact with patients, breaking down work into lists of tasks
- Promoting the detachment and denial of feelings
- Attempting to minimise the number and variety of decisions a nurse must make by ritualised task-performance
- Reducing the weight of responsibility in decision-making by introducing checks and counter-checks

It could be argued that with high risk personality disordered offenders, some strategies to manage anxiety are a crucial component of management structures: for example, efforts to achieve consistency in risk assessment do involve a rather ritualised adherence to risk assessment tools, and this in turn reduces the responsibility that an individual has to take in terms of decisions, that is, standardising defensible decision-making. Furthermore, the shared care of patients – within reasonable limits – is considered to be good practice (Bateman and Tyrer, 2002); and emotional detachment is necessary for survival, and often achieved by adherence to intellectual and 'scientific' approaches. However, it is also easy to see how such structures may result in the fragmentation of services, which mirrors the objectification of the offender, with poor communication between agencies; how an emphasis on organisational rituals might lead to paralysis in the individual practitioner, with an associated inability to think or act independently; and how preoccupations with repeated risk assessments of the offender may mask underlying professional and organisational anxieties in relation to feelings of helplessness in the face of overwhelming psychological dysfunction.

This section on containment has been approached from a psychoanalytical point of view. However, it is important to note that, in our view, there is no inherent contradiction between the main theoretical approaches – just the use of different descriptive terminology, and a difference in emphasis. For example, schema-focused therapy, from a cognitive-behavioural perspective, would also pay detailed attention to the patient–therapist relationship. The core, unconditional, beliefs related to disconnection and rejection (abandonment/instability, mistrust/abuse, emotional deprivation, defectiveness/shame, and social isolation/alienation) would be likely to manifest themselves in expressive acts and interpersonal strategies which involve highly dysfunctional responses to the intervention of practitioners and agencies involved in the management plan. These are alluded to in Chapter 6 in the section on personality traits.

Conclusion

There is no one model of management for personality disordered offenders which has superiority over others, given the absence of a comparative evidence-base. We would propose that any management structure needs to stem from a coherent formulation of the personality disordered offender's difficulties and anticipated behaviours, and that this formulation must integrate the psychological need, offending behaviour, and social functioning of the offender. The agency structure should mirror the formulation, and the extent to which the structure is efficacious is likely to be based on the extent to which all members of the multi-agency forum subscribe to a shared model of management. Within such a structure, different agencies and practitioners are likely to have disparate competencies and roles, but they need to be contained by the overarching philosophical framework. Management can then utilise a range of tools which stem from the offender's own strengths and from the external controls available to the agencies. It is likely that excessive reliance on either internal or external controls may lead to problems, particularly with higher risk offenders; likewise, adopting a range of tools without reference to the underlying psychosocial paradigms may lead to incoherent and inconsistent management plans. Core elements of a plan are likely to include consideration of attachment issues and behavioural and situational concerns, the emphasis being on the consistent application of transparent decision-making in collaboration, as far as possible, with the offender.

Chapter 6

Personality traits and strategic approaches

In this chapter we consider how the three strategies for intervention in the community described in the previous chapter impact on various personality types. Attachment-based interventions are likely to be problematic in cases where deceitfulness, detachment or a strong paranoid response are encountered. Nonetheless they offer the best prospects of the individual gaining internal control of their behaviour and offer the best hope that positive changes will generalise to new environments. Behavioural control interventions include supervision and surveillance and the use of orders and prohibitions to set limits and interrupt chains of behaviour leading towards offending. Environmental planning strategies address the situational determinants of behaviour, and try to minimise/eliminate the triggers associated with the individual's maladaptive or antisocial behaviour. An important component of this dimension is appropriate accommodation including the availability of specialist hostel facilities.

An assumption of this framework is that these strategies can be superimposed on each other in ways which can act synergistically or potentially conflict with each other. Agencies have tended to see themselves focusing on perhaps one of these approaches and not the others. However, modern multi-agency interventions such as the Intensive Surveillance and Support Programmes (Little *et al.*, 2004) explicitly combine intensive surveillance with an emphasis on access to good treatment resources. In this context arrest and breach are not seen as failure but rather as potentially successes and as worthy an outcome as treatment progress.

In order to think theoretically about how various interventions impact on personality disordered individuals, it is helpful to be familiar with particular characteristics of each disorder. Table 6.1 is helpful in orienting the reader to key aspects such as self-image, dominant schemas (see Chapter 2), characteristic view of others, the way in which behaviour is characteristically executed, and dominant interpersonal strategies. We have chosen to focus on four diagnostic patterns within this DSM-based framework, which are particularly pertinent to offenders. Examples of successful and less successful interventions are included.

Table 6.1 Particular characteristics of personality disorders

Personality type	Self-schemas Self-image[1]	Others/world schemas	Expressive acts	Regulatory mechanism	Interpersonal strategy Conduct
Paranoid	Right/noble *Inviolable*	Malicious/intricate	Defensive	Projection	Suspicious *Provocative*
Schizoid	Self-sufficient *Complacent*	Intrusive/ unimportant	Impassive	Intellectualisation	Isolated *Unengaged*
Schizotypal	Varies *Estranged*	Varies/varies	Eccentric	Undoing	Varies *Secretive*
Antisocial	Strong/alone *Autonomous*	Exploitative/ a jungle	Impulsive	Acting out	Deceive/manipulate *Irresponsible*
Borderline	Bad/vulnerable *Uncertain*	Malevolent/ dangerous	Spasmodic	Regression	Attach/attack *Paradoxical*
Histrionic	Inadequate *Gregarious*	Seducible/ manipulable	Dramatic	Dissociation	Charm/exaggerate *Attention-seeking*
Narcissistic	Worthless *Admirable*	Threatening/ dangerous	Haughty	Rationalisation	Demand/compete *Exploitative*
Avoidant	Inadequate/ worthless *Alienated*	Critical/ demanding	Fretful	Fantasy	Avoid *Aversive*
Dependent	Weak/helpless *Inept*	Strong/ overwhelming	Incompetent	Introjection	Attach *Submissive*
Obsessive-compulsive	Responsible/ competent *Conscientious*	Irresponsible, incompetent/needs order	Disciplined	Reaction formation	Control *Respectful*

[1] All italics derive from Millon et al. (1994), all normal script derives from Padesky (teaching handout).

Borderline pattern

Features of presentation

The borderline offender presents with a particularly confusing picture to those around him, characterised by a pattern of chaotic and contradictory behaviours and reactions. Such offenders have core beliefs that they are both bad and vulnerable and that others are malevolent and the world is a dangerous place; their behaviour is spasmodic and unpredictable, and they are prone to regression (to a more infantile state); they have paradoxical – i.e. apparently conflicting – interpersonal strategies of both attaching to others and then attacking others. Their impulsive and disorganised style of offending reflects the instability of their inner world, and can often serve the function of reducing emotional dysregulation.

Management approaches

Attachment-based interventions

Modern attachment theory asserts a fundamental role for attachments in the development of an ability to recognise and modulate emotions and thereby to reduce the tendency to impulsive behaviour. The partial hospitalisation model described by Bateman and Fonagy (1999) involves the patient developing an attachment to professionals and staff within the programme, allowing a second chance to develop these so-called 'mentalisation' abilities which have been compromised in borderline and other personality disordered individuals.

Borderline patients are typically 'attachment hungry' and establish rapid and intense transference to professional workers and teams. Problems for teams can arise here, especially in terms of the time and resources required to contain the individuals and the level of dependence they can engender. Because of the inner vacillation of their moods and attitudes, these patients can also be experienced as demanding and manipulative, and if this is not processed, it can lead to negative counter-transference developments in staff and the wish to distance and reject them.

It is particularly important in both hospital and community settings to be able to identify splitting and related dynamics and know how to respond appropriately. Confident management of splitting can reduce the likelihood of tensions between members of staff involved with the patient, or inadvertent sabotage of the treatment programme, and assists in maintaining the patient's sense of containment and security.

Most treatment models emphasise the importance of establishing a clear treatment contract, as well as the importance of supervision and consultation (Kernberg *et al.*, 1989; Linehan, 1993). Acting out in the treatment needs to be anticipated and managed within this contract. Dialectical behaviour therapy, for example, emphasises balancing the need to emotionally validate the patient's experience with a challenge for them to attempt behavioural change (Linehan, 1993). It is also important to be able to make sense of the conflicting and alternating positions that one is pushed into by these patients. Again DBT incorporates a way of structuring the nature of the attachment and interaction with the client. This involves not allowing the patient to incapacitate the therapist through adopting positions of 'apparent competence', 'active passivity', 'unrelenting crises' etc.

It remains important for treatment providers to be clear and realistic about how much flexibility they can offer borderline patients. Some services, for example, have discovered that patients need greater containment than they can offer (Morant *et al.*, 1999), or that other comorbid paranoid or antisocial traits limit the extent to which containment can progress to actual treatment (Karterud *et al.*, 2003). We have encountered a number of these individuals in local forensic services, and it is often clear that outpatient treatment on its own is unlikely to limit their tendency to offend, or to decline in social functioning. Typically these individuals started their treatment in the general adult mental health services, where they were often regarded with considerable ambivalence. The degree of containment that the general services could offer was often insufficient to prevent their emotional and social instability from escalating, culminating eventually in a serious, usually aggressive – or firesetting – offence, which led to secure care in a prison or forensic hospital. However, as the example below shows, residential hostel placement can provide a more robust set of therapeutic attachments which can diffuse the high level of dependency and potential acting out of these patients.

Case example

Stephen had a history of impulsive violent behaviour in the context of alcohol use. He had previously lived a very chaotic life and as a result had found it difficult to engage with any treatment services. Following his conviction for a violent homophobic offence, he was placed in a supported hostel. He was able to form good relationships both with staff in the hostel and with his community-based social worker. He proved very demanding to look after, however, as he was prone to feelings of rejection and loneliness, and frequently behaved provocatively and was tempted to drink again. However his attachment needs were well dispersed across a range of people so that no one individual felt over-burdened. These therapeutic relationships allowed him the space to talk through his powerful emotions, and over time think more reflectively about how to approach situations less impulsively. There is also the important consultative task of helping staff teams develop and maintain their own emotional resilience and insight when faced with these dynamics.

Behavioural control interventions

Behavioural control interventions are important in setting boundaries and limits to individuals who are unable to maintain normal social boundaries around dependency, emotional expression and aggression. Dialectical behaviour therapy explicitly incorporates a behavioural focus in terms of reinforcing appropriate rather than maladaptive behaviour, and in its emphasis on seeking positive behavioural change. More explicit setting of limits by the criminal justice system may be needed to supplement that provided within treatment approaches.

However, the issue of splitting can also manifest itself here in relation to confusion between health and criminal justice responses. Specifically, health and justice responses are sometimes seen as mutually incompatible, such that intervention by one agency is seen as making the other redundant. This is seen most commonly in decisions to either prosecute a borderline individual or detain him in hospital under the Mental Health Act. Such splitting between agencies is important to address as it clearly undermines the sense of containment required by these patients.

Compulsory admission to a psychiatric ward has often been used to control the behaviour of these individuals at times of acute emotional disturbance. This intervention has been criticised in the recent guidelines for the management of borderline patients issued by the American Psychiatric Association (2001). It is argued by many clinicians that compulsory admission contravenes most of the principles of psychological treatment which may be effective in treating BPD. In addition, drug treatment is not so unequivocally effective as to warrant compulsory treatment. The APA guidelines recommend that admission only be used at times of psychotic decompensation or serious suicidal intent.

Having said that, we are of the view that there should be facilities in the community, mental health or otherwise, where individuals can go for greater emotional support and containment at times of stress and crisis. It is important, however, to avoid the typical battles of control that occur around such 'admissions', and the tendency to focus only on the patient presenting with the right symptom (e.g. self-harm, alcohol use) rather than the patient's underlying emotional instability.

Case example

Alison was referred for assessment by the forensic mental health services. She was at the time being case-managed by her local general adult team. She had a long-standing history of deliberate self-harm (including cutting and burning herself), but in recent months this had progressed to setting small fires outside her flat. This pattern appeared to be escalating in frequency and she also disclosed at assessment that she was having urges to put lighted papers through her neighbours' letterboxes. She had already been charged and put on a probation order.

Although she had a good relationship with both her consultant and care co-ordinator, her impulsiveness and alcohol use appeared to be escalating. The clinical team took the decision to offer Alison informal admission to hospital when she felt she needed it, and not after she had set a fire or self-injured. However, it was made clear that the admission was time-limited to seventy-two hours. It was also very important to meet with the nursing team on the ward and explain the thinking behind this plan so that they felt clear about the purpose of this intervention, maintained a focus on the patient's emotional distress as well as her behaviour, and could see that admission was strictly time-limited.

The effect of this intervention was that Alison felt more in control of admissions and was able to avoid being in a position where she felt not responsible for her behaviour any more. Over about six months the incidences of firesetting and self-injury reduced.

It is acknowledged that many acute mental health (and forensic) services are reluctant to use hospital beds with this sort of flexibility, but it is likely that the overall multi-agency cost is less, and such interventions do not have the effect of needing the patient to escalate their behaviour to offending or self-injury in order for someone to offer them more containment.

There may be a reluctance to use criminal prosecution with these patients, particularly given their often extensive histories of contact with mental health services. Their more bizarre and pathological behaviours such as self-harm seem to mark them out as psychiatric in the eyes of the criminal justice system, and police officers may assume they are mentally ill.

Case example

David was admitted to an acute general ward due to fears about his self-harm. There was some suggestion he might be depressed. He had recently set fire to his flat which had become uninhabitable. The police seemed undecided about charging him for the fire which had clearly posed some risk to other residents in the block. The fact that David was in hospital seemed to dissuade them. He was referred to the local personality disorder service and attempts were made to engage him voluntarily in assessment and consideration for a more supported hostel placement. However David proved unwilling or unable to engage, and also became more parasitic and exploitative on the ward. Eventually the police were persuaded that he needed to be charged in order to provide a more robust and criminal justice oriented framework for managing him in the future.

Unfortunately, although he was charged and remanded in custody, the case had to be dropped through lack of evidence. David was released but had no accommodation and in many ways was in a worse position than at the time he committed the alleged offence.

This case illustrates the potential confusion and splitting between mental health services and criminal justice agencies. Admission to a ward and referral to a specialist service were seen as the primary interventions, and prosecution for a relatively serious offence was deferred. The mental health services were right to rely on the criminal justice system to help manage the risk. On the other hand, simply locking someone up for a period of time can make it even more difficult on release to secure the stable social circumstances that are particularly necessary for borderline individuals.

Environmental planning interventions

In terms of environmental interventions, many borderline individuals report difficulties of feeling lonely, but also finding it difficult to live at close quarters with other adults. Because of their rapidly changing moods and impulsiveness, Stone (1990) has suggested that certain social structures and communities provide necessary containment, structure and identity for borderline individuals. Although this is discussed particularly in the context of religious cults, the principles can be extended to other natural or artificial 'therapeutic communities' such as a day centre, hostel, workplace or church. In Stone's (1990) long-term follow-up study of borderline patients, those who engaged with Alcoholics Anonymous tended to do well. In general, the provision of some structure and daytime occupation is likely to be helpful in many of these cases. It particularly helps to contain the anxiety in these individuals. We have found that residential hostel placements, where available, provide an important level of structure and containment for many individuals in the community who need much more than one or two outpatient treatment sessions per week to manage them.

In this context it is particularly worth noting the potential success of partial hospitalisation for this group (Bateman and Fonagy, 1999, 2001). This approach provides a structure and social support system for patients in the community, which on the one hand offers considerably more containment than outpatient therapy on its own, and on the other reduces the potential for regression and other potentially malignant processes that can take place during protracted inpatient admissions.

Antisocial pattern

Features of presentation

The antisocial offender sees himself as strong and independent, others as exploitative, and the world as a jungle in which he has to survive against the odds. His behaviour is predominantly impulsive, and he is unable or unwilling to contain and process his feelings, preferring to act them out; his primary strategies are to deceive and manipulate others in an irresponsible manner, largely as a result of his belief system and early experiences.

Management approaches

Attachment-based interventions

Antisocial personality disorder has generally been seen to be very difficult to treat. This is not difficult to understand given the personality traits that lead to the diagnosis, such as deceitfulness, impulsiveness and irresponsibility. The value of any presumed attachment of the offender is therefore immediately questionable. Indeed therapists need to be very wary of the potential to be manipulated. This is, however, usually tempered with the qualification that there is a spectrum of severity in antisocial personality, with the psychopathic group being at the 'severe' end of this continuum.

In regard to the latter, some previous studies have suggested that the wrong kind of treatment can even increase the risk of future offending despite apparent treatment progress (Rice et al., 1992; Seto and Barbaree, 1999). High PCL-R factor 1 traits are considered particularly difficult to deal with in terms of the conning, manipulative, deceitful pattern of behaviour, as well as the potential in these patients to demonstrate misleading displays of affect and emotion. Meloy (1988) helpfully suggests a number of psychological characteristics that may also be associated with a high factor 1 score and untreatability:

- Sadistic aggressive behaviour in the patient's history
- A complete absence of any remorse, justification or rationalisation of such behaviour
- Intelligence greater or lower than two standard deviations from the mean
- A historical absence of any capacity or inclination to form a bond or emotional attachment to another person
- An atavistic fear of predation felt by experienced clinicians when in the patient's presence without overt behaviour precipitating such a counter-transference reaction

Accepting that this end of the spectrum is untreatable, most authors acknowledge that at the mild end of the antisocial spectrum there may be some potential for movement. This may be associated with favourable life conditions, maturation and a new motivation to give up the criminal life. Even the presence of depression here may be a sign of treatability (Woody et al., 1985).

A number of different interventions have been proposed, with most modern approaches focusing on cognitive skills deficits rather than the emotional functioning of the offender. The evidence for the effectiveness of these approaches is considered in Chapter 5. However it is useful to be aware of Gabbard's (1990) criteria for effective work with antisocial or psychopathic populations. He has suggested that any potential therapist must:

- Be incorruptible, stable and persistent
- Confront repeatedly the patient's denial or minimisation of his anti-social behaviour
- Help the patient connect his actions with his internal (emotional/attitudinal) states
- Confront the here and now behaviours
- Monitor counter-transference so as to avoid inappropriate responses
- Avoid excessive expectations for improvement

It is important for clinicians to recognise and deal with their own emotional responses to and expectations of this group. One of the most important aspects of this is the fear of being manipulated and deceived by the patient. To some extent this can never be avoided with a really antisocial patient, but it is important not to feel too defensive or humiliated if this proves to be the case (Doren, 1987).

There is a general consensus that there is little hope of the psychopathic offender developing any sense of remorse or guilt about his pattern of offending (Doren, 1987; Hare and Wong, 2003). It seems that an approach centred on what has been described as 'enlightened self-interest' or 'social-ised hedonism' is much more likely to be effective (Hare and Wong, 2003). This style of therapy avoids attempts to develop empathy or remorse in the offender and instead involves motivational techniques to identify more legitimate ways of meeting their own needs, at the same time clarifying the cost/benefit ratio in their offending. Tackling impulsivity and problem-solving skills may form part of this approach (Doren, 1987).

It is acknowledged that there is little likelihood the patient will ever truly internalise a higher moral value system, where better choices would be made without external coaxing. Although some therapists may see this approach as inherently naive, and in danger of making some psychopaths even more manipulative, it is defended by Hare and Wong (2003) and Doren (1987) as the 'best hope' for this population. It is, however, at present unclear whether this approach does offer anything fundamentally new to the existing cognitive skills programmes *in situ*, and whether it really does mean that the boundaries of treatability can be shifted up the antisocial spectrum.

Two examples of the enlightened self-interest approach are described below.

Case examples

Ian had originally been detained in a maximum secure hospital under the legal category of Psychopathic Disorder following his third conviction for rape. Clinically he had strong antisocial and narcissistic characteristics and his PCL-R score was 29. He had originally been detained under a Home Office Restriction Order, but then subsequently persuaded a tribunal that he was probably untreatable. He was released into the community where he was offered voluntary aftercare consisting of review by a psychiatrist and contact with a psychologist.

The patient had a history of repeated rape offences against adult women. In the community he developed various relationships with women where conflicts always emerged relating to his underlying entitlement and exploitativeness, exacerbated by stimulant use. The psychologist was very flexible about seeing Ian and was able to persuade Ian at times to end or distance himself from relationships, thus de-escalating a potential for further violence.

Another psychopathic patient, James, lived on a difficult local estate. A pattern of escalating conflict with neighbours and housing professionals developed and James was clearly behaving in a racist and provocative manner. At times he appeared to enjoy this. However, he was encouraged to reflect on the fact that he was putting his tenancy in serious jeopardy, something that also threatened his rather cosy arrangement of sub-letting his property in exchange for drugs. In this way the costs of his behaviour were highlighted and this appeared to be effective in James reducing his intimidating and provocative behaviour.

Despite the hope offered by some of these potential interventions, it must be acknowledged that some individuals are too arrogant, manipulative or perverse to work with meaningfully. In some ways they may need a rather devious and paranoid approach from the police to manage them effectively, a mindset that few clinicians are encouraged to develop. Thornton (2003), for example, has suggested that devious and psychopathic sex offenders might be most effectively supervised by probation staff high in Machiavellianism (a personality trait that has some conceptual similarity with certain PCL-R factor 1 traits).

Behavioural control interventions

Meloy (1988) suggests that in many psychopaths, the behavioural control intervention is the only feasible mode of interaction. These interventions, to some extent, rely on having some ability to monitor behaviour effectively in the community, which may require the use of supervised hostels and strict reporting conditions as well as, increasingly, new surveillance technology such as tagging. While psychopaths have traditionally been seen as failing to learn from experiences of punishment and deterrence, a strict behavioural approach in the community offers a framework for managing these individuals consistently and may eventually encourage a willingness to look at the cost-benefit analysis of their behaviour. Emphasis on 'enlightened self-interest' or 'socialised hedonism' may be able to capitalise on these factors.

A behavioural approach can be considered here in two contexts. First, as a framework for management it allows sanctions to be imposed in a proportionate and flexible way with the ultimate sanction of deprivation of liberty in a secure setting. Controls will be imposed based on an understanding of risk factors – for example, substance misuse, association with criminogenic peers, placing oneself in high risk situations. This management framework does not require the consent of the individual and may involve minimal dialogue with him. It does, however, depend on having access to adequate collateral information, for example surveillance, observation by hostel staff, information from other offenders, complaints by the public, etc.

A second component of the behavioural approach may be that it involves the imposition of contingencies in order to punish antisocial behaviour and 'shape' compliance. In other words there is a hope that some sort of useful conditioning process may take place. Psychopaths may be particularly insensitive to the effects of punishment as a result of their temperament and/or conditioning history. There are some experimental studies supporting this problem of 'response perseveration' (Newman *et al.*, 1987). It may be that punishment needs to satisfy the requirements described by Hollin (2002) if it is to be effective, i.e. immediate, inevitable and intensive.

It may be that in relation to psychopaths, supervising officers need to be focused on the behavioural approach and there is a danger of emphasising the individual rehabilitation needs of the client. Thornton (2003) gives an interesting example of how more devious inmates may be less likely to offend in a highly structured prison regime where there is little attempt to individualise treatment, rather than one that focuses on the individual needs of the individual. Key supervision decisions, such as decisions about recall to prison, may also need to be taken by those not directly involved with the psychopathic individual. The Damien Hanson Inquiry, referred to in Chapter 1, is an example of where such an individual was given far too much freedom to dictate the parameters of his parole licence, and where each failure to respond to his pushing of the boundaries probably convinced him that he was too clever for the authorities to stop him.

There is a widespread perception in the UK media that the authorities are too soft, despite a lot of new legislation; and the effectiveness of the 'Broken Windows' approach in New York (where even minor antisocial behaviour is addressed) is being seen as something that London as a comparable major city needs to consider. The following case study illustrates the need for this very rigorous approach to supervision.

Case example

Paul, a 40-year-old man, was discharged from medium security after a pattern of serious sexual assaults involving adolescent and young adult males. In some senses these assaults appeared to represent the re-enactment of a pattern of sadistic sexual abuse experienced by the offender in his own development. Whilst in hospital, the presence of entitlement, manipulativeness and deceitfulness had clearly been in evidence.

On discharge to the community, it was considered important to have a clear plan of risk management led by MAPPPs but encompassing strict conditions within a Home Office Restriction Order. These included residence at a supervised hostel, a system for checking on Paul's whereabouts, careful diary planning around activities and initially periods of surveillance by the police.

Paul found this level of supervision and control quite difficult and intrusive and it seemed important for him to be able to discuss this with the psychologist. At one point Paul went to see a friend of a previous victim and the local police were notified. Paul's subsequent and rapid recall to hospital served as a reminder that there would be severe consequences to any behaviour that looked like grooming. After this he was better able to think about his long-term goals in the psychology sessions and question his own sense of entitlement to have contact with young men. As a result he was more able to focus on how he might develop an appropriate homosexual relationship where concerns about his intentions and potential grooming would be lessened.

This case clearly illustrates how a firm behavioural approach with rapid consequences to non-compliant or high risk behaviour gave a clear message that the authorities were not naive or lethargic. At the same time, such clear contingencies can then be used as the basis for an enlightened self-interest approach in 'therapy'.

Environmental planning interventions

Environmental planning strategies in this group may include support and protection of potential victims and vulnerable adults within the psychopath's environment, and minimising the opportunities for predatory behaviour in these individuals. Psychopaths are easily bored and have a strong need for dominance and self-assertion. It seems unlikely, therefore, that many of them are ever going to settle in conventional nine to five employment. There may be some jobs, such as sales, lorry driving or bar work, that give them a relative degree of independence from supervisors and generate their own sense of novelty or excitement. However, this may come into conflict with the behavioural control paradigm and the wish to limit the movement of these offenders.

Another area which may be worth highlighting here is family inter-ventions. Salekin's (2002) review of effective interventions for psychopathic individuals included a role for family-based interventions. Although pri-mary psychopaths may have no respect for the public at large or wider cultural values, they may have some residual loyalty and respect for family, particularly if there is a strong narcissistic interest, for example with their son. This may be capitalised on, in terms of raising their motivation to change towards more pro-social behaviours.

Paranoid pattern

Features of presentation

The paranoid offender sees himself as righteous and inviolable, others as malicious, and the world as complex; he presents primarily as defensive, projecting negative aspects of himself into the world around him, which is perceived as hostile and conspiratorial; his interpersonal strategy is pri-marily suspiciousness of others and he takes a provocative stance by appearing unamenable to any form of rational discussion about his griev-ances. Such individuals can be particularly difficult to manage, not least because they demand intervention but reject offers of assistance, and their suspicious and rigid attributions towards others can be intolerable for practitioners, who retreat behind official procedures and resort to secretive communications with others about the offender. Unfortunately this con-firms the paranoid offender's beliefs and can lead to long-lasting self-righteous outrage.

Management approaches

Attachment-based interventions

Attachments are fundamentally problematic for paranoid individuals. A dominant aspect of their interaction is a need to project an internalised persecutory figure onto those around them, which is then defensively controlled and manipulated by the individual. Workers are prone to feel uncomfortable dealing with these projections, and it is important that workers feel able to contain the feelings engendered without behaving reactively and defensively towards them. This may manifest itself in the form of counter-control, defensiveness or withdrawal.

Workers should have modest aims in forming attachments with these individuals, together with an understanding that a relatively distant approach may be more beneficial. They should avoid doing anything to unnecessarily heighten the already fragile sense of autonomy and persecution for these individuals. Individuals and teams frequently make mistakes by trying to have too much contact or therapy with these individuals, who may find a relatively intense or regular pattern of treatment quite overwhelming. Paranoid individuals should be allowed a degree of control and autonomy where possible in setting up treatment contracts.

Case example

Leroy represents a relatively benign outcome to paranoid difficulties. This 32-year-old man was originally convicted of an assault on the partner of an ex-girlfriend. On admission to hospital there was a differential diagnosis of paranoid personality and paranoid psychosis. During the admission he was at one point restrained and injected with antipsychotic medication, and thereafter developed homicidal ideas and fantasies about the consultant and senior nurse involved. In the community the evidence for a long-standing paranoid personality accumulated.

Leroy remained very guarded and suspicious. However a new consultant was able to develop an alliance with the patient, provided the consultant was not too intrusive and only wanted to see him every four weeks or so. The patient within this relationship was willing to take oral antipsychotic medication, which seemed to have benefits in reducing his level of arousal and paranoid irritability. Leroy also inherited his own independent property after his mother died. Although he continued to be assaultative occasionally in the community, his grievance and preoccupation with the professional staff appeared to slowly subside.

This case illustrated the importance of respecting the offender's need for control and distance in the therapeutic relationship. The fact that Leroy had a stable independent residence − effectively control of his own living space − also seemed important.

In some cases, strong paranoid grievances develop towards professionals and teams themselves, which require management. Here there may need to be a consideration of whether the value of being in contact with the patient is outweighed by the risk of further provoking them by such contact. In a different context, Young and Gibb (2001) discuss how, for some individuals, offers to resolve and work through grievances are used perversely to further stimulate their sense of anger and injustice. With patients who have been locked into a relationship with services (for example, through a Home Office Restriction Order), the sense of mutual claustrophobia can exacerbate this dynamic. In the context of enquiries it can be difficult to discharge the patient or reduce contact, and some considered review and documentation will be needed if that is decided. Generally these cases appear difficult to resolve, and there appear to be few examples in the literature of strategies that are successful.

Behavioural control interventions

Behavioural control interventions, by their very nature, run the risk of threatening the fragile sense of autonomy that these individuals have. The patient can easily experience such interventions as provoking feelings of powerlessness, persecution and humiliation, which will then lead to an intensification of the defensive processes of the individual, primarily based around projection. In this way, there could even be a degree of paradoxical increase in risk by trying to control such an individual with overly coercive intervention.

Similarly, orders for contact and supervision need to be careful not to set up expectations for the individual of too much contact. A particular sensitivity to feelings of shame and humiliation is important to consider here, in that certain restrictions and controls could easily be perceived as belittling and infantalising.

Case example

Samuel was released from prison having served for an offence of GBH against a female partner. He was still angry with her and had continued to make threats about revenge which had inevitably led to the parole board deferring release until relatively late. On release on parole he was required to live for a number of months in a probation hostel, and was also subject to tagging and curfew. He had a very paranoid personality, almost certainly related to poor attachments and a history of abuse as a child. He found the entire process of parole supervision persecutory and provocative, and he frequently made threats to others in response to these feelings, which often made things worse and certainly delayed any early relaxation of his supervision conditions.

He was referred at an early stage of release to a specialist personality disorder service. His case worker approached the situation in a very flexible manner and initially sought to help him with social issues such as benefits and work. The latter proved problematic as he was simply too paranoid and irritable around other employees. However, he did respond to the dedication and flexibility of the case worker, who increasingly saw that whatever social 'goodies' could be obtained for Samuel, sooner or later he had to learn not to provoke, reject or otherwise sabotage his interactions with agencies he depended upon, especially the criminal justice system.

He came extremely close to recall on several occasions but finally completed his parole licence, enabling him to secure independent accommodation where he had more privacy and felt less provoked by his environment.

This case illustrates several points. First, the need to be flexible and dedicated to making an impact on the inevitably difficult release situation, perhaps initially focusing on social issues that can reduce the environmental stressors impinging on the individual. Second, there needs to be a realisation that whatever might be done 'for' the personality disordered client, he sooner or later needs to be shown how to deal with other agencies and professionals in a less self-defeating manner. This is very skilled work which needs to be a focus in both casework and any concurrent therapy. The worker has to be able to anticipate and neutralise the dysfunctional interactions with other agencies – particularly difficult in a context where the criminal justice system is 'coming down hard' on the offender. Third, there may be a need to point out to other agencies what is experienced as so provocative by the client so that he is not unnecessarily provoked and antagonised. In this context, using a combination of relatively intrusive supervision measures may need to be rethought with this kind of offender.

The form of intervention used may depend a lot on the level of threat posed by the individual. Some offenders are content to make repeated complaints or write threatening letters. Others develop a more active and confrontational attitude which may amount to stalking. Violence may be more likely where there are comorbid antisocial traits and substance misuse. A risk assessment is therefore essential at this point and may itself influence the type of intervention pursued (White and Cawood, 1998). In the context of stalking, White and Cawood note that 'threat management is far from a science and far from perfect. . . . The poles of argument tend to be "come down hard and swift on them" (e.g. strictly enforced protective orders, arrest, imprisonment) versus "quietly disappear" (better to relocate since it is so hard to control a violence-inclined stalker).' Currently it is difficult to predict which of these strategies is likely to be better with any particular case.

At the more benign and mild level, there is often some possibility of resolving or at least modulating the individual's grievance by an empathic response, a channelling into some official process of investigation and/or third party mediation. The personal safety of others may not be threatened. Where threats have been made, sometimes these can be dealt with by reporting them to the police and authorities, in a way that seems to helpfully set limits for the patient. It is important to avoid being secretive in response to the paranoid individual. For example, clinicians should be willing to share all documentation with the patient except in exceptional circumstances.

In more severe and intractable cases, it is much less clear how to proceed. Sometimes it is essential to involve the police, and this can lead on to an injunction being taken out to manage the risk.

Case example

Michael represented a much more difficult trajectory. This patient met the criteria for both paranoid and antisocial personality disorder. He had a long and serious history of violence towards others, which encompassed both instrumental and reactive aggression. He had been detained under a hospital order and recalled twice under a Home Office Restriction Order. In the community there had been the development of a very malignant and rigid paranoid transference to the consultant who had shared some information about him during a previous prison remand. This grievance appeared to transfer and extend to any other staff who became associated with the consultant. He became increasingly threatening, indicating he knew the home addresses of various staff members and would take his revenge at his own time, including on their families.

He appeared very aroused and rigid in his thinking. Despite attempts to meet with the patient and resolve the situation, eventually it was decided that an injunction needed to be taken out to manage the risks. The patient flouted this, and the police were persuaded to arrest him for breaching the injunction, although he was eventually convicted for 'Threats to Kill' and given a short prison sentence. It was decided at this point that the risks of any mental health team trying to engage the patient, particularly under a restriction order, outweighed any potential benefits of contact. He was therefore discharged. A subsequent discussion at the local MAPPP meeting agreed that he needed to be monitored and dealt with by the police, who ultimately had the power of arrest, and who in some ways appeared to be less provocative to the patient than mental health services.

This case proved difficult because of the combination of paranoid and comorbid antisocial traits, and also because the patient felt he had been irreparably injured by a previous therapeutic intervention. In these cases it is also easy to see how a vicious cycle develops where professional teams become (understandably) more defensive and secretive in order to manage the risk, and this tends to further provoke the offender.

Environmental planning interventions

Environmental control options are likely to be particularly relevant to this group, given the difficulties in attachment. Placing the individual in a situation with too much contact with other adults may be provocative – for example, placement in a supported flat may be preferable to placement in a hostel. In particular, contact with too many other paranoid individuals can lead to potential escalation and needs to be avoided. Paranoid individuals may be particularly troubled in dealing with other agencies. Their coping skills, despite good intelligence, are often limited because they are so distracted by their suspicious and combative approach. In general, the individual should be given as much control as possible over their environment.

Schizoid/avoidant offenders

Features of presentation

These offenders may present an essentially pro-social law-abiding life, with little evidence of alcohol or drug misuse or previous contact with mental health services. Their long-term psychological functioning may well have been stable but limited in terms of its capacity for involvement with others and emotional spontaneity. The schizoid group may be those who show by nature little inclination for deep involvement with others; whilst in avoidant personalities, the desire for social contact is there but is conflicted and ambivalent due to fear of rejection, criticism or humiliation. The risk of these individuals committing a serious violent or sexual offence may be very low and essentially not possible to predict.

Management approaches

Attachment-based interventions

In attachment-related terms, many of these offenders are avoidant or even schizoid by nature. This implies that they will have either a highly conflicted or an absent need for attachment. There may, however, be a superficial willingness to engage in therapy or supervision, but this often lacks any meaningful spontaneity or emotional contact.

Such individuals may therefore be experienced for long periods as rather compliant and passive, if not boring, and the risks correspondingly seem very minimal. It is more difficult, however, to identify potential triggers or grievances in these individuals which could potentially lead on to sudden destabilisation. Over-controlled individuals themselves can be subdivided into those who react to provocation without any angry feelings whatsoever, and those who do feel angry but tend to over-control their reactions, leaving them under-assertive and frustrated as a result.

The goals with these offenders may therefore be to encourage them to be more assertive, and to tolerate their aggressive feelings towards others without becoming immobilised by them. Such individuals may show difficulties in dealing with interpersonal situations where the other person is experienced as intrusive or rejecting, and any new relationships need to be carefully considered in the context of the dynamics of the index offence.

It is also possible that the current emphasis on cognitive-behavioural interventions does not serve this group particularly well. Providers of such treatment interventions often report that the offender has been compliant but has intellectualised the therapy, and may be seen as 'going through the motions'. Psychodynamic therapy, with its emphasis on accessing the spontaneous feelings of the individual, may be necessary to get past the repression and intellectualisation of these offenders. An approach that may have some relevance is Intensive Short Term Dynamic Psychotherapy (Malan and Coughlin Della Selva, 2005). The case studies in Malan and Coughlin Della Selva's work provide some good illustrative examples of the kind of approach and technique needed to get past these often apparently successful defences.

Case example

Peter had been convicted of a number of contact sexual offences against children in his early twenties. He was only convicted some twenty years later when one of the victims came forward. Although he completed SOTP in prison, he felt he had little real understanding of himself or what the true nature of his difficulties was. He had never been able to establish an intimate relationship with another adult, despite being reasonably intelligent and successful in his employment. What he did feel clear about was that he did not have a fixated interest in children; he had turned to them as a sexual outlet because he felt a complete failure with other adults.

He was not schizoid in the sense that he seemed to genuinely want to understand why women kept rejecting him. He said he wished that women would give him some direct feedback as to where he was going wrong. The therapist felt that he tended in conversation to retreat into intellectual discussion of his needs and feelings and had largely lost touch with his spontaneous ability to feel things. It became clear in the process of the therapy that on the few occasions he had made some contact with a potential partner, he tended to quickly become obsessive and dependent, probably leading to the woman rejecting him and experiencing him as possessive and clingy. His rather aloof and avoidant veneer therefore concealed and defended against a much more needy and dependent self. This issue subsequently manifested itself in the transference and the therapist was able to help Peter stay more in touch with the feelings and express them in a genuine but not over-whelming manner. Follow-up revealed that he had been able to establish a rela-tionship with a woman and he was much less prone to emotional withdrawal and fantasy.

This case illustrates that personality disorder diagnoses may not be as fixed as they sometimes seem. An initially avoidant or obsessional personality may, for example, be seen as someone who uses a dominant defence pattern that can be toned down and used less rigidly.

Behavioural control interventions

Behavioural control interventions are rarely needed in this group, because they are rather passive and compliant. It is only when the often rigid defences break down that they may be suddenly precipitated into emotional turmoil, impulsivity and dangerousness. They may then, of course, require rapid control and limit-setting.

Environmental planning interventions

Environmental interventions are also somewhat redundant here. Individuals may, however, be targeted by more antisocial peers, as well as generally feeling frustrated and provoked by the control and restrictions needed for antisocial personalities, which are not necessary for them. This may lead to an undermining of rapport with professional workers and teams. The relative trustworthiness of these individuals may need to be recognised by giving them appropriate freedom and responsibilities which could not be given to more antisocial and impulsive individuals.

Case example

George had been convicted of grievous bodily harm towards a female colleague. Following a transfer from prison to hospital under Section 47 of the Mental Health Act, he was subsequently placed in supported accommodation and followed up by a community forensic team. He got to know a woman who lived in one of the nearby flats and appeared to strike up a friendly but non-sexual relationship with her. In view of the previous offence which appeared to reflect his inability to deal with feelings about women, the team decided that George needed to make a disclosure to the woman about his offence.

   He had some weeks to prepare this, and the consultant psychiatrist subsequently met with both George and the woman to check that the disclosure had been made and to consider the way forward. The woman felt able to continue the relationship with George, making it clear that she did not consider the relationship likely to proceed to an intimate one. At two-year follow-up George was still coping effectively in the community, had gained a part-time job in a charity shop and had not had any further depressive episodes. He continued to see the woman, though somewhat less frequently than before.

Conclusions

The above examples illustrate the potential impact of various interventions on different types of offender personality. It is important to recognise that in any individual case, one type of intervention is probably more appropriate than others but that all should be considered in a flexible, problem-solving mode. Ideally, approaches in the three highlighted domains should complement and support each other in managing risk. In other situations, it is quite easy to see how different types of intervention can clash and potentially come into conflict with each other.

At present, multi-agency panels, being dominated by criminal justice agencies, tend to focus on behavioural control and environmental options, although the latter are often limited. It is a somewhat confusing time at the moment in that a whole range of new legislative options have been brought into place and yet many offenders are still offending whilst on supervision. It is unclear whether this is due to poor resources in actually implementing and enforcing these, or whether there is still an emphasis in some areas on the human rights and rehabilitation of the offender rather than public protection. There is a widespread call in the conservative media for more prisons and an end to the early release of any offenders who have committed a serious offence.

There is perhaps potential to do more work in thinking about how different neighbourhoods may be more risky than others. The insights derived from the burgeoning field of offender profiling could be relevant here. An understanding of 'the psychology of place' helps to understand why certain locations are favoured by criminals. Similarly there are important findings about the way in which serious serial offenders evolve their strategy and choice of where to offend. As Canter (2003: 8, 9) notes:

> The opportunities for crime where there are possible victims or ready access and escape, will of course shape the pattern of offence behaviour. If an offender's predilections are for a particular type of victim then he will be drawn to locations in which those sorts of people are available. . . . Offenders' journeys have two surprising features – pointers to their criminal nature – that have been found over and over again in studies of serial offenders. One is the way in which the home, or at least where criminals are based, acts as a focus for their actions. The other is the geographical scale over which they operate.

There could thus be greater consideration of where criminals might choose to offend, and appropriate targeting of dangerous environments.

Chapter 7

Where are we now?

Good practice

For a number of years, there have been isolated pockets of good practice, both in the UK and abroad: individual mental health practitioners with a special interest in personality disorder have set up modest treatment services, usually for non-offending populations; criminal justice agencies have developed accredited programme approaches to targeting key crimino-genic problems. Rarely, comprehensive service provision – such as the Henderson Hospital and Cassell Hospital therapeutic community – has provided complete philosophical and clinical care to a tiny group of patients. However, until 2003/4, it was probably only in the Netherlands that there was a complete systemic approach to the assessment and treat-ment of high risk personality disordered offenders.

In the UK, the conceptual development of DSPD, with associated financial underpinning, has resulted in a new range of services being piloted. The four centres – two in high secure hospitals and two in the high secure prison estate – now provide 300 beds for a group of severely personality disordered men who have a history of seriously violent inter-personal offences often associated with an institutional history of markedly challenging and destructive behaviour. These services are soon to be supplemented by a small prison development for DSPD women. In parallel with these developments, the guidance paper on personality disorder (NIHME, 2003) from the Department of Health has led to complementary developments within the health service, located within the community and medium secure provision. The aim of these community projects is to provide a more local service for a wider group of personality disordered offenders; to enhance the confidence and skills of general mental health and criminal justice staff; and to provide a pathway of care for a very small group of DSPD offenders who have benefited from treatment and can embark on the slow process of rehabilitation into the community.

To date, there are four community pilots underway – with seventy-five beds – all of which are open for business. These include:

- East London medium secure unit (MSU) and discharge hostel
- South London MSU, hostel and community team
- Newcastle MSU and community team
- South East London hostel and community contact team

Each pilot has been developed with its own philosophical and theoretical approach, designed to complement the existing services within the area, and to match the anticipated needs of its clients. All are funded by the Department of Health and the Home Office, and collaborate with each other in terms of some key principles. These principles include:

1   All pilot services are developed in the light of the known evidence-base, as detailed in the earlier chapters of this book.
2   All offer assessment, treatment and consultation/training services to their relevant catchment area.
3   All target a client group with personality disorder as a primary diagnosis, and provide a personality disorder specific service.
4   All take clients who are offenders, who have engaged in significant interpersonal violence, and who continue to pose a moderate or high level of risk to either specific victim groups or the wider community.
5   All the pilots are utilising the same core psychometric assessments, and are adhering to a common database for the purposes of service evaluation; these measures target personality and risk variables.

A good deal of learning has been taking place over the past one to two years, in implementing these new services. It seems worthwhile to reflect on this learning process and, in light of the book's focus on community management, particularly in respect of those services which have an independent provision for community clients. The authors have intimate knowledge of two of the services with which they are connected, but there are a further two services which are also considered here.

DHP

DHP is a partnership project between social care (Turning Point) and forensic mental health services in South East London, run with the support of the probation service. It is centred on the residential provision – six self-contained bedsit-type flats with shared communal lounge and kitchen – and manages a small community contact team for those individuals who have moved on from the residential provision, or who are living outside the project. It has been developed to enhance existing long-standing forensic psychology provision in the area, including strong consultative relationships with the probation service.

Theoretical underpinnings and clinical interventions

The single overarching aim of the service is to achieve successful integration into the community for the service users, enabling them to maintain an improved quality of life, with the appropriate levels of support, the least possible restrictions, and minimising the potential harm to the public. The service model is based on the premise that the client group presents with severe interpersonal difficulties which have previously led to community failure. The primary aim is to provide a physical – residential – environment which provides emotional as well as physical containment; that is, impulses to manage emotional turmoil and interpersonal stress by means of acting out are contained, thereby promoting a capacity for reflection and self-awareness.

In the absence of a single coherent theory explaining the aetiology and treatment of personality disorder and offending, the project has emphasised an integrative model of care which addresses tensions, splits and fragmentation, which can be understood at many levels:

- Between mental health and criminal justice responsibilities
- Between the care programme approach and risk management approaches
- Between addressing risk and psychological need
- Between social inclusion and protecting the public

Key theoretical elements include: psychoanalytic and attachment ideas in order to understand individual/group/institutional dynamics and inform thinking on problem relationships; and psychosocial ideas – social problem solving, cognitive-behavioural interventions, and meaningful social roles – to inform the residential programme of interventions.

The model of intervention holds as its central tenets, a shared philosophy, a well articulated model of care, and adherence to a coherent set of interventions. There is an emphasis on staff understanding psychodynamic principles, including defence mechanisms and transferential issues; the development of skills in delivering a social problem-solving approach to clients; and maximising the role of meaningful service user collaboration and engagement in all aspects of their care, including risk management.

Personality disordered offenders who pose a high risk of harm to others tend to be characterised by lists of risk factors and associated restrictions, which impoverish their quality of life and, paradoxically, can raise the risk of reoffending. The project has adopted an assessment and treatment planning approach which is highly individualised, but also explicitly based on a 'good lives' model (Ward and Brown, 2003) which reframes risk management in terms of the promotion of approach (rather than avoidance) behaviours: thus, offending can be understood as previously dysfunctional attempts to obtain primary goods, and risk factors are viewed as potential obstacles to the attainment of prioritised goals and meaningful social roles.

Referrals are gate-kept by the forensic mental health team, but are taken to a joint project referral meeting as soon as it is determined that the person referred broadly meets the criteria for the service. Time scales vary according to the situation, but decisions about admission to the project can be made within four weeks if necessary (more usually it takes over two months). Clients may be in prison or hospital, or breaking down in the community, and can be referred by any agency. They must, however, reside – at least in principle – within the catchment area, and the local authority must agree to retain ongoing responsibility. If the resident has been in receipt of inpatient hospital care, and possibly also subject to a restriction order under the Mental Health Act, they will have a consultant forensic psychiatrist as responsible medical officer; for those who reside at the project as part of a criminal justice order (licence or community sentence), they will be case co-ordinated by the probation service, and in practice the seconded probation officer to the project will be the responsible case manager. However, the project philosophy is to avoid the parallel systems of risk management and care programme approach, and one single integrated procedure is followed in all cases: individual formulation, risk/needs assessment, and identified interventions with associated goals, all of which are reviewed and amended on a regular basis.

Specific interventions include: twice weekly key work sessions, community trips (escorted initially), a modest programme of activities, weekly community meetings, hostel jobs/access to the specialist work project, and access to outpatient psychological interventions off-site.

The original plan – prior to finding an appropriate building for the service – was to provide care to eight to twelve residents. With a smaller residential service, the project developed an additional community contact service for four to six non-residents who were living within the catchment area, and who met the criteria for the residential project (or, in due course, who had progressed from the residential facility into semi-independent or independent accommodation). The aim of the community contact team is to provide intensive social care to highly vulnerable and isolated personality disordered offenders who are already engaged in psychological work with the wider forensic team, but for whom traditional outpatient contact is insufficient to contain and manage their needs. This model has drawn heavily from the ideas developed by religious communities in North America who have been implementing Circles of Support for such offenders, although it does not involve the use of community volunteers.

Staffing profile and training

The staff role is pivotal in providing consistent, nurturing and boundaried responses to the residents which model pro-social functioning. Staff are provided with a basic level of induction training which amounts to almost twenty days, spread over a period of three to six months, and includes skills training (motivational interviewing, psychosocial practice), problem-specific training (managing violence, substance misuse) and theoretical models (risk assessment, Good Lives). More advanced training is then provided which focuses on counselling skills, social problem solving, and mentalisation and attachment. The senior staff are encouraged to undertake formal post-graduate courses in forensic mental health and psychotherapy. Staff support is organised in a variety of ways, including weekly staff group support meetings, access to confidential staff counselling, debriefing following incidents, and weekly clinical work discussions.

The staffing profile comprises a part-time senior service manager and full-time deputy, managing eleven senior project workers (social care); the forensic mental health team is co-ordinated by a full-time consultant clinical psychologist, with additional part-time staff, including a consultant forensic psychiatrist, psychologist, occupational therapist, community psychiatric nurse, and full-time probation officer (seconded to the team). The social care team and the majority of the mental health team are situated together on-site. The community contact service is divided into two teams: each comprises a number of the project workers and one mental health team member, and each team has responsibility for the care of up to three community clients, in addition to their responsibilities to the project residents.

Learning points

The project has now been open for eighteen months, and there has been time for reflection. One of the key learning points has been to appreciate, in retrospect, just how long it takes a new service to find its feet – about one year in fact. This appears to reflect an underlying process of maturation which runs fairly independently from overt procedures such as the recruitment of staff and the development of operational policies. Associated with this was an obvious difficulty in recruiting good staff to a very new project when the philosophy of care and intervention was somewhat hesitant. There was a high turnover from the first recruitment drive. The second round of staff were of a very high calibre and well integrated into the project. The project also changed its training programme, from an over-ambitious six-week induction, to a much more gradual programme with more emphasis on generic skill building rather than specialised knowledge (which is so quickly forgotten). This has had an obvious benefit in enhancing staff confidence in dealing with clients, and revisiting and re-learning core competencies over a period of months.

Finally, it is worth pointing out that managing personality disordered offenders in the community is a chaotic and risky business, as the probation service know only too well. Services need to have a robust managerial structure which can contain risk, supporting rather than persecuting their staff, and understanding that the baseline for placement breakdown and antisocial behaviour is very high (in an urban environment at least). A significant incident within the first nine months of the project reminded the team of this, and there was no doubt that a long history of providing community forensic services stood the team (and the management) in good stead.

FIPTS

Theoretical underpinnings and clinical interventions

The Forensic Intensive Psychological Therapy Service (FIPTS) comprises both an inpatient (medium secure) service for fifteen beds and hostel/community provision. There are six high support hostel beds and four low support, provided at two different locations. The service has built on the limited experience that some members of the staff team had already gained with personality disordered offenders in generic forensic mental health services. The service set out to develop a strong clinical psychology component, as it was felt that this staff group had the most interest in and experience of delivering relevant interventions for this client group.

In developing an overarching treatment for this client group, the service was particular impressed by the Violence Reduction Programme (VRP) in Canada, a programme specifically designed to address the problems of working with psychopathic offenders (Wong and Hare, 2001). The VRP offers a helpful framework, focusing on the need to establish the current motivation to change and the need to systematically address a range of dynamic risk factors identified on an associated risk prediction instrument. The programme incorporates three phases, reflecting where the client is in terms of their cycle of change: looking in the mirror, breaking the cycle and relapse prevention. Although the VRP has developed programme guidelines for each of these phases, there is a recognition that these are general phases of change, and more individual treatment components may need to be included in this overarching framework. These could easily include elements of a sex offender treatment programme, substance misuse, anger management work and other therapeutic approaches such as dialectical behaviour therapy (DBT).

The fact that the service includes an inpatient programme to some extent dictates that the community caseload will derive from this. Furthermore, the fact that we are able to progress patients initially from secure conditions to supported hostel conditions, and finally to more independent living in the community, means the level of support and supervision can be tailored to the individual and progressively relaxed.

The service also recognises that within the broad spectrum of personality disordered offenders, there is clearly a more borderline (emotionally unstable) group, together with a more psychopathic group. The service has therefore also invested in training some staff in dialectical behaviour therapy. Although DBT is now seen as one of the treatments of choice for borderline presentations, the service feels that many of the skills and principles of supervision/consultation can be applied to more antisocial and psychopathic offenders.

Referrals are processed through the central forensic services referral meeting and then allocated at a separate weekly FIPTS meeting. At present, referrals can take anything between one and three months to be seen, although there is an attempt to prioritise, recognising that individual circumstances vary.

The community service distinguishes between four levels of intervention:

1   Assessment/consultation only (this provides baseline assessments of risk and personality disorder diagnosis, as well as a clinical formulation and recommendations regarding management/treatment).
2   Specialist psychological interventions without a case management function (the main interventions are the VRP group programmes comprising five two-hour treatment sessions per week; individual DBT sessions with a weekly DBT skills training session; and individual schema-based therapy).
3   Full case management in association with therapeutic interventions (case management typically comprises flexible contact with the client, CPA keyworker roles and liaison with other agencies. Frequency of contact can be very variable depending on the client's presentation and whether they are in crisis. A zoning system is used which was developed by the community forensic (mental illness) team).
4   Residential (hostel) provision alongside case management and treatment (the hostel provides keyworker sessions and twenty-four-hour supervision in high support. There is support for community rehabilitation and links with local education/employment agencies).

Again, the service is therefore able to offer a range of levels of intervention as well as potentially tease out the relative contributions of residential provision case management and psychological treatment in addressing the needs of personality disordered offenders.

Staffing profile and training

The community team consists of: one senior nurse/social worker team leader, three community psychiatric nurses/social workers, 1.5 clinical psychologists and 0.5 consultant forensic psychiatrist. In addition to this, a number of other staff members based primarily in the inpatient service contribute to the community team. This is seen as important in establishing continuity across different settings within the service.

The hostel team is completely separate and consists of both trained and untrained staff. Nine staff cover two daytime shifts, and a separate team of four staff cover the night shift in the high support setting. The hostel provision is provided by Penrose Housing, a separate organisation with whom the forensic services have already established close links, and which has considerable experience in previous management of sex offenders as well as, to some extent, personality disordered offenders.

The development of a new service offered the opportunity for a fundamental rethink on recruitment procedures. In particular, it was considered, given the needs of this client group, that attention to both analytic and interpersonal skills was necessary in the recruitment of staff. Recruitment was therefore 'multimodal' and included four elements: individual interview, written exercise, group discussion and psychometric testing (of personality traits).

Not surprisingly, this procedure generated an enormous amount of data, some of which we are still digesting. Nonetheless, it was felt extremely helpful to have this range of evidence available in making recruitment decisions, and the procedure certainly highlighted the potential independence of interpersonal qualities and analytic skills in the workforce.

At the beginning of this service, an intensive six-week induction programme was delivered for as many of the staff as were available. This included a range of theoretical, experiential and practical sessions and we sought to involve experts from outside the service where possible. A central component of the training was a two-week module delivered by Steve Wong and Audrey Gordon, originators of the VRP in Canada. This led to the designation of two clinical psychologists in the service as responsible for the development and delivery of the VRP within FIPTS. They are hoping to establish their own accreditation to train other services in the VRP in the future.

Learning points

The community service to some extent has been overshadowed by the need to get the inpatient service up and running. Due to the high level of initial demand in establishing the VRP, as well as in managing a series of quite difficult patients, there has been something of a drain of community resources into the inpatient service, which needs to be corrected in time. Furthermore, there have been a large number of referrals for assessment coming from probation/MAPPPs at a time when the number of assessors available has been small, and there have been delays to the assessment process – including screening out inappropriate referrals – which have led to some frustration in the referring agency and unhappiness with the service provision. There has been further disruption to the assessment process in some referrals where the offender has been resident in a local probation hostel, and subject to eviction or breach proceedings, which has interfered with FIPTS being able to carry out the work.

The experience thus far would suggest that there may be a role for a short-stay residential facility, although it is unlikely that one setting could provide for all needs: for example, some personality disordered offenders might need to be admitted on section briefly for stabilisation without requiring medium security, whilst others might be admitted voluntarily (something difficult to manage in a medium secure unit) while an assessment is completed; other short-term residential needs include one or two crisis beds (which could be in the community), where clients under the care of FIPTS could seek temporary respite, particularly at times of social instability and breakdown.

Another important issue has been the relationship between the new treatment service and the local MAPPP/Jigsaw team. Initially there was quite a lot of curiosity and expectation from MAPPP. A number of FIPTS clinicians had already developed good working relationships with the Jigsaw (PPU) team prior to the development of the service. However, there was a significant change in PPU personnel about a year into the project, which perhaps was also associated with a slightly tougher approach to public protection. The FIPTS clinicians' perception was that the Jigsaw team became more suspicious and critical of their role, at times accusing them of withholding information and co-operation. This was particularly focused on two high risk paedophiles being managed in the community.

The FIPTS view was that the Jigsaw team needed to understand that there were necessarily differences in approach to the police, and issues of confidentiality and treatment alliance to appreciate, although clearly there is a common goal of public protection.

Tensions appear to have been eased through a few diplomatic phone calls.

Newcastle

Theoretical underpinnings and clinical interventions

The aim of the community personality disorder team is to provide care and treatment to personality disordered offenders from within health and social services rather than allowing the criminal justice system to take sole responsibility for their management. It is based on the premise that mentally disordered offenders should be dealt with as far as possible in the community, in such a way as to maximise their rehabilitation and chances of sustaining an independent life, and as near as possible to their own homes or families, if appropriate.

The purpose of the service is to provide effective and meaningful assessment, treatment and management of men with personality disorders in whom there are concerns about their risk of sexual or violent behaviour towards others, the primary goal being to reduce the risk of causing harm to others.

Alongside the community team, a pilot medium secure personality disorder service is now in operation, albeit opening much more recently, and there will clearly be strong links between the two services. The community service covers a very wide geographical area in the north east of England, encompassing nineteen Primary Care Trusts, and this has informed the model of care delivery. Concerned not to develop a service characterised by intensive work with a small group of patients who are shadowed by an increasingly long waiting list, the team emphasises collaboration with local services and community mental health teams (CMHTs), and the delivery of service at three different tiers:

1   *Consultation* – as a one-off, ongoing management advice, or initial assessment and/or reassurance.
2   *Provision of specific treatment* whilst the patient continues to be managed by the local service – this will focus on social types of intervention, in line with the ten evidence-based criteria for Home Office accreditation of offending behaviour programmes; it includes a combination of group and individually based treatments aimed at addressing underlying psychopathology, including affect regulation, social problem solving, interpersonal relationships, cognitive processing, and problem-specific behaviours such as anger and sexual offending.
3   *Joint working* with higher risk complex cases, in which local providers remain responsible for the patient's day-to-day management, but the specialist personality disorder team work closely alongside, and treatment responsibilities are shared between the two providers.

Entry criteria to the service are in line with the other pilots. The aim is for referrals to be seen within twenty-five days and for assessments to take no longer than three months to complete. Referrals are gate-kept by the local community mental health teams; care co-ordination and RMO responsibilities rest throughout with the CMHT, and must be agreed before an intervention from the specialist team can commence. Patients can be de-selected from the service on the grounds that they are too disruptive to respond to treatment, they interfere with the treatment of others, or they are thought to be too dangerous to be managed safely. In such cases, the patient will be discharged, in consultation with MAPPPs, or transferred to medium (or even high) security specialist personality disorder (and DSPD) units, if appropriate.

Staffing profile and training

The community team is staffed by nine multi-disciplinary team members. This includes a half-time team leader (nurse), a full-time community psychiatric nurse, a seconded probation officer, an approved social worker, a senior occupational therapist, and a psychology assistant. Additionally there are eight sessions of psychology – of which four are at consultant grade – and four sessions of psychiatry. Each team member has 'link' responsibilities, providing an interface between the team and a particular geographical area and set of local providers. The team is organised into interchangeable co-working pairs, each individual carrying a caseload of up to ten cases (all co-worked). As experienced mental health staff, the team have a number of shared core skills and individual professional skills; these are enhanced by access to locally and centrally provided training opportunities, including expertise in risk and personality assessment, and the administration and interpretation of associated psychometric tools. There are ongoing monthly consultation sessions with an external consultant in which the focus is on the dynamics of the team and the emotional impact of the work on staff.

Learning points

The community team has now been in operation for over two years. There were difficulties in recruiting psychology staff, who joined the team much later. A strong case management ethos has developed, and there is now confidence in the assessment process and in ongoing liaison with local providers, attendance at reviews and input into local MAPPPs. However, the specialist treatment component of the service has been slow to develop, because the majority of the staff team – albeit experienced – do not have specific therapy training or a background in treatment delivery to personality disordered offenders. With the recruitment of psychology staff, this is beginning to change, but is hampered by the sessional input of these members to the team. The team has also had to adapt to providing a service to a wide geographical area, which can be an impediment to the service users, involves time-consuming travel for staff, and also requires the establishment of relationships with an extraordinarily large group of local providers. The CMHT response to the service has been variable, some co-operating fully and others refusing to accept responsibility for participation in the care of personality disordered offenders, hampering the development of appropriate care pathways or joint working. Related to this is a particular difficulty with those offenders who also present with learning difficulties, falling between adult mental health and learning disability services.

North East London Forensic Personality Disorder Service (FPDS) and Look Ahead Health Trust (LAHT)

The FPDS is based within a newly developed pilot medium secure personality disorder service, and has joined with social care (LAHT) to develop a hostel facility in the local area. There are eight supported tenancies, comprising *en suite* bedroom facilities with communal kitchen (allowing for self-catering or supported catering) and living areas. The project is based on the shared aim of returning personality disordered offenders safely to independent lives in the community.

Theoretical underpinnings and clinical interventions

All the project residents will have had experiences of not being able to continue ordinary lives in the community as a result of their offending histories and the risks they may pose to others; the fundamental task of the LAHT team is to support the residents in trying to break their offending patterns. Sophisticated risk assessments and formulations of mental health and criminogenic factors tailored to the needs of a personality disorder client group will be a foundation upon which the safe working of the project will depend.

A clear link between the client's personality disorder and their offending behaviour is a key criterion and interventions and management strategies aimed to address this link will be central to the model of care. There is an emphasis on the role of chronic distress, poor self-esteem and severe difficulties with interpersonal relationships, both in relation to risk to others, and to self-defeating patterns. The first task is therefore to engage the resident in a collaborative relationship, and then to provide an emotionally containing environment – as well as the necessary physical containment – to create a sense of safety for the resident. This will be done by providing consistent support, empathy and validation within the context of predictable, boundaried relationships. Staff will seek to resist the pressure to respond with punishment or abandonment when confronted with challenging and provocative behaviour from residents, and thus seek to break the cycles of rejection that so many residents will have experienced. Instead, staff will respond in ways that maintain collaborative relationships and in doing so demonstrate that emotional turmoil and interpersonal stress do not have to be 'acted out' through destructive behaviour. It is anticipated that this model of care will promote a capacity for reflection and self-awareness in residents that will enhance the quality of their relationships.

The hostel programme will include opportunities to reflect individually and as a community group, and there is a weekly programme of events and meetings.

The FPDS is responsible for screening all referrals, and assessing diagnosis, risk and social care needs. The CPA care plan and risk management strategy are developed jointly with LAHT, and underpin the LAHT client support plan. Post-admission decisions are taken in partnership between the two teams, on a weekly basis, and client cases are reviewed fortnightly. Referrals from mental health must have an identified community mental health team who will retain primary resonsibility for care co-ordination under the CPA. Referrals from prison and probation without prior contact with mental health services will be linked to the CMHT in the client's home borough; however, if this is not possible to facilitate, the FPDS will assume care co-ordination responsibility.

Entry into the project is determined by the criteria shared by all the projects, including a willingness to engage with the service on the part of the client. Tenancies can, of course, be terminated due to a range of presenting behaviours, including serious and/or repeated threats of harm, violation of statutory conditions of release, offending behaviour, substance misuse, and so on. If such action has to be taken, a number of possible management solutions are available, depending on the circumstances, and need to be determined in a joint planning meeting. As a general rule, it is hoped that residents will be prepared to progress to less supported accommodation within a two-year period, although it is recognised that this time frame is tentative given the long-standing nature of the residents' difficulties.

Staffing profile and training

In recruiting staff to the project, the social care team recognises that staff will need to develop interpersonal skills, capacities for self-reflection, realistic expectations of residents and trusting collegial relationships. Individuals with personality disorder can provoke great anxiety in all involved in their care, and staff will need to understand that residents may engage in various forms of challenging behaviour, and that the dynamics of the residents' internal worlds will from time to time seek to express itself in team functioning and team dynamics.

The LAHT staff will have access to a programme of continuous training and education, much of which is organised from within the specialist personality disorder medium secure unit. Various forms of formal and informal staff support are also available on a regular basis.

The LAHT staff team comprises a full-time project manager and deputy manager, and eight senior support workers. The FPDS contribution to the project does not involve dedicated staff, but there will be approximately one (half-day) session per week provided to the project from each discipline of the multi-disciplinary team based at the medium secure unit.

In summary, there is now a growing body of experience emerging from these four community pilots, and the services are constantly reviewing and revising their practice as a result. These brief outlines should be read very much as work in progress. Three of the four projects have embarked on a specialist partnership between forensic mental health and social care: North East London has developed something of a traditional medium secure pathway to the community, using a hostel, with some additional flexibility; the FIPTS hostel provides back-up to both the community team and the medium secure service; and DHP is a stand-alone residential facility with a community contact team but no formal access to specialist hospital beds. All have developed slightly different therapeutic models of intervention, but with similar goals; all have tried to grapple with the issues of risk management, CPA and clinical responsibility, and have come up with slightly differing solutions.

Some obvious initial successes to the pilots include the enthusiasm with which models of care have been developed, and the creative thinking associated with the development of new treatment services. Recruitment of staff – initially thought of as an obstacle – has been a surprisingly smooth process, albeit with a few hiccups in the first instance. This is partly due to the relatively modest size of the services, but also persistence with recruitment processes and a willingness to be flexible about roles and responsibilities to a certain extent. This issue is explored further in the section below.

Some of the difficulties and learning points of the projects have been described above. There is, however, one shared – and somewhat unexpected – difficulty encountered by all the projects. This has been the matter of referrals: difficulties in accessing appropriate referrals, difficulties in getting referrals with sufficient warning and planning time; difficulties in filling beds quickly; and difficulties in retaining clients to the end of their assessment or treatment. A number of reasons have been put forward for this:

1   Some of the most difficult personality disordered offenders create chaos and uncertainty in those around them, and this underpins the rushed and poorly planned nature of some of the referrals, many of which are instigated after the client has already fallen into crisis. None of the projects provide an emergency service which might act as a bridge to a more organised and reflective community service.
2   Despite articulating the entry criteria to the services very clearly, a large number of unsuitable referrals have been sent to the pilot services.

Unsuitability includes comorbid mental illness, offenders with significant learning disability and/or marked autistic spectrum disorder, and
intransigent offenders who refuse to engage at any level in a discussion
of potential personal change.

3   There can be obstacles and delays to the process of admission to the
community services which lie outside the control of the teams. These
include delays in tribunals and parole board hearings, delays within the
courts and unexpected decisions made by judges, anxious patients not
wanting to leave conditions of medium security instigating crises which
delay transfer, and the emergence of hostile inter-agency dynamics
which result in destructive envy and the projection of blame elsewhere.

These issues have led to frustratingly slow progress in filling the services to
capacity, but they seem to be an inevitable part of the maturational process.
The maturational process is also central to the issue of culture and
philosophy, which is difficult to establish in new services, and which is of
crucial importance to the efficacy of any intervention for personality disordered services (Bateman and Tyrer, 2002). A culture requires several
years to develop and necessitates key 'culture carriers' – whether it be staff
or patients – who hold and adhere to the philosophy of care, and who
guide newcomers within its framework. This is what happens in families,
whose role is to prepare and nurture their offspring, ready for integration
into wider society; and it is mirrored within services, such as those described
above. During the maturational phase, these personality disordered offender services will inevitably encounter resistance from within the staff and
the patient group, the latter especially (but not exclusively) resorting to
habitual patterns of dealing with anxiety, that is, 'acting out' conflicts
within the immediate social environment. Destructive, aggressive incidents
are to be expected, and it is the capacity of the services to contain and
reflect upon these incidents which will ultimately determine whether they
can mature into a secure therapeutic environment.

Staff competencies

The issue of staff competencies has been alluded to already. In the community, competencies relate to the structure and remit of the team, as
described in general terms in Chapter 4. For the high secure DSPD sites,
who have had to recruit very large numbers of staff and train them in
preparation for the opening of a much larger number of beds than in the
community pilots, staff competencies have been a major focus of the
organisational work.

To a greater or lesser extent, the pilot projects at all levels have been
guided by the Personality Disorder Capabilities Framework (NIMHE,
2003), which was drawn up specifically to complement the development of

personality disorder services generally in England and Wales. But before outlining the recommendations of this framework, it is worth considering some work with nurses which has been undertaken in high secure hospital personality disorder services. Bowers (2002) undertook some research with the aim of identifying the factors underlying and maintaining nurses' positive therapeutic attitudes to patients with severe personality disorder, in order to inform a support and training strategy to nurture such attitudes. He sent a questionnaire to all the nurses in the three high secure hospitals (2,503) – 25 per cent of whom replied – and randomly selected a stratified subgroup of 121 nurses to interview. Although this research was specific to high secure nurses, the findings are undoubtedly applicable to staff working in community settings (albeit the organisational and staff–patient dynamics perhaps being less intense) and across disciplines and agencies. Essentially, Bowers concluded that there was a range of traits/mechanisms/cognitions which were repeatedly associated with positive attitudes to personality disordered patients and, ultimately, linked to positive outcomes in terms of the therapeutic environment and progress of the patients.

Bowers described a *psychiatric philosophy* as a particular set of beliefs about psychiatry and nursing, including a commitment to the importance of psychosocial factors in the cause of personality disorder, the efficacy of treatments, and understanding behaviour in a psychological way, with a focus on the individuality of patients. Positive attitude nurses held a set of *moral commitments*, including honesty, bravery, a lack of superiority, non-judgementalism, and a belief in univeral humanity, seeing themselves as fulfilling a parental role towards personality disordered patients, especially in the provision of care and nurturance. Techniques of *cognitive-emotional self-management* helped nurses to see the patients as they were now rather than in terms of what they had done in the past, wanting to know them before finding out about their offences and drawing a distinction between the person and his behaviour. Interpersonal skills – *technical mastery* – allowed nurses to stay calm and reason with aroused patients, give neutral feedback, and turn conflict into therapeutic learning. Demonstrating *teamwork skill* was a positive feature, including using colleagues for ventilating feelings and support, and achieving consistency in relation to rules. Vitally, *organisational support* in the form of clear policies, clinical supervision and specialist training seemed to be crucial.

These positive mechanisms were associated with a positive appreciation of the patients as valued individuals, and compassion for their difficulties. *Emotional regulation* allowed these nurses to be able to suppress and set aside their natural responses towards the past and present behaviours of the patients, and therefore deal more calmly with difficult situations; they were also able to provide a more *effective structure* for ward life, including a meaningful routine for patients and consistent application of necessary rules. As a result of these positive approaches, the morale of nurses was higher; they enjoyed their work and felt secure, and they were less damaged by their work and grew in confidence and self-awareness. Such nurses spent more time interacting with patients, created opportunities for therapy and were more likely to organise other therapeutic approaches; there was less conflict overall, with fewer incidents, a more stable ward environment, and less recourse to overt containment measures such as seclusion and increased medication.

Bowers emphasised that his findings did not support the premise that there are good nurses and bad nurses; rather he worked with the assumption that personality disordered patients – particularly serious offenders – inevitably provoke difficult thoughts and feelings in staff, but that some staff have found ways of overcoming these obstacles to therapeutic working. The Capabilities Framework mirrors some of Bowers's work, identifying four key areas:

- Promoting social functioning/obtaining social support
- Improving psychological well-being
- Assessing and managing risk to self and others
- Management and leadership

The necessary capabilities are organised into four career/skill stages:

- Pre-employment
- Vocational education
- Professional training
- Continuing professional development

In an ideal world of heavy competition for staff posts, accurate interviewing, and continuous personal development, these capabilities would reflect the workforce of the world of personality disorder. However, an imperfect world means that not all candidates have all the pre-employment capabilities, and sometimes promoting change within staff can be difficult. Teams are likely to be faced with two broad dilemmas: first, the question of which skills to prioritise. There is a tendency to drift towards the delivery of knowledge-based training (for example, theories of personality disorder, the role of the Mental Health Act, the nature of treatment models) or the delivery of technical skills (in particular, the administration and interpretation of psychometric tests). These are tangible and concrete goals, which can be demonstrably taught and used. It seems much less clear whether many core belief systems can be taught (and if so, in what format), whether they are instrinsic to the staff member's personality makeup, or whether they can evolve slowly over time with maturation. Yet these core skills are likely to form the backbone of any personality disordered offender team and probably the essential component of any successful service.

The second dilemma is the question of generic or specialist team roles and responsibilities. For community services, where teams are small, generic working may well enhance team cohesion and promote a sense of personal investment in and commitment to the service; individual clinical responsibility means that team members are pushed into practising their learnt technical skills, such as psychometric assessments, and broaden their range of experience. However, generic working can be demoralising or frustrating for staff who identify strongly with a set of identifiable skills or training, and it may frustrate particular strengths (or pander to particular weaknesses); certain complex areas of work, perhaps the delivery of specialist psychological therapies, either cannot be delivered, or may be delivered inadequately. Specialist team roles – more likely than not reflecting the professional backgrounds of the staff – can lead to inequalities within the team and stereotypical and stagnant ways of working, and envy may arise as some skills are perceived as more worthy than others. However, specialist working does allow for individual staff to identify an area of particular strength and knowledge, to hone a skill, and thereby enhance the overall creativity and quality of the team.

The experience of the community pilots is variable in relation to these two dilemmas, and the different projects have adopted a variety of approaches to the formation of the staff group and its training. It seems clear that although technical skills can be seductive, it does require constant practice to maintain this knowledge base, and staff can lose confidence very quickly; thus, small independent teams working fairly generically are best placed to retain these skills. It has also been found that core beliefs and attitudes within the social care staff have been at the heart of the residential provision success, and there has been a shift in favour of less formal learning, and more generic skills development via consultation and supervision. Specialist psychological treatment provision, particularly but not exclusively in group format, has fallen increasingly to a small group of experienced staff, usually psychologists but not necessarily so. This is illustrated by the difficulty in transferring skills from a formal intensive teaching block and manualised treatment programme to the reality of treatment provision for a group of highly disordered offenders who already have a track record of community failure. Whilst it must be acknowledged that the prison service have managed to deliver psychological interventions to a large number of fairly challenging offenders, relying on relatively inexperienced staff, the containment of the physically secure environment does facilitate the process in a way that is not available in the community.

We would argue that preliminary experience from the development of community personality disordered offender services would suggest that staffing – recruitment, training and roles – should be thought about in terms of a hierarchy of priorities.

1   The crucial core traits (as suggested by Bowers, 2002) are likely to reflect something intrinsic to the personality of staff, and are both difficult to elicit in traditional forms of recruitment interview, and also likely to be resistant to change (although both the best and worst of staff traits can be greatly influenced by the quality of supervision and management staff receive). For these reasons, these professional qualities are a priority for staff recruitment.

2   Early training opportunities should probably focus on two areas: the introduction of the culture and philosophy of care intrinsic to the service; and the development of confident but basic key interpersonal skills.

3   Early on in their employment, staff learning needs to be integrated within clinical care, with the use of a variety of forms of reflective practice, including attention to supervision and case consultation.

4   It is only at this point that specific 'technical' learning needs to take place, which might include more advanced training in personality disorder and risk, including the understanding of psychometric tools and formal treatment interventions.

5   Roles and responsibilities are likely to be determined by the nature of the service and the size of the team. However, it seems reasonable to suggest that there should probably be consideration of a flexible mix of generic and specialist roles, which are largely determined by professional background or experience; however, it may well be appropriate to provide opportunities for personally chosen roles (and skills) to develop out of annual professional appraisal systems, which maximises the potential of highly motivated staff.

Tools to take away

This book has focused primarily on the practical aspects of managing personality disordered offenders in the community. In doing so, we recognise that practitioners work in very different settings, with differing access to specialists, limited resources, and various professional backgrounds and statutory duties. We have tried to cover the material in line with the evidence-base to date, albeit largely from a psychological perspective. However, if we were to offer a more personal selection of the key aspects of assessment, treatment and management, then we would suggest the following twelve points:

1   The prevalence of personality disorder in offender populations is very high; and there is a close relationship between the features of personality

disorder, the details of the offending, and future risk of violence that an offender might pose.

2   Certain psychological/personality traits are particularly important to identify in terms of risk to others; these include psychopathy and sadism.

3   The dominant theoretical model for understanding personality disorder incorporates biological vulnerabilities, developmental experiences and the social context.

4   Actuarially based approaches to risk prediction play a *necessary* role in assessment but are not *sufficient* in themselves; however, risk assessments which are not anchored within the main evidence-based domains for sexual and violence risk prediction *will* result in unnecessary mistakes being made.

5   There is a spectrum of treatability across the personality disorder classificatory system; there is some evidence for responsiveness within the cluster B personality traits, with a great deal more uncertainty about the cluster A traits, which may require alternative approaches.

6   There is no one single treatment model which has evident superiority to the others; however, there are shared elements to all the treatment models which have been shown to have some efficacy: the central component is a shared team and client understanding of philosophy and care.

7   Personality disordered offenders have difficulties which span the domains of offending behaviour, mental health needs and social functioning; it is therefore unlikely that any one agency should take individual responsibility for all aspects of care.

8   Management structures need to be thought of in terms of parallel and integrative models, both of which have implications for risk responsibilities and professional control; it is probably preferable to develop a mixed management model of partial integration.

9   It is probably impossible to run a successful service for personality disordered offenders without having a provisional formulation of the inter-agency dynamics.

10 Good management is likely to draw on three paradigms – attachment, behavioural and environmental approaches – which may differ in importance according to the personality difficulties of the offender.

11 There is little indication that mental health services are likely to provide a superior service as an alternative to the criminal justice system, but there is evidence for the role of mental health in partnership with or as an adjunct to a criminal justice approach.

12 More than with any other mental disorder, staff working with personality disordered offenders need to be recruited on the grounds of their core personality traits, rather than traditional approaches to professional background and experience.

A final word – the omnipotent fantasy

It seems reasonable to finish as we started, considering the social and political environment in which services for personality disordered offenders are being developed. We noted that the probation service has really only come under fierce public and media scrutiny since it explicitly reframed itself as a public protection service rather than an offender welfare service. It is unlikely that this is coincidental. This raises the question as to whether the explicit, government-funded, development of treatment services for personality disordered offenders will also ultimately result in the same phenomenon; that is, failures in such treatment (which have always existed) will now be experienced by the public as a betrayal incurring their wrath.

What, in fact, are the criteria for success? It would be naive to assume that the public – and the government who represent them – would have much interest in or empathy for an offender's reduction in personal traumatisation or an increase in his quality of life. These may be secondary benefits to the primary intervention, that is, the protection of the public. Therefore there needs to be a significant reduction in serious reoffending. Let us suppose for one moment that we are treating or managing 100 personality disordered offenders, all of whom are considered reasonably high risk for violent reconviction. A high base rate is good, in terms of demonstrating treatment efficacy, so maybe we might be able to reduce the reconviction rate by 30 per cent (a gold standard percentage). For men with more than a 50 per cent likelihood of reconviction, this means halving their risk to 20–30 per cent; even more optimistically, we might be able to keep the reconviction rate just below 10 per cent (as would be expected in a population of released patients restricted under the Mental Health Act); at best, we might match the parole board (where 5 per cent of released discretionary lifers committed further grave offences), so that only five of our men seriously fail. Do we live in a society in which the ninety-five relative successes are celebrated, or should we anticipate five front-page headlines, depending of course on the age and social status of the victims? Good practice and success flourish within a supportive and facilitating environment, and this necessitates a courageous political and social response.

Where will we be in ten years' time? Evaluation is clearly an important component to any answer. Centrally funded treatment projects – both in secure settings and in the community – are resource-intensive, and it seems unlikely that in the UK they will be rolled out nationally. Despite this, there will always be a need for specialist interventions within secure settings for a relatively small group of offenders, many of whom will be managed on indeterminate sentences. However, these developments in the UK and elsewhere have attracted considerable professional interest and have resulted in creative clinical developments, and an increased task force of experienced individuals. The learning is likely to be disseminated wider into criminal justice, mental health and social care settings, improving practice generally. We would argue that there now needs to be a shift in emphasis from a top-down approach (starting with high security), to a bottom-up approach: this involves maximising the potential of the community agencies, at the heart of which sits the MAPPA – generally considered to be one of the most successful developments of the past few years, despite having been denied significant additional resources for their own management. There is scope to develop consultancy as an important intervention in its own right, and increase the range of semi-secure and semi-residential settings. This latter point acknowledges the gulf between hospital- and prison-based interventions, and outpatient or probation community provision. It seems to us that there is considerable scope for an interim stage, providing respite and rehabilitation, taking as its model the relative success of open prisons, specialist hostel provision, and personality disorder treatment day centres.

Finally, although the human predicament has always been complex, and we will never be able to obtain supreme control over behaviour and the environment, we are cautiously optimistic. Risk can be reduced and managed; personality disorder – whatever the limits of classification and diagnosis – is interesting to understand; working closely in teams can be stimulating and rewarding; and individuals can respond to care and treatment so that their lives become more meaningful.

References

Abel, G. G., Mittleman, M., Becker, J., Rathner, J. and Rouleau, J. (1988). Predicting child molesters' response to treatment. In R. A. Prentky and V. L. Quinsey (eds), *Annals of the New York Academy of Science* (pp. 223–235). New York: New York Academy of Science.

Adshead, G. (1998). Psychiatric staff as attachment figures. *British Journal of Psychiatry*, *172*, 64–69.

Ainsworth, M. D. S., Blehar, M. C., Waters, E. and Wall, S. (1978). *Patterns of Attachment: A Psychological Study of the Strange Situation*. Hillsdale, NJ: Erlbaum Associates.

American Psychiatric Association (1987). *Diagnostic and Statistical Manual of Mental Disorders* (4th edn). Washington, DC: American Psychiatric Association.

American Psychiatric Association (1997). *Structured Clinical Interview for DSM-IV Axis I Disorders*. Washington, DC: American Psychiatric Association.

American Psychiatric Association (1999). *Dangerous Sex Offenders: A Task Force Report*. Washington, DC: American Psychiatric Association.

American Psychiatric Association (2001). Practice guidelines for the treatment of patients with borderline personality disorder. *American Journal of Psychiatry*, *158*, 1–52.

Andrews, D. A., Bonta, J. and Hoge, R. D. (1990). Classification for effective rehabilitation: rediscovering psychology. *Criminal Justice and Behavior*, *17*, 19–52.

Aristotle (2002). *Nichomachean Ethics*. Translation, Introduction, Commentary by Christopher Rowe. Oxford: Oxford World Classics.

Ball, S. A. (1998). Manualized treatment for substance abusers with personality disorders: dual focus schema therapy. *Addictive Behaviors*, *23*, 883–891.

Bartholemew, K., Kwong, M. J. and Hart, S. D. (2001). Attachment. In W. J. Livesley (ed.), *Handbook of Personality Disorders* (pp. 196–230). New York: Guilford Press.

Bateman, A. and Fonagy, P. (1999). The effectiveness of partial hospitalization in the treatment of borderline personality disorder – a randomised controlled trial. *American Journal of Psychiatry*, *156*, 1563–1569.

Bateman, A. and Fonagy, P. (2001). Treatment of borderline personality disorder with psychoanalytically oriented partial hospitalisation: an 18-month follow-up. *American Journal of Psychiatry*, *158*, 36–42.

Bateman, A. and Fonagy, P. (2004). *Psychotherapy for Borderline Personality Disorder: Mentalization-based Treatment*. Oxford: Oxford University Press.

Bateman, A. and Tyrer, P. (2002). *Effective Management of Personality Disorder*. www.nimhe.org.uk.

Beckett, R. (1994). Assessment of sex offenders. In T. Morrison, M. Erooga and R. C. Beckett (eds), *Sexual Offending Against Children – Assessment and Treatment of Male Abusers* (pp. 55–79). London: Routledge.

Beckett, R., Beech, A., Fisher, D. and Fordham, A. (1994). *Community-based Treatment for Sex Offenders: An Evaluation of Seven Treatment Programs*. London: HMSO.

Bedarf, A. (1995). Examining sex offender community notification laws. *California Law Review, 83*, 885–939.

Beech, A. (1998). A psychometric typology of child abusers. *International Journal of Offender Therapy and Comparative Criminology, 42*, 319–339.

Beech, A., Fisher, D. and Beckett, R. (1999). *An Evaluation of the Prison Sex Offender Treatment Programme*. London: HMSO.

Beech, A., Erikson, M., Friendship, C. and Ditchfield, J. (2001). *A Six-year Follow-up of Men Going Through Probation-based Sex Offender Treatment Programmes*. London: HMSO.

Beech, A., Friendship, C., Erikson, M. and Hanson, K. (2002). The relationship between static and dynamic risk factors and reconviction in a sample of UK child abusers. *Sexual Abuse: A Journal of Research and Treatment, 14*, 155–167.

Berkowitz, L. (1993). *Aggression: Its Causes, Consequences, and Control*. Philadelphia: Temple University Press.

Berry, A., Duggan, C. and Larkin, E. (1999). The treatability of psychopathic disorder: how clinicians decide. *Journal of Forensic Psychiatry, 10*, 710–719.

Berzins, L. G. and Trestman, R. L. (2004). The development and implementation of dialectical behavior therapy in forensic settings. *International Journal of Forensic Mental Health, 3*, 93–103.

Black, D. W. (1999). *Bad Boys, Bad Men: Confronting Antisocial Personality Disorder*. Oxford: Oxford University Press.

Black, D. W., Baumgard, C. H. and Bell, S. E. (1995). A 16–45 year follow-up of 71 males with antisocial personality disorder. *Comprehensive Psychiatry, 36*, 130–140.

Blackburn, R. (1975). An empirical classification of psychopathic personality. *British Journal of Psychiatry, 127*, 456–460.

Blackburn, R. (1996). Psychopathy and personality disorder: implications of interpersonal theory. In D. J. Cooke, A. E. Forth, J. Newman and R. D. Hare (eds), *International Perspectives on Psychopathy* (Vol. 24, pp. 18–23). Leicester: British Psychological Society.

Blackburn, R. (1997). Psychopaths: are they mad or bad? *Issues in Criminological and Legal Psychology, 22*, 97–103.

Blackburn, R. and Coid, J. (1999). Empirical clusters of DSM-III personality disorders in violent offenders. *Journal of Personality Disorders, 13*, 18–34.

Blair, R. J. R. (2005). *The Psychopath: Emotion and the Brain*. Oxford: Blackwell.

Blair, R. J. R., Jones, L., Clark, F. and Smith, M. (1997). The psychopathic individual: a lack of responsiveness to distress cues? *Psychophysiology, 34*, 192–198.

Bland, R. and Orn, H. (1986). Family violence and psychiatric disorder. *Canadian Journal of Psychiatry*, *31*, 129–137.

Blud, L. (2003). Introduction: Accreditation of offender behaviour programmes and recent developments in What Works initiatives in HM Prison Service. *Legal and Criminological Psychology*, *8*, 65–67.

Bollas, C. (1995). *Cracking Up: The Work of Unconscious Experience*. London: Routledge.

Bouchard, T. (1997). The genetics of personality. In K. Blum, E. P. Noble, R. S. Sparkes and T. H. J. Chen (eds), *Handbook of Psychiatric Genetics* (pp. 273–296). Boca Raton, FL: CRC Press.

Bowers, L. (2002). *Dangerous and Severe Personality Disorder: Response and Role of the Psychiatric Team*. London: Routledge.

Buchanan, A. and Leese, M. (2001). Detention of people with dangerous severe personality disorders: a systematic review. *The Lancet*, *358*, 1955–1959.

Butcher, J. (2005). *The Minnesota Report: Adult Clinical System-Revised* (4th edn). University of Minnesota: Pearson Assessments.

Cann, J., Falshaw, L., Nugent, F. and Friendship, C. (2003). *Understanding What Works: Accredited Cognitive Skills Programmes for Adult Men and Young Offenders* (No. 226). London: Home Office.

Canter, D. (2003). *Mapping Murder: The Secrets of Geographical Profiling*. London: Virgin Books.

Cartright, D. (2002). *Psychoanalysis, Violence and Rage-Type Murder*. Hove: Brunner-Routledge.

Casey, P. and Tyrer, P. (1986). Personality, functioning and symptomatology. *Journal of Psychiatric Research*, *20*, 363–374.

Chaffin, M. (1992). Factors associated with treatment completion and progress among intrafamilial sexual abusers. *Child Abuse and Neglect*, *16*, 251–274.

Chiesa, M., Fonagy, P. and Holmes, J. (2002). Health service utilisation costs by personality disorder following specialist and non-specialist treatment: a comparative study. *Journal of Personality Disorders*, *16*, 160–173.

Choca, J. P. (2004). *Interpretive Guide to the Millon Clinical Multi-axial Inventory* (3rd edn). Washington, DC: American Psychological Association.

Clark, D. (2000). *The Use of the Hare Psychopathy Checklist Revised to Predict Offending and Institutional Misconduct in the English Prison System*. London: Correctional Services Standards Unit.

Cleckley, H. (1976). *The Mask of Sanity* (5th edn). St Louis, MO: Mosby.

Coid, J. (1992). DSM-III diagnosis in criminal psychopaths: a way forward. *Criminal Behaviour and Mental Health*, *2*, 78–89.

Coltart, N. (1987). Diagnosis and assessment for suitability for psycho-analytical psychotherapy. *British Journal of Psychotherapy*, *4*, 127–134.

Cooke, D. J. (1998). Psychopathy across cultures. In D. J. Cooke, A. E. Forth and R. D. Hare (eds), *Psychopathy: Theory, Research, and Implications for Society* (pp. 13–45). Dordrecht: Kluwer.

Cooke, D. J. and Hart, S. D. (2004). Personality disorders. In E. V. Johnstone *et al.* (eds), *Companion to Psychiatric Studies* (8th edn) (pp. 502–526). Edinburgh: Churchill Livingstone.

Cooke, D. J. and Michie, C. (1999). Psychopathy across cultures; an item response theory comparison of Hare's Psychopathy Checklist-Revised. *Journal of Abnormal Psychology*, *108*, 58–68.

Cooke, D., Forth, A. and Hare, D. D. (1998). *Psychopathy: Theory, Research, and Implications for Society*. Dordrecht: Kluwer.

Cooke, D. J., Michie, C., Hart, S. D. and Hare, R. D. (1999). The functioning of the screening version of the Psychopathy Checklist-Revised: an item response theory analysis. *Psychological Assessment*, *11*, 3–13.

Cooke, D. J., Michie, C., Hart, S. D. and Clark, D. A. (2004). Reconstructing psychopathy: clarifying the significance of antisocial and socially deviant behavior in the diagnosis of psychopathic personality disorder. *Journal of Personality Disorders*, *18*, 337–357.

Copas, J. and Marshall, P. (1998). The offender group reconviction scale: a statistical reconviction score for use by probation officers. *Applied Statistics*, *47*, 159–171.

Cornell, D. G., Warren, J., Hawk, G., Staford, E., Oram, G. and Pine, D. (1996). Psychopathy in instrumental and reactive violent offenders. *Journal of Consulting and Clinical Psychology*, *64*, 783–779.

Correctional Services of Canada (2003). *Circles of Support and Accountability: Guide to Project Development*. Ottawa: Correctional Services of Canada.

Costa, P. and McCrae, R. (1992). *Revised NEO Personality Inventory (NEO-PI-R) and the NEO Five-Factor Inventory (NEO-FFI) Professional Manual*. Odessa, FL: Psychological Assessment Resources.

Craig, L., Beech, A. and Browne, K. (2006). Cross-validation of the Risk Matrix 2000 Sexual and Violent scales. *Journal of Interpersonal Violence*, *16*, 205–221.

Craissati, J. (1998). *Child Sexual Abusers: A Community Treatment Approach*. Hove: Psychology Press.

Craissati, J. (2003). Personality disordered offenders in a community context. *Forensic Issues*, *4*, 54–64.

Craissati, J. (2004). *Managing High Risk Sex Offenders in the Community: A Psychological Approach*. Hove: Brunner-Routledge.

Craissati, J. and Beech, A. (2001). Attrition in a community treatment program for child sexual abusers. *Journal of Interpersonal Violence*, *16*, 205–221.

Craissati, J. and Beech, A. (2003). A review of dynamic variables and their relationship to risk prediction in sex offenders. *Journal of Sexual Aggression*, *9*, 41–55.

Craissati, J. and Beech, A. (2004). The characteristics of a geographical sample of convicted rapists: sexual victimisation and compliance in comparison to child molesters. *Journal of Interpersonal Violence*, *19*, 225–240.

Craissati, J. and Beech, A. (2005). Risk prediction and failure in a complete urban sample of sex offenders. *Journal of Forensic Psychiatry and Psychology*, *16*, 24–40.

Craissati, J. and McClurg, G. (1994). Sex offenders and the criminal justice system. *Justice of the Peace*, *158*, 689–691.

Craissati, J., McClurg, G. and Browne, K. (2002). The parental bonding experiences of sex offenders: a comparison between child molesters and rapists. *Child Abuse and Neglect*, *26*, 909–921.

Craissati, J., Webb, L. and Keen, S. (2006). The relationship between developmental variables, personality disorder and risk in an urban community sample of child molesters and rapists. *In submission.*

Cramer, V., Torgersen, S. and Kringlen, E. (2003). Personality disorders, prevalence, socio-demographic correlations, quality of life, dysfunction and the question of continuity. *PTT: Personlichkeitstorunger Theorie und Therapie, 7,* 189–198.

Crittenden, P. A. (2000). A dynamic-maturational approach to continuity and change in pattern of attachment. In P. A. Crittenden and A. H. Claussen (eds), *The Organisation of Attachment Relationships: Maturation, Culture and Context* (pp. 343–357). Cambridge: Cambridge University Press.

Daniel, A. E., Robins, A. J., Reid, J. C. and Wilfley, D. E. (1988). Lifetime and six-month prevalence of psychiatric disorder among sentenced female prisoners. *Bulletin of the American Academy of Psychiatry and the Law, 16,* 333–342.

Davey, L., Day, A. and Howell, K. (2005). Anger, over-control and serious violent offending. *Aggression and Violent Behaviour, 10,* 624–635.

Davidson, K. M. (1996). Cognitive therapy for antisocial and borderline personality disorders: single case study series. *British Journal of Clinical Psychology, 35,* 413–429.

Davies, R. (1996). The inter-disciplinary network and the internal world of the offender. In C. Cordess and M. Cox (eds), *Forensic Psychotherapy: Crime, Psychodynamics and the Offender Patient* (pp. 133–144). London: Jessica Kingsley.

Davies, W. (2001). *The RAID Manual.* Leicester: APT Press.

Davison, S., Leese, M. and Taylor, P. (2001). Examination of the screening properties of the personality diagnostic questionnaire 4+ (PDQ-4+) in a prison population. *Journal of Personality Disorders, 15,* 180–194.

Dept. of Health (2004). The Multi-Agency Public Protection Arrangements (the MAPPA) and the 'Duty to Co-operate' (Vol. LASSL (2004)3). London: HMSO.

Dept. of Health and Home Office (1999). *Managing Dangerous People with Severe Personality Disorder: Proposals for Policy Development.* London: Home Office and Department of Health.

Derogatis, L. R. (2003). *Brief Symptom Inventory – Revised.* www.pearsonassessments.com

De Zulueta, F. (1996). Theories of aggression and violence: mainly theory. In C. Cordess and M. Cox (eds), *Forensic Psychotherapy: Crime, Psychodynamics and the Offender-Patient* (Vol. 1), (pp. 175–186). Philadelphia: Jessica Kingsley.

Digman, J. M. (1990). Personality structure: emergence of the five-factor model. *Annual Review of Psychology, 41,* 417–440.

Dolan, B. and Coid, J. (1993). *Psychopathic and Antisocial Personality Disorders: Treatment and Research Issues.* London: Gaskell.

Dolan, B. and Evans, C. (1992). Therapeutic community treatment for personality disordered adults: changes in neurotic symptomatology on follow-up. *International Journal of Social Psychiatry, 38,* 243–250.

Dolan, B., Warren, F. and Menzies, D. (1996). Cost-offset following specialist treatment of severe personality disorders. *Psychiatric Bulletin, 20,* 413–417.

Dolan, B., Warren, F. and Norton, K. (1997). Change in borderline symptoms one year after therapeutic community treatment for severe personality disorder. *British Journal of Psychiatry, 171,* 272–279.

Dolan, M. (2003). *Neurobiological Approaches to Disorders of Personality*. Liverpool: Department of Health.

Doren, D. M. (1987). *Understanding and Treating the Psychopath*. New York: John Wiley and Sons.

Dorr, D. (1998). Psychopathy in the pedophile. In T. Millon, E. Simonsen, M. Birket-Smith and R. D. Davis (eds), *Psychopathy: Antisocial, Criminal and Violent Behaviour* (pp. 304–320). New York Guilford Press.

Douglas, K. S. and Webster, C. D. (1999). The HCR-20 violence risk assessment scheme: concurrent validity in a sample of incarcerated offenders. *Criminal Justice and Behavior*, *26*, 3–19.

Douglas, K. S., Ogloff, J. R., Nicholls, T. L. and Grant, I. (1999). Assessing risk for violence among psychiatric patients: the HCR-20 risk assessment scheme and the Psychopathy Checklist: Screening Version. *Journal of Consulting and Clinical Psychology*, *67*, 917–930.

Douglas, K., Guy, L. and Weir, J. (2005). *HCR-20 Violence Risk Assessment Scheme: Overview and Annotated Bibliography*. Lutz, FL: Psychological Assessment Resources Inc. www.parinc.com.

D'Silva, K., Duggan, C. and McCarthy, L. (2004). Does treatment really make psychopaths worse? A review of the evidence. *Journal of Personality Disorders*, *18*, 163–178.

DSPD Programme, Dept. of Health, Home Office, HM Prison Service (2005). *Forensic Personality Disorder Medium Secure and Community Pilot Services: Planning and Delivery Guide*. London: Home Office.

Duggan, C. (2004). Does personality change and, if so, what changes? *Criminal Behaviour and Mental Health*, *14*, 5–16.

Epperson, D. L., Huot, S. J. and Kaul, J. D. (1999). *Minnesota Sex Offender Screening Tool – Revised (MnSOST-R)*. Minnesota: Department of Corrections.

Evans, K., Tyrer, P., Catalan, J. *et al.* (1999) Manual-assisted cognitive–behaviour therapy (MACT): a randomised controlled trial of a brief intervention with bibliotherapy in the treatment of recurrent deliberate self harm. *Psychological Medicine*, *29*, 19–25.

Exner, J. E. (1993). *The Rorschach: A Comprehensive System* (3rd edn, Vol. 1). New York: Wiley.

Exner, J. E. and Weiner, I. B. (1995). *The Rorschach: A Comprehensive System* (2nd edn, Vol. 3). New York: Wiley.

Eysenck, H. J. (1990). Biological dimensions of personality. In L.A. Pervin (ed.), *Handbook of Personality* (pp. 244–270). New York: Guilford Press.

Eysenck, H. J. (1998). Personality and crime. In T. Millon, E. Simonsen, M. Birket-Smith and R. D. Davis (eds), *Psychopathy: Antisocial, Criminal and Violent Behaviour* (pp. 40–49). New York: Guilford Press.

Farrall, S. (2004). *Rethinking What Works with Offenders: Probation, Social Context and Desistance from Crime*. Collumpton, Devon: Willan Publishing.

Farrington, D. P. and West, D. J. (1990). The Cambridge Study in Delinquent Development: a long-term follow-up of 411 males. In H. J. Kerner and G. Kaiser (eds), *Criminality: Personality, Behaviour and Life History* (pp. 115–138). Berlin: Springer-Verlag.

Finn, P. (1997). *Sex Offender Community Notification*. Washington, DC: National Institute of Justice, Office of Justice Programs, Research in Action.

Fitch, K. (2006) *Megan's Law: Does it Protect Children? (2). An updated review of evidence on the impact of community notification as legislated for by Megan's Law in the United States*. London: NSPCC.

Forth, A. and Kroner, D. (1995). The factor structure of the Revised Psychopathy Checklist with incarcerated rapists and incest offenders. Unpublished manuscript.

Forth, A. E., Kosson, D. and Hare, R. D. (2003). *The Hare Psychopathy Checklist: Youth Version*. Toronto: Multi-Health Systems.

Freedman, D. (2001). False prediction of future dangerousness: error rates and Psychopathy Checklist-Revised. *Journal of the American Academy of Psychiatry and Law, 29*, 89–95.

Freud, S. (1916). *The Path to Symptom Formation. S.E. Volume 1* (Vol. 15). London: Pelican Freud Library.

Friendship, C., Blud, L., Erikson, M. and Travers, R. (2002). *An Evaluation of Cognitive Behavioural Treatment for Prisoners* (No. 161). London: Home Office.

Frodi, A., Dernevik, M., Sepa, A., Philipson, J. and Bragesjo, M. (2001). Current attachment representations of incarcerated offenders varying in degree of psychopathy. *Attachment and Human Development, 3*, 269–283.

Gabbard, G. O. (1989). Splitting in hospital treatment. *American Journal of Psychiatry, 146*, 444–451.

Gabbard, G. O. (1990). *Psychodynamic Psychiatry in Clinical Practice*. Washington, DC: American Psychiatric Press.

Gacono, C. B. and Meloy, J. R. (1994). *The Rorschach Assessment of Antisocial and Psychopathic Personalities*. Hillsdale, NJ: Lawrence Erlbaum Associates.

Gacono, C., Meloy, R., Speth, E. and Roske, A. (1997). Above the law: escapes from a maximum security forensic hospital and psychopathy. *Journal of the American Academy of Psychiatry and the Law, 25*, 547–550.

Gallwey, P. L. G. (1985). The psychodynamics of borderline personality. In D. P. Farrington and J. Gunn (eds), *Aggression and Dangerousness* (pp. 127–151). London: John Wiley & Sons.

George, C., Kaplan, N. and Main, M. (1987). The attachment interview. Unpublished manuscript, University of California, Berkeley.

Gilligan, J. (1996). *Violence: Our Deadly Epidemic and its Causes*. New York: G. P. Putnam & Sons.

Glasser, M. (1996). The assessment and management of dangerousness: the psychoanalytical contribution. *Journal of Forensic Psychiatry, 7*, 271–283.

Glasser, M. (1998). On violence: a preliminary communication. *International Journal of Psycho-Analysis, 79*, 887–902.

Gondolf, E. W. (1998). *Assessing Woman Battering in Mental Health Services*. Thousand Oaks, CA: Sage Publications.

Grann, M., Langstrom, N., Tengstrom, A. and Kullgren, G. (1999). Psychopathy (PCL-R) predicts violent recidivism among criminal offenders with personality disorders in Sweden. *Law and Human Behavior, 23*, 205–217.

Grubin, D. (1998). *Sex Offending Against Children: Understanding the Risk* (No. 99). London: Home Office.

Gudjonsson, G. H. and Sigurdsson, J. F. (2000). Differences and similarities between violent and sex offenders. *Child Abuse and Neglect, 24*, 363–372.

Gunn, J. (1998). Psychopathy: an elusive concept with moral overtones. In T. Millon, E. Simonsen, M. Birket-Smith and R. D. Davis (eds), *Psychopathy:*

Antisocial, Criminal and Violent Behaviour (pp. 32–39). New York: Guilford Press.

Hamberger, L. K. and Hastings, J. E. (1988). Characteristics of male spouse abuser consistent with personality disorders. *Hospital and Community Psychiatry, 39,* 763–770.

Hamberger, L. K. and Hastings, J. E. (1990). Recidivism following spouse abuse abatement counseling; treatment program implications. *Violence and Victims, 5,* 157–170.

Hanson, K. (1997). *The Development of a Brief Actuarial Risk Scale for Sexual Offense Recidivism* (No. 97–04). Ottawa: Department of the Solicitor General.

Hanson, K. and Harris, A. (1998). *Dynamic Predictors of Sexual Recidivism.* Ottawa: Department of the Solicitor General.

Hanson, K. and Harris, A. (2000). *The Sex Offender Need Assessment Rating (SONAR): A Method for Measuring Change in Risk Levels* (No. 1998–01). Ottawa: Department of the Solicitor General.

Hanson, K. and Harris, A. J. R. (2001). A structured approach to evaluating change among sexual offenders. *Sexual Abuse: A Journal of Research and Treatment, 13,* 105–122.

Hanson, K. and Thornton, D. (1999). *Static 99: Improving Actuarial Risk Assessments for Sex Offenders.* Ottawa: Department of the Solicitor General.

Hanson, K. and Thornton, D. (2000). Improving risk assessments for sex offenders: a comparison of three actuarial scales. *Law and Human Behaviour, 24,* 119–136.

Hanson, R., Gordon, A., Harris, A., Marques, J., Murphy, W., Quinsey, V. *et al.* (2002). First Report of the Collaborative Outcome Data Project on the Effectiveness of Psychological Treatment for Sex Offenders. *Sexual Abuse: A Journal of Research and Treatment, 14,* 169–194.

Hare, R. D. (1991). *Manual for the Revised Psychopathy Checklist.* Toronto: Multi-Health Systems.

Hare, R. D. (1998). Psychopaths and their nature: implications for the mental health and criminal justice systems. In T. Millon, E. Simonsen, M. Birket-Smith and R. D. Davis (eds), *Psychopathy: Antisocial, Criminal and Violent Behaviour* (pp. 188–214). New York: Guilford Press.

Hare, R. D. and Jutai, J. (1983). Criminal history of the male psychopath: some preliminary data. In K. van. Dusen and S. Mednick (eds), *Prospective Studies of Crime and Delinquency* (pp. 146–151). Boston: Kluner Mijhoff.

Hare, R. D. and McPherson, L. M. (1984). Violent and aggressive behaviour by criminal psychopaths. *International Journal of Law and Psychiatry, 7,* 35–50.

Hare, R. D. and Wong, S. (2003). *Program Guidelines for the Institutional Treatment of Psychopaths.* Toronto: Multi-Health Systems.

Hare, R. D., McPherson, L. M. and Forth, A. E. (1988). Male psychopaths and their criminal careers. *Journal of Consulting and Clinical Psychology, 56,* 710–714.

Harpur, T. J. and Hare, R. D. (1994). Assessment of psychopathy as a function of age. *Journal of Abnormal Psychology, 103,* 604–609.

Hechtman, L. and Weiss, G. (1983). Long-term outcome of hyperactive children. *American Journal of Orthopsychiatry, 53,* 532–541.

Hemphill, J. F., Hare, R. D. and Wong, S. (1998). Psychopathy and recidivism: a review. *Legal and Criminological Psychology, 3,* 139–170.

Henderson, D. K. (1939). *Psychopathic States.* London: Chapman & Hall.

Hering, C. (1997). Beyond understanding? Some thoughts on the meaning and function of the notion of 'evil'. *British Journal of Psychotherapy, 14*, 209–220.

Herman, J. L., Perry, J. C. and van-der-Kolk, B. A. (1989). Childhood trauma in borderline personality disorder. *American Journal of Psychiatry, 164*, 490–495.

Hilton, N. Z. and Harris, G. T. (2005). Predicting wife assault: a critical review and implications for policy and practice. *Trauma, Violence and Abuse, 6*, 3–23.

Hinshelwood, R. D. (1999). The difficult patient. *British Journal of Psychiatry, 174*, 187–190.

Hiscoke, U. L., Langstrom, N., Ottosson, H. and Grann, M. (2003). Self-reported personality traits and disorders (DSM-IV) and risk of criminal recidivism: a prospective study. *Journal of Personality Disorders, 17*, 293–305.

HM Inspectorate of Probation (2006a). *An Independent Review of a Serious Further Offence Case: Damien Hanson and Elliot White.* London: Home Office. www.inspectorates.homeoffice.gov.uk/hmiprobation/.

HM Inspectorate of Probation (2006b). *An Independent Review of a Serious Further Offence Case: Anthony Rice.* London: Home Office. www.inspectorates. homeoffice.gov.uk/hmiprobation/.

HM Prison Service (2005). The Structured Assessment of Risk and Need (Sexual Offenders). Manual version 2. Internal document, Offending Behaviour Programmes Unit, HM Prison Service.

Hollin, C. (2002). Does punishment motivate offenders to change? In M. McMurran (ed.), *Motivating Offenders to Change* (pp. 235–250). Chichester: John Wiley & Sons.

Hollin, C., Palmer, E., McGuire, J., Hounsome, J., Hatcher, R., Bilby, C. *et al.* (2004). *Pathfinder Programmes in the Probation Service: A Retrospective Analysis.* London: HMSO.

Holt, S., Meloy, J. R. and Strack, S. (1999). Sadism and psychopathy in violent and sexually violent offenders. *Journal of the American Academy of Psychiatry and the Law, 27*, 23–32.

Home Office (2002). *Offender Assessment System (OASys): User Manual Version Two.* London: National Probation Directorate, Home Office.

Home Office (2005a). *Annual Report for MAPPA (London).* London: Home Office.

Home Office (2005b). Forensic Personality Disorder Medium Secure and Community Pilot Services: Planning and Delivery Guide. Internal document, Home Office, DSPD Programme.

Home Office (2006). *MAPPA – The First Five Years: A National Overview of the Multi-agency Public Protection Arrangements 2001–2006.* London: Home Office. www.probation.homeoffice.gov.uk.

Hough, M., Clancy, A., McSweeney, T. and Turnbull, P. J. (2003). *The Impact of Drug Treatment and Testing Orders on Offending: Two-year Reconviction Results* (No. 184). London: Home Office.

Howard, P., Clark, D. and Garnham, N. (2006). *An Evaluation of the Offender Assessment System (OASys) in Three Pilots 1999–2001.* London: Home Office.

Hyler, S. E., Rieder, R. O., Williams, J. B., Spitzer, R. L., Hendler, J. and Lyons, M. (1988). The Personality Diagnostic Questionnaire: development and preliminary results. *Journal of Personality Disorders, 2*, 229–237.

Jackson, H. J. and Burgess, P. M. (2004). Personality disorders in the community: results from the Australian National Survey of Mental Health and Well-Being

Part III: relationships between specific type of personality disorder, Axis I mental disorders and physical conditions with disability and health consultations. *Social Psychiatry and Psychiatric Epidemiology*, *39*, 765–776.

Kamphuis, J. H. and Emmelkamp, P. M. G. (2000). Stalking – a contemporary challenge for forensic and clinical psychiatry. *British Journal of Psychiatry*, *176*, 206–209.

Kantojarvi, L., Veijola, J., Lasky, K., Jokelainen, J., Herva, A., Karvonen, J. T., *et al.* (2004). Comparison of hospital-treated personality disorders and personality disorders in a general population sample. *Nordic Journal of Psychiatry*, *58*, 357–362.

Karterud, S., Pedersen, G., Bjordal, E., Braband, J., Friis, S., Haaseth, O., *et al.* (2003). Day treatment of patients with personality disorders: experiences from a Norwegian treatment research network. *Journal of Personality Disorders*, *17*, 243–262.

Kemshall, H., Mackenzie, G., Wood, J., Bailey, R. and Yates, J. (2005). *Strengthening Multi-Agency Public Protection Arrangements (MAPPAs)*. Home Office Development and Practice Report, No. 45. London: Home Office.

Kernberg, O. F. (1984). *Severe Personality Disorders: Psychotherapeutic Strategies*. New Haven: Yale University Press.

Kernberg, O. F., Selzer, M. A., Koeningerg, H. W., Carr, A. C. and Appelbaum, A. H. (1989). *Psychodynamic Psychotherapy of Borderline Patients*. New York: Basic Books.

Knight, R. A. and Prentky, R. A. (1990). Classifying sexual offenders: the development and corroboration of taxonomic models. In W. L. Marshall, D. R. Laws and H. E. Barbaree (eds), *Handbook of Sexual Assault: Issues, Theories and Treatment of the Offender* (pp. 23–52). New York: Plenum Press.

Knock, K. (2002). *The Police Perspective on Sex Offender Orders: A Preliminary Review of Policy and Practice* (No. 155). London: Home Office.

Krawitz, R. (1997). A prospective psychotherapy outcome study. *Australian and New Zealand Journal of Psychiatry*, *31*, 465–473.

Kray, K. (2002). *Hard Bastards*. London: Blake Publishing Ltd.

Kropp, P. R. and Hart, S. D. (2000). The Spousal Assault Risk Assessment (SARA) Guide: reliability and validity in adult male offenders. *Law and Human Behavior*, *24*, 101–118.

Kropp, P. R., Hart, S. D., Webster, S. and Eaves, D. (1994). *Manual for the Spousal Assault Risk Assessment Guide* (2nd edn). Vancouver: British Columbia Institute of Family Violence.

Lees, J., Manning, N. and Rawlings, B. (1999). *Therapeutic Community Effectiveness. A systematic international review of therapeutic community treatment for people with personality disorders and mentally disordered offenders* (No. CRD Report 17). York: University of York.

Linehan, M. M (1993). *Cognitive-Behavioral Treatment of Borderline Personality Disorder*. New York: Guilford Press.

Linehan, M. M., Heard, H. L. and Armstrong, H. E. (1993). Naturalistic follow-up of a behavioral treatment for chronically parasuicidal borderline patients. *Archives of General Psychiatry*, *50*, 971–974.

Linehan, M., Schmidt, H. L., Dimeff, L. A., Craft, J. C., Kanter, J. and Comtois, K.

A. (1999). Dialectical behavior therapy for patients with borderline personality disorder and drug-dependence. *American Journal on Addictions*, *8*, 279–292.

Linehan, M., Dimeff, L. A., Reynolds, S. K., Comtois, K., Welch, S. S. and Heagerty, P. (2002). Dialectical behavior therapy versus comprehensive validation therapy plus 12-step for the treatment of opioid dependent women meeting criteria for borderline personality disorder. *Drug and Alcohol Dependence*, *67*, 13–26.

Little, M., Kogan, J., Bullock, R. A. and Van der Laan, P. (2004). ISSP: an experiment in multi-systemic responses to persistent young offenders known to children's services. *British Journal of Criminology*, *44*, 225–240.

Livesley, W. J. (2001). *Handbook of Personality Disorders. Theory, Research and Treatment*. New York: Guilford Press.

Livesley, W. J. (2003). *Practical Management of Personality Disorder*. New York: Guilford Press.

Looman, J., Abracen, J., Serin, R., Marquis, P. and Maillet, G. (2004). Psychopathy, treatment change and recidivism in high risk high need sexual offenders. *Journal of Interpersonal Violence 19*, 177–190.

Losel, F. (1998). Treatment and management of psychopaths. In J. Cooke, A. Forth and R. Hare (eds), *Psychopathy: Theory, Research, and Implications for Society* (pp. 303–355). Dordrecht: Kluwer.

Low, G., Jones, D. and Duggan, C. (2001). The treatment of deliberate self-harm in borderline personality disorder using dialetical behaviour therapy: a pilot study in a high security hospital. *Behavioural and Cognitive Psychotherapy*, *29*, 85–92.

Lykken, D. (1995). *The Antisocial Personalities*. Hillsdale, NJ: Erlbaum Associates.

Maden, A., Williams, J., Wong, S. and Leis, T. A. (2004). Treating dangerous and severe personality disorder in high security: lessons from the Regional Psychiatric Centre, Saskatoon, Canada. *Journal of Forensic Psychiatry and Psychology*, *15*, 375–390.

Maden, A., Rogers, P., Watt, A., Lewis, G., Amos, T., Gournay, K. and Skapinakis, P. (2005). *Assessing the Utility of the Offenders Group Reconviction Scale-2 in Predicting the Risk of Reconviction within 2 and 4 Years of Discharge from English and Welsh Medium Secure Units (MRD 12/58)*. Report to the National Forensic Mental Health R&D Programme. www.nfmhp.org.uk/publications.htm.

Maden, T., Swinton, M. and Gunn, J. (1994). Psychiatric disorder in women serving a prison sentence. *British Journal of Psychiatry*, *164*, 44–54.

Maguire, M., Kemshall, H., Noaks, L., Wincup, E. and Sharpe, K. (2001). *Risk Management of Sexual and Violent Offenders: The Work of Public Protection Panels* (No. 139). London: Home Office.

Maier, W., Lichtermann, D., Klingler, T. and Heun, R. (1992). Prevalences of personality disorders in the community. *Journal of Personality Disorders*, *6*, 187–196.

Main, M., Kaplan, N. and Cassidy, J. (1985). Security in infancy, childhood, and adulthood: a move to the level of representation. In I. Bretherton and E. Waters (eds), *Growing Points of Attachment Theory and Research* (Vol. 50 (1–2 Serial No. 209), pp. 66–104). Monographs of the Society for Research on Child Development. Chicago: University of Chicago Press.

Malan, D. and Coughlin Della Selva, P. (2005) *Lives Transformed: A Revolutionary Method of Dynamic Psychotherapy*. London: Karnac Books.

Mann, R. (1996). *Motivational Interviewing with Sex Offenders: A Practice Manual*. Hull: NOTA Publication.

Marshall, P. (1997). *A Reconviction Study of HMP Grendon Therapeutic Community* (No. 53). London: Home Office.

Marshall, W. and Marshall, L. E. (2000). The origins of sexual offending. *Trauma, Violence and Abuse, 1*, 250–263.

May, C. (1999). *Explaining Reconviction Following a Community Sentence: The Role of Social Factors* (No. 192). London: HMSO.

McCann, R. A., Ball, E. A. and Ivanoff, A. (2000). The effectiveness of dialectical behaviour therapy in reducing burnout among forensic staff. *Cognitive and Behavioural Practice, 5*, 447–456.

McClurg, G. and Craissati, J. (1997). Public opinion and the sentencing of perpetrators of CSA. *Journal of Sexual Aggression, 3*, 30–34.

McMurran, M. (2003). *Personality Disorders*. Liverpool: Department of Health.

McMurran, M., Fyffe, L. M., Duggan, C. and Latham, A. (2001). 'Stop & Think!': social problem-solving therapy with personality disordered offenders. *Criminal Behaviour and Mental Health, 11*, 273–285.

Megargee, E. I. (1966). Undercontrolled and overcontrolled personality types in extreme antisocial aggression. *Psychological Monographs, 80*, 1–611.

Meloy, J. R. (1988). *The Psychopathic Mind: Origins, Dynamics and Treatment*. Northvale, NJ: Jason Aronson.

Meloy, J. R. (1997). *Violent Attachments*. Northvale, NJ: Jason Aronson.

Meloy, J. R. (ed.) (2001). *Psychology of Stalking: Clinical and Forensic Perspectives*. San Diego: Academic Press.

Meloy, J. R. and Gacono, C. B. (1998). The internal world of the psychopath. In T. Millon, E. Simonsen, M. Birkey-Smith and R. D. Davis (eds), *Antisocial, Criminal, and Violent Behavior* (pp. 95–109). New York: Guilford Press.

Menninger, K. and Mayman, M. (1956). Episodic dyscontrol as third order of stress adaptation. *Bulletin of the Menninger Clinic, 20*, 153–165.

Menzies, I. (1988). The functioning of social systems as a defence against anxiety. In *Containing Anxiety in Institutions* (Vol. 4, pp. 43–85). London: Free Associations.

Miller, W. R. (1983). Motivational interviewing with problem drinkers. *Behavioural Psychotherapy, 1*, 147–172.

Miller, W. R. and Rollnick, S. (1991). *Motivational Interviewing: Preparing People to Change Addictive Behaviour*. New York: Guilford Press.

Millon, T. and Davis, R. O. (1996). *Disorders of Personality: DSM-IV and Beyond* (2nd edn). Chichester, UK: John Wiley and Sons.

Millon, T., Millon, C. and Davis, R. D. (1994). *Millon Clinical Multi-axial Inventory – III*. Minneapolis: National Computer Systems.

Moran, P. (1999). *Antisocial Personality Disorder: An Epidemiological Perspective*. London: Gaskell.

Morant, N., Dolan, B., Fainman, D. and Hilton, M. (1999). An innovative outreach service for people with severe personality disorders: patient characteristics and clinical activities. *Journal of Forensic Psychiatry, 10*, 84–97.

Morey, L. (1991). *Personality Assessment Inventory – Professional Manual*. Lutz, FL: Psychological Assessment Resources, Inc.

Morton, N. and Browne, K. D. (1998). Theory and observation of attachment and its relation to child maltreatment: a review. *Child Abuse and Neglect, 22,* 1093–1104.

Mulder, R. T., Joyce, P. R. and Cloninger, C. R. (1994). Temperament and early environment influence comorbidity and personality disorders in major depression. *Comprehensive Psychiatry, 35,* 225–233.

Mullen, P. E., Pathe, M., Purcell, R. and Stuart, G. W. (1999). Study of stalkers. *American Journal of Psychiatry, 156,* 1244–1249.

Mullen, P. E., Pathe, M. and Purcell, R. (eds). (2000). *Stalkers and their Victims.* Cambridge: Cambridge University Press.

Murphy, C. and Vess, J. (2003). Subtypes of psychopathy: proposed differences between narcissistic, borderline, sadistic and antisocial psychopaths. *Psychiatric Quarterly, 74,* 11–29.

Murphy, G. H. (1990). Analysis of motivation and fire-related interests in people with a mild learning difficulty who set fires. Paper presented at the International Congress on Treatment of Mental Illness and Behavioural Disorders in Mentally Retarded People, Amsterdam.

NHS London (2006). *Report of the Independent Inquiry into the Care and Treatment of John Barrett.* London: NHS London.

NHS South East Coast (2006). *Report of the Independent Inquiry into the Care and Treatment of Michael Stone.* South East Coast Strategic Health Authority, Kent County Council, Kent Probation Area. www.southeastcoast.nhs.uk.

National Institute for Mental Health Evaluation (2003). *The Personality Disorder Capabilities Framework.* Leeds: NIMHE.

National Probation Service (2003). *MAPPA Guidance: Multi-Agency Public Protection Arrangements. Protection Through Partnership.* London: Home Office.

National Probation Service (2006). *Putting Risk of Harm in Context: An Inspection Promoting Public Protection.* www.inspectorates.homeoffice.gov.uk.

Nestadt, G., Samuels, J. F. *et al.* (1992). The relationships between personality and DSM-I disorders in the population: results from an epidemiological survey. *American Journal of Psychiatry, 149,* 1228–1233.

Newman, J. P., Patterson, C. and Kosson, D. (1987). Response perseveration in psychopaths. *Journal of Abnormal Psychology, 96,* 145–148.

Ogloff, J., Wong, S. and Underwood, A. (1990). Treating criminal psychopaths in a therapeutic community program. *Behavioural Sciences and the Law, 8,* 81–90.

Olver, M. E. (2003). The development and validation of the Violence Risk Scale: Sexual offender version (VRS:SO) and its relationship to psychopathy and treatment attrition. Unpublished manuscript, University of Saskatchewan.

Palmer, E. J., Caulfield, L. S. and Hollin, C. R. (2005). *Evaluation of Interventions with Arsonists and Young Firesetters.* London: Office of the Deputy Prime Minister.

Paris, J. (1996). *Social Factors in the Personality Disorders: A Biopsychosocial Approach to Etiology and Treatment.* Cambridge: Cambridge University Press.

Paris, J. (2000). Childhood precursors of borderline personality disorder. *The Psychiatric Clinic of North America, 23,* 77–88.

Perry, J. C. and Bond, M. (2000). Empirical studies of psychotherapy for personality disorders. In J. G. Gunderson and G. O. Gabbard (eds), *Psychotherapy for Personality Disorders* (pp. 1–31). Washington, DC: American Psychiatric Press.

Perry, J. C., Banon, E. and Ianni, F. (1999). Effectiveness of psychotherapy for personality disorders. *American Journal of Psychiatry*, *156*, 1312–1321.

Pincus, H. A., Frances, A. J., Davis, W. W., First, M. B. and Widiger, T. A. (1992). DSM-IV and new diagnostic categories: holding the line on proliferation. *American Journal of Psychiatry*, *149*, 112–117.

Pines, M. (1978). Group-analytic psychotherapy of the borderline patient. *Group Analysis*, *11*, 115–126.

Plotnikoff, J. and Woolfson, R. (2000). *Where Are They Now?: An Evaluation of Sex Offender Registration in England and Wales* (No. 126). London: Home Office.

Porter, S., Fairweather, D., Drugge, J., Herve, H., Birt, A. and Boer, D. (2000). Profiles of psychopathy in incarcerated sexual offenders. *Criminal Justice and Behavior*, *27*, 216–233.

Powis, B. (2002). *Offenders' Risk of Serious Harm: A Literature Review* (No. 81). London: Home Office.

Prentky, R. A. and Burgess, A. W. (2000). *Forensic Management of Sexual Offenders*. New York: Kluwer Academic/Plenum Publishers.

Quinsey, V., Rice, M. and Harris, G. (1995). Actuarial prediction of sexual recidivism. *Journal of Interpersonal Violence*, *10*, 85–105.

Quinsey, V. L., Harris, G., Rice, M. and Cormier, C. (1998). *Violent Offenders: Appraising and Managing Risk*. Washington, DC: American Psychiatric Association.

Raine, A. (1988). Antisocial behaviour and social psychophysiology. In H. Wagner (ed.), *Social Psychophysiology and Emotion: Theory and Clinical Application* (pp. 231–253). London: Wiley.

Raine, A. (1993). *The Psychopathology of Crime*. San Diego: Academic Press.

Ranger, M., Methuen, C., Rutter, D., Rao, B. and Tyrer, P. (2004). Prevalence of personality disorder in the case-load of an inner city assertive outreach team. *Psychiatric Bulletin*, *28*, 441–443.

Reich, J., Boerstler, H., Yates, W. and Dduaquba, M. (1989). Utilisation of medical resources in persons with DSMIII personality disorders in a community sample. *International Journal of Psychiatry in Medicine*, *19*, 1–9.

Ressler, R. K., Burgess, A. W. and Douglas, J. E. (1988). *Sexual Homicide: Patterns and Motives*. Lexington, MA: Lexington Books.

Rice, M. and Harris, G. (1997). Cross-validation and extension of the violence risk appraisal guide for child molesters and rapists. *Law and Human Behaviour*, *21*, 231–241.

Rice, M. E., Harris, G. T. and Cormier, C. (1992). An evaluation of a maximum-security therapeutic community for psychopaths and other mentally disordered offenders. *Law and Human Behavior*, *16*, 399–412.

Risk Management Authority (2006). *Risk Assessment Tools Evaluation Directory*. Paisley, Scotland: RMA.

Robins, C. J. and Chapman, A. L. (2004). Dialectical behavior therapy: current status, recent developments, and future directions. *Journal of Personality Disorders*, *18*, 73–89.

Robins, L. N. (1966). *Deviant Children Grown Up*. Baltimore: Williams and Watkins.

Robins, L. N., Tipp, J. and Przybeck, T. (1991). Antisocial personality. In L. N.

Robins and D. Regier (eds), *Psychiatric Disorders in America* (pp. 258–290). New York: Free Press.

Rogers, R. and Dickey, R. (1991). Denial and minimization among sex offenders: a review of competing models of deception. *Annals of Sex Research*, *4*, 49–63.

Rosenfeld, B. (2003). Recidivism in stalking and obsessional harassment. *Law and Human Behaviour*, *27*, 251–265.

Ryle, A. (1997). *Cognitive Analytic Therapy and Borderline Personality Disorder: The Model and the Method*. Chichester: John Wiley & Sons.

Ryle, A. and Golynkina, K. (2000). Effectiveness of time-limited cognitive analytic therapy of borderline personality disorder: factors associated with outcome. *British Journal of Medical Psychology*, *73*, 197–210.

Salekin, R. T. (2002). Psychopathy and therapeutic pessimism. Clinical lore or clinical reality? *Clinical Psychology Review*, *22*, 79–112.

Saulsman, L. M. and Page, A. C. (2003). Can trait measures diagnose personality disorders. *Current Opinion in Psychiatry*, *16*, 83–88.

Saunders, D. G. (1996). Feminist cognitive behavioural and process psychodynamic treatment for men who batter: interaction of abuser traits and treatment models. *Violence and Victims*, *11*, 393–414.

Schlesinger, L. (1996). The catathymic crisis, 1912–present: a review and clinical study. *Aggression and Violent Behaviour*, *1*, 307–316.

Schneider, K. (1950). *Psychopathic personalities* (9th edn, English trans.). London: Cassell (first published 1923).

Schore, A. N. (2001). Effects of a secure attachment relationship on right brain development, affect regulation, and infant mental health. *Infant Mental Health Journal*, *22*, 7–66.

Schram, D. and Milloy, C. (1995). *Community Notification: A Study of Offender Characteristics and Recidivism*. Seattle: Urban Policy Research.

Seto, M. and Barbaree, H. E. (1999). Psychopathy, treatment behavior and sex offender recidivism. *Journal of Interpersonal Violence*, *14*, 1235–1248.

Siever, L. and Davis, K. L. (1991). A psychobiological perspective on the personality disorders. *American Journal of Psychiatry*, *148*, 1647–1658.

Singleton, N., Meltzer, H. and Gatward, R. (1998). *Psychiatric Morbidity among Prisoners in England and Wales*. London: Statistical Office.

Stevenson, H. C., Castillo, E. and Sefarbi, R. (1989). Treatment of denial in adolescent sex offenders and their families. *Journal of Offender Counseling, Services and Rehabilitation*, *14*, 37–50.

Stone, M. H. (1990). *The Fate of Borderline Patients*. New York: Guilford Press.

Stone, M. H. (2000). Gradations of antisociality. In J. Gunderson and G. O. Gabbard (eds), *Psychotherapy of Personality Disorders* (pp. 95–130). Washington, DC: American Psychiatric Press.

Stone, M. H. (2001). Natural history and long-term outcome. In W. J. Livesley (ed.), *Handbook of Personality Disorders: Theory, Research and Treatment* (pp. 259–276). New York: Guilford Press.

Strand, S., Belfrage, H., Fransson, G. and Levander, S. (1999). Clinical and risk management factors in risk prediction of mentally disordered offenders: more important than actuarial data? *Legal and Criminological Psychology*, *4*, 67–76.

Taylor, R. (1999). *Predicting Reconvictions for Sexual and Violent Offences Using the*

Revised Offender Group Reconviction Scale. Home Office Research Findings No. 104. London: Home Office.

Taylor, R. (2000). *A Seven-year Reconviction Study of HMP Grendon Therapeutic Community* (No. 115). London: Home Office.

Thomas, A. and Chess, S. (1977). *Temperament and Development*. New York: Brunner/Mazel.

Thomas-Peter, B. (2002). *Forensic Service Models*. London: Dept. of Health.

Thornton, D. (2002). Constructing and testing a framework for dynamic risk assessment. *Sexual Abuse: A Journal of Research and Treatment, 14*, 139–153.

Thornton, D. (2003). The Machiavellian sex offender. In A. Matravers (ed.), *Sex Offenders in the Community: Managing and Reducing the Risks* (pp. 144–152). Cullompton, Devon: Willan Publishing.

Thornton, D., Mann, R., Webster, S., Blud, L., Travers, R., Friendship, C., *et al.* (2003). Distinguishing and combining risks for sexual and violent recidivism. *Annals of the New York Academy of Science, 989*, 225–235.

Twemlow, S. W. and Sacco, F. C. (1996). Peacekeeping and peacemaking: the conceptual foundations of a plan to reduce violence and improve the quality of life in a Jamaican city. *Psychiatry, 59*, 156–175.

Tyrer, P. (2000). Improving the assessment of personality disorders. *Criminal Behaviour and Mental Health, 10*, 551–565.

Tyrer, P., Sensky, T. and Mitchard, S. (2003). Principles of Nidotherapy in the treatment of persistent mental and personality disorders. *Psychotherapy and Psychosomatics, 72*, 350–356.

Vennard, J., Hedderman, C. and Sugg, D. (1997). *Changing Offenders' Attitudes and Behaviour: What Works?* (No. 61). London: Home Office.

Verheul, R., Van den Brink, W. and Koeter, M. W. (1998). Temporal stability of diagnostic criteria for antisocial personality disorder in male alcohol dependent patients. *Journal of Personality Disorders, 12*, 316–331.

Verheul, R., Van den Bosch, L. and Van den Brink, W. (2002). A Dutch 12 month clinical trial of Dialectical Behaviour Therapy for women with Borderline Personality Disorder. Paper presented at the 5th ISSPD European Congress on Personality Disorders – Abstracts, Munich, Germany.

Ward, T. and Brown, M. (2003). The good lives model and conceptual issues in offender rehabilitation. *Psychology, Crime and Law, 10*, 243–257.

Ward, T., Polaschek, D. and Beech, A. (2005). *Theories of Sexual Offending*. London: John Wiley & Sons.

Warren, F., Preedy, K., McCauley, G., Pickering, A., Norton, K., Geddes, J. R., *et al.* (2001). *Review of Treatments for Dangerous and Severe Personality Disorder*. London: Home Office.

Webster, C. D., Douglas, K. S., Eaves, D. and Hart, S. D. (1997). *HCR-20: Assessing the Risk for Violence* (2nd edn). Vancouver: Mental Health, Law, and Policy Institute, Simon Fraser University.

White, S. G. and Cawood, J. S. (1998). Threat management in stalking cases. In J. R. Meloy (ed.), *The Psychology of Stalking* (pp. 335–342). San Diego: Academic Press.

Widiger, T. A. (1994). Conceptualising a disorder of personality from the five-factor model. In P. T. Costa (ed.), *Personality Disorders and the Five-factor Model of Personality* (pp. 311–317). Washington, DC: American Psychiatric Association.

Widiger, T. A. and Trull, J. (1994). Personality disorders and violence. In J. Monahan and H. Steadman (eds), *Violence and Mental Disorder: Developments in Risk Assessment* (pp. 203–226). Chicago: Chicago University Press.

Wong, S. and Gordon, A. (1996). *Violence Risk Scale Experimental Version I.* Department of Psychiatric Research, Regional Psychiatric Centre, Saskatoon, Sask.

Wong, S. and Gordon, A. (2000). *Violence Risk Scale.* Saskatoon, Sask.

Wong, S. and Hare, R. (2001). *Program Guidelines for the Institutional Treatment of Violent Psychopathic Offenders.* Toronto: Multi-Health Systems.

Woody, G. E., McLelland, T. and Luborsky, L. L. (1985). Sociopathy and psychotherapy outcome. *Archives of General Psychiatry, 42,* 1081–1086.

World Health Organization (1989). *International Classification of Diseases. Mental and Behavioural Disorders (including Disorders of Psychological Development)* (Vol. 10). Geneva: WHO.

Young, J. E. (1999). *Cognitive Therapy for Personality Disorders: A Schema-Focused Approach* (Vol. 3). Sarasota, FL: Professional Resource Exchange.

Young, J. E. and Brown, G. (1990). *Young Schema Questionnaire.* New York: Cognitive Therapy Center of New York.

Young, J. E. and Brown, G. (2001). *Young Schema Questionnaire: Special Edition.* New York: Schema Therapy Institute.

Young, J. E., Klosko, J. S. and Weishaar, M. E. (2003). *Schema Therapy: A Practitioner's Guide.* New York: Guilford Press.

Young, L. and Gibb, E. (2001). Trauma and grievance. In C. Garland (ed.), *Understanding Trauma* (pp. 81–95). London: Duckworth.

Zevitz, R. and Farkas, M. (2000a). Sex offender community notification: examining the importance of neighborhood meetings. *Behavioral Sciences and the Law, 18,* 393–408.

Zevitz, R. and Farkas, M. (2000b). Sex offender community notification: managing high risk criminals or exacting further vengeance? *Behavioral Sciences and the Law, 18,* 375–391.

Index